UNDERSTANDING FOODSERVICE FINANCIAL MANAGEMENT

Jeannie Sneed, PhD, RD
University of Tennessee
Knoxville, Tennessee

Kathryn Henderson Kresse, MBA
Consultant
Strategic Planning and
Financial and Operations Management

AN ASPEN PUBLICATION®
Aspen Publishers, Inc.

1989

Rockville, Maryland
Royal Tunbridge Wells

Library of Congress Cataloging-in-Publication Data

Sneed, Jeannie.
Understanding foodservice financial management/Jeannie Sneed,
Kathryn Henderson Kresse.
p. cm.
"An Aspen publication."
Bibliography: p.
Includes index.
ISBN: 0-87189-795-4
1. Food service--Finance. 2. Food service management.
I. Kresse, Kathryn Henderson. II. Title.
TX911.3.F5S64   1988   647'.95'0681--dc19   88-22321
CIP

Aspen Publishers, Inc., is not affiliated with the American
Society of Parenteral and Enteral Nutrition.

Editorial Services: Marsha Davies

Library of Congress Catalog Card Number: 88-22321
ISBN: 0-87189-795-4

Printed in the United States of America

1 2 3 4 5

Table of Contents

Preface

Financial management of foodservice operations is becoming increasingly critical to the success and, perhaps, to the very existence of such operations. At the very time when financial management is so critical, research shows that employers feel that dietitians are not as prepared in this arena as they should be.

There is a paucity of literature focusing on the financial management of institutional foodservice operations. While the management of these operations is becoming more similar to that of commercial operations, they have unique characteristics and issues that must be addressed.

We strongly believe in approaching management using a systems perspective and, therefore, chose to approach the writing of this book using that perspective. Marketing, production, financial, and human resource strategies must work together cohesively for the organization to be successful. We tried to integrate and apply all of these areas as they relate to financial management. We hope we can help foodservice managers design and implement strategies that will maximize the performance of their operation. We provide guidelines for tracking, analyzing, and changing components of the operation to ensure that goals and objectives are met.

The environment will remain competitive, so we challenge managers to hone their financial management skills so they will be on the competitive edge. The marketplace will be challenging, but it will also be exciting and rewarding for the astute manager.

We are grateful to the many people who provided support and assistance to us in the writing of this book. Special thanks are extended to Jim Rose, M.S., R.D., D.H.C.F.A., L.D., National Dietary Director for ARA Living Centers. It was at Jim's suggestion that we accepted the challenge to write this book. We appreciate his many ideas; they truly improved the quality of the finished product.

We are extremely appreciative to the many professionals with whom we have studied and worked who have contributed to our knowledge, perspectives, and motivation. We especially thank Sisters Miriam Patrick Cooney and Jeanette Lester of St. Mary's College for their insights on using quantitative tools to develop creative, competitive solutions in a changing environment. Also, thanks to Drs. Betty Ruth Carruth and Jean Skinner of the University of Tennessee, Knoxville, for their professional mentorship and friendship.

Thanks to Andrea Little of Methodist Hospital, St. Louis Park, Minnesota, who reviewed the manuscript and provided valuable input. Also, a big thanks goes to Michael Brown, Vice President–Publisher, Sandy Cannon, Senior Developmental Editor, Marsha Davies, Assistant Editor, and Nancy Weisgerber, Promotions Manager, at Aspen Publishers, Inc. Their expert guidance made this book a reality.

A special note of appreciation is extended to our families and friends. Without their love, support, patience, and understanding, this book could not have been written. We especially thank Jeanette Sneed; Jim Kresse; and David and Patricia Barry Henderson. We also thank Michael, Patrick, Crystal, Joni, and Jennifer, and Adam Henderson; and Bonnie, Rick, Bill, and Bobby Kresse.

Chapter 1

Introduction to Financial Management in Foodservice Operations

Today, more than ever before, financial management is the key ingredient in the recipe for a successful foodservice operation. Terms such as diagnosis-related groups (DRGs), financial accountability, and cost containment are in the everyday vocabulary of today's foodservice managers in health care settings. The objective of this book is to hone the financial and accounting skills of operation managers so they can meet the increasingly complicated financial management demands of their job. This should lead to improved decision making by the manager, resulting in more efficient and effective operations.

SYSTEMS APPROACH TO MANAGEMENT

The systems approach to management provides a framework for viewing the foodservice operation as a whole as well as its interaction with the larger organization and with the environment. This approach is valuable for looking at the financial considerations of a foodservice operation.

A *system* is a set of interrelated elements that are coordinated to meet common goals and objectives. On the departmental level, there are clinical dietitians working with patients and administrative dietitians operating the food production area, which is comprised of many functional areas such as purchasing, receiving, vegetable preparation, salads, bakery, entree preparation, trayline, pot and pan washing, dishroom, and others. These work together to achieve the common goals and objectives of the department. An overall goal might be to provide nutritious food to patients and cafeteria customers within the budgetary guidelines established by the department. Other objectives might address issues such as nutrition education, a safe and satisfying work environment for employees, productivity levels, and specific profitability levels.

At the hospital level, administrators, physicians, and employees in diverse departments such as nursing, dietary, pharmacy, respiratory therapy,

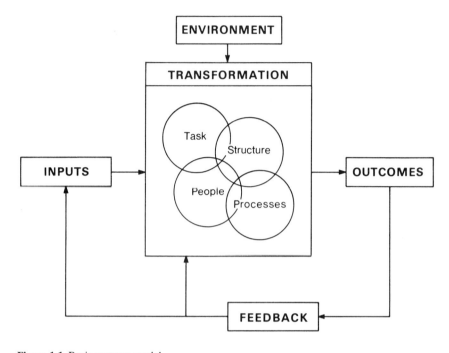

Figure 1-1 Basic systems model

radiology, and a host of others work together toward the common goal of providing health care at a competitive, cost-effective level. All components are important and must be integrated and coordinated in order to reach the common goal.

The *basic systems model* shown in Figure 1-1 has five components: inputs, transformation (or process), outcomes, feedback, and the environment. Each of these components and their interrelations must be considered for system evaluation, problem identification, change implementation, and decision making.

This basic systems model can be adapted specifically for use in foodservice (see Figure 1-2). A close examination of this model shows that financial management is related to and important in each component.

Inputs

Inputs are those resources that are brought into the system and that contribute to the production of the goods and/or services of the operation. Inputs include human resources (direct and indirect labor), material re-

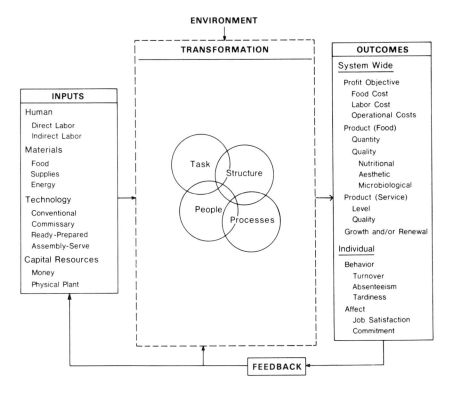

Figure 1-2 Foodservice systems model

sources (food, supplies, energy), capital resources (money, physical facility, equipment), and the technology of production. *Technology* is defined here as the materials and methods employed for production and includes the four basic production technologies in foodservice: conventional, commissary, ready-prepared, and assembly-serve.

Each input has a direct influence on the financial management of the organization. The number and skills of employees affect the dollars spent for labor. The quality, quantity, and type of food drastically affect the food cost. The specific food production system (conventional, commissary, ready-prepared, or assembly-serve) used in the operation also has a major impact on food and labor costs and costs associated with equipment, storage, and transportation.

Transformation

Transformation is the process by which the resources are changed into the desired products and/or services that meet the objectives of the operation. Basically, the transformation is what occurs in the foodservice operation. There are four basic components of the transformation stage of the foodservice system: task, people, structure, and processes.

Within the structure of the operation, several control mechanisms are in place. An effective foodservice system has established financial and record keeping systems, which are examples of one type of control mechanism, as shown in Figure 1-3.

There are many processes within a foodservice operation. Financial management is directly related to many of them, especially decision making, problem solving, planning and goal setting, and evaluation and control.

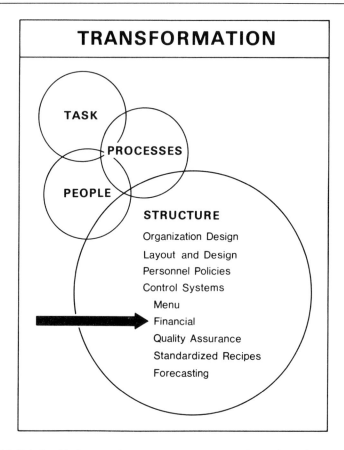

Figure 1-3 Relationship between financial control systems and transformation phase of systems model

Outcomes

Outcomes are the results of the transformation process. In foodservice operations, the outcomes include meals served, service provided to customers, profit, and employee satisfaction (to name just a few).

All foodservice operations have a profit objective. Some actively seek to make a profit, while others seek only to break even. Some operations may be subsidized. For example, some hospitals sell food to employees at cost as an employee benefit. The labor and operational costs are subsidized by administration.

Whatever the profit objective, a well-established financial control system must be in place. Financial records must be kept to provide management with information to be used for planning, evaluating the effectiveness of the operation, and making decisions about future courses of action.

Feedback

Feedback is information obtained about the performance (outcomes) of the operation that will affect future decisions about inputs and transformation. For example, if an operation makes less profit than planned, this information will be used to evaluate the inputs and transformations of the operation. Perhaps too much food was purchased, resulting in waste. Perhaps employees were not trained properly and served portions that were too large to customers. Any number of problems might exist that should be changed to improve the cost-effectiveness of the operation.

Environment

The final major component of the basic systems model is the environment. There are many factors external to the foodservice operation that have an impact on the operation. One of the major influences in the environment is related to the customer, client, or patient served. Demographic characteristics of the customer group, such as age, income, educational level, employment status, number of children, and religion, influence the values, expectations, and decisions made by the group. Public policy and the government agencies that enforce policies have a major impact on foodservice operations. Wage and hour laws, child labor laws, tip reporting, and taxation are all public policy issues that affect foodservice operations. Sanitation inspectors, who routinely inspect foodservice facilities, represent another environmental impact.

The Joint Commission on Accreditation of Healthcare Organizations (Joint Commission) is an external agency that inspects hospitals for quality standards. Other groups, such as the National Institute for the Foodservice Industry (NIFI), National Restaurant Association (NRA), American School Food Service Association (ASFSA), National Association of College and University Food Service (NACUFS), and the American Public Health Association (APHA), provide standards and self-monitoring guidelines for foodservice.

The systems model provides a systematic way to view an organization to identify problems, determine possible causes for problems, and establish strategies for correcting problems. The use of this model can help foodservice managers reach the goals and objectives of their operation.

FUNCTIONS OF MANAGEMENT

Planning, organizing, staffing, leading, and controlling are the basic functions of management. Successful financial management of a foodservice operation is related to each management function and requires a manager to perform all of them (see Figure 1-4).

Figure 1-4 Relationship between financial management and managerial functions

Planning

Budgeting is the basic planning mechanism in the financial management of the foodservice operation. A *budget* is a financial plan that projects the income, expenditures, and profit for a specified period of time. When well planned, the budget provides a guide for making financial decisions. Budgets are usually developed for one year, with breakdowns for each month. This is especially helpful when the volume of business (or patient census) has seasonal variations.

Staffing

Staffing is the function whereby the foodservice manager determines the number and skills of employees needed to perform the work required to reach the goals and objectives of the organization. It also includes recruiting, selecting, and orienting employees.

Scheduling is another staffing function of managers. Since labor is the largest cost in most foodservice operations, scheduling has a big impact on financial performance. In fact, high labor costs were the impetus to the development of alternate food production systems such as the commissary and ready-prepared systems. The consideration of these systems may be necessary for some managers, especially those located in areas where there is a shortage of labor.

Leading

Leading is the human relations function of the manager. Employee motivation is one of the challenges the foodservice manager faces in the leading function of management. Employee motivation is related to productivity, which has a direct effect on labor cost. *Goal setting with feedback* is a motivation technique that has been shown to have a positive impact on performance, energy conservation, safety behavior, and job satisfaction of employees.

Controlling

Controlling is the management function concerned with ensuring that plans are achieved. Feedback from the system is used to evaluate performance and, if goals and objectives are not being met, will indicate changes that will improve progress toward those goals.

In the planning process, the desired performance for the system is identified and measurement standards are set for performance. In the controlling process, actual performance is compared with desired performance. If the deviation or variance between actual and desired performance is beyond acceptable limits, corrective action must be taken to redirect efforts toward goal accomplishment.

To facilitate the control process, foodservice operations have several control systems in place. The most basic is the menu. The menu influences many decisions, including purchasing, staffing, production, equipment needs, and pricing. Standardized recipes are a necessity in foodservice to provide a product at a consistent quality, quantity, and price. Quality assurance systems are in place in most operations to insure the consistent quality and safety of products and services. Forecasting systems provide information upon which to base decisions such as purchasing, production quantity, number and scheduling of staff, and budgeting. Financial control systems are the focus of this book. These control systems are interrelated, and all must be in place to ensure goal attainment.

It is the purpose of this book to provide the reader with the theoretical and practical knowledge required to implement or use financial systems in the management of an effective and efficient foodservice operation. Specific tools are suggested for use in record keeping so that the manager will have the data necessary for decision making. Practical examples and suggestions for the use of these data are also provided.

Chapter 2

Performance and Expense Reports

Using the systems approach, the *performance* of a dietary department refers to the outcomes of the transformation process. According to the systems model presented in chapter 1, there are important outcomes at both the system-wide and individual levels. System-wide performance includes profit, food quality and quantity, service quality, and growth or renewal. At the individual level, there are both behavioral and affective outcomes.

Sink[1] identified seven performance measures for organizations: (1) efficiency, (2) effectiveness, (3) profitability, (4) productivity, (5) innovation, (6) quality of work life, and (7) quality. Performance is multidimensional, and these dimensions overlap. For example, productivity levels and efficiency affect profitability. Quality of work life affects absenteeism and turnover, which have a direct impact on costs. Thus, it is important to consider each dimension when evaluating the overall performance of an operation.

Because of the focus of this book, emphasis is given to those measures that relate most to direct costs. This chapter presents the important dimensions of cost, discusses the various costs in a dietary department, and provides guidelines for record keeping and expense reporting.

DIMENSIONS OF COST

Cost is the price incurred by the dietary department in providing goods and services. There are many costs involved, including costs for food, labor, supplies, energy, water, maintenance and repairs, printing, telephones, and many more. A knowledge of the actual cost of operating is important for making many decisions, such as planning operating budgets, purchasing equipment, renovating, and pricing goods and services. Therefore, it is

9

imperative that foodservice managers understand costs and be able to determine the actual costs for their department.

Cost Categories

Costs are usually classified into three categories: fixed, variable, and semivariable. These costs are categorized by their relation to the sales or business volume (Figure 2-1). *Fixed costs* are costs that do not vary with the volume of business or sales. They include overhead (occupation costs such as mortgage or rent, taxes, and insurance), advertising, maintenance and repairs, administrative, office, and depreciation expenses. While these expenses vary over time, they are not affected by the sales volume.

Variable costs are those costs that vary directly with the volume of sales (number of covers, number of patients, number of cafeteria meals, and/ or amount of catering). Food costs are directly related to the volume of sales and fit into the category of variable costs. Paper supplies (plates, bowls, cups) would be a variable cost if used for serving meals. Variable costs increase as sales increase and decrease as sales decrease.

Some costs have both a fixed and a variable component. These costs are called *semivariable costs*. Labor cost is the best example. The dietary department has a number of full-time equivalent (FTEs) employees that are always on the payroll. As the number of patients and/or customers (business or sales volume) increases, employees may be added. Thus, those full-time permanent employees represent the fixed labor cost, and the added employees (who are often temporary or part-time) represent the variable cost. For example, if a 200-bed hospital were to operate at only

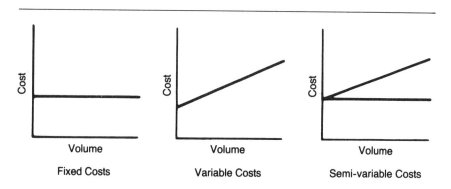

Figure 2-1 Relationship of cost to sales volume

50 percent occupancy, there would be some fixed-cost employees, including a department director, a clinical dietitian, a secretary, two cooks, and employees to work in salad preparation, vegetable preparation, trayline, cafeteria service, pots and pans, dishroom, and sanitation. The number of employees that would be employed regardless of volume is the fixed cost. If occupancy were to increase to 100 percent, more employees would be needed to meet the requirements of the additional number of meals that had to be produced and served. This is the variable portion of labor cost.

Controllable Costs

Another important cost concept is that some costs can be controlled while others cannot. *Controllable costs* are those costs a manager can change in the short run. Many costs in foodservice are controllable, including food, supply, labor, advertising, office expenses, postage, telephone, and energy. Notice that some of these controllable expenses are fixed and some are variable and semivariable.

Food costs can be controlled by purchasing less-expensive items, decreasing portion size, changing the menu to reflect lower-cost items and seasonal items, reducing waste, reducing spoilage, introducing controls to reduce theft, and training employees to improve food-handling skills. Labor costs can be controlled by reducing staff, decreasing turnover and absenteeism, training employees, scheduling, and production planning. These are only a few examples of how a manager can influence costs. By carefully tracking costs and implementing control systems, the manager can improve the operation's profitability.

Noncontrollable Costs

Noncontrollable costs are costs the manager cannot change in the short run. Overhead costs and depreciation expenses are examples. Overhead costs are usually dictated by administration as a percentage of usage or as a percentage of square footage of the facility occupied. The depreciation expense could change if assets were to increase, but the depreciation expense is predetermined by the depreciation method chosen.

Prime Costs

The *prime cost* refers to the total cost of food, beverages, and labor (including payroll, payroll taxes, and benefits). The prime cost is the largest percentage of cost in a foodservice operation and are costs that can be controlled by the manager. As a result, managers should focus the most attention on tracking and controlling these costs in order to affect the profitability of their operation or department.

FOODSERVICE COSTS

Awareness of and concern for costs vary among foodservice operators. The success of commercial operators has depended on their ability to determine and control costs. Conversely, for many years, managers of dietary departments in health care were not very concerned with determining the actual costs of running their department or with the realistic allocation of those costs to the appropriate cost centers. As a result, patient foodservice costs were artificially inflated. The cafeteria in many operations was operated at a loss, with prices for food based on raw food costs only.

It is a new day in health care. The increased accountability for health care costs brought about by DRGs has revolutionized hospitals. These changes have already had a major impact on dietary departments. Pressures to control costs and increase revenues will continue. As a result, record keeping and control systems to evaluate performance are critical to the success of the dietary department.

Food Costs

Food costs are a controllable expense; therefore, it is important to know actual food costs as compared with desired or projected food costs. Food cost is routinely determined in most foodservice operations in order to monitor performance and allocate costs. The allocation of these costs to the appropriate area may not always be done accurately.

The total food costs for a department may be determined on a daily, weekly, monthly, or yearly basis. For most dietary departments, food costs are determined on a monthly basis, and these figures are later used for preparation of monthly and end-of-year financial statements. Calculating food costs less often than monthly is not recommended because corrective action could not be taken soon enough if costs were too high.

Monthly food costs are determined as follows:

$$
\begin{array}{l}
\text{Beginning inventory} \\
+\,\text{Purchases} \\
\hline
\text{Total food available for use} \\
-\,\text{Ending inventory} \\
\hline
\text{Monthly food cost}
\end{array}
$$

To calculate monthly food costs, accurate records must be kept of food purchases. An inventory of foods on hand must also be taken on a monthly basis. A *perpetual inventory* is a continuous record of purchases and issues of food and supplies. This provides the manager with up-to-date information on the amount of product on hand. A *physical inventory* is an actual physical count of products on hand done on a periodic basis. Even if a perpetual inventory is maintained, it is recommended that a physical inventory be taken on a monthly basis to verify the perpetual inventory and provide an accurate determination of food cost for the period.

Physical Inventory

A physical inventory should be taken the last working day of each month. All foods should be included in the inventory, including those in dry storage, frozen storage, and refrigerated storage. A value is determined for the physical inventory using the inventory valuation method selected for the operation. This inventory value is used as the cost of the ending inventory for the month just passed and as the cost of the beginning inventory for the upcoming month. There are several methods of inventory valuation, each offering advantages and disadvantages.

Purchase Price Method. This method is based on the actual purchase price of the product. To use this method, the receiving clerk or stores clerk must write the actual purchase price on each food item received. As the physical inventory is taken, the number and price of each item are recorded. The value of the inventory is determined simply by adding the value of all products on hand. While it appears to be time-consuming on first impression, it may save time on the valuation calculation because all the cost information is readily available. Another advantage of this method is that it provides an actual value of the inventory based on the actual purchase price of the product.

Weighted Average Purchase Price Method. This method is based on an average price paid for products. To calculate the weighted average purchase price, multiply the number of units of each product in the opening inventory and those purchased during the month by the purchase price. Add these prices to find the total value of all units for a particular product, and divide by the total number of units. The major disadvantage with this method is that it is time-consuming and necessitates extensive records for each product.

First-In, First-Out Method (FIFO). This method assumes that the stock was rotated during the inventory period. In other words, the first unit of a product purchased was the first unit issued and used. To calculate the value of the inventory using this method, a count is taken of each product. The last price paid for the product is multiplied by the number of units on inventory.

Last-In, First-Out Method (LIFO). This method values the inventory by using the oldest price paid for each item in inventory. In other words, the latest purchase price (usually the most expensive, since prices usually increase) is used to determine the food cost. This method usually overestimates food cost and underestimates the value of the current inventory.

Latest Purchase Price Method. This method values the inventory based on replacement costs of items. Thus, the method uses the last purchase price for a product to determine the total value for those products.

Comparing Inventory Valuation Methods. A short case study illustrates the effects of the five methods on the value of the inventory. A foodservice operation's inventory records showed the following information for canned peach halves:

2/1 Opening inventory	7 units at $3.04 each
2/4 Purchased	12 units at 3.39 each
2/10 Purchased	12 units at 4.27 each
2/18 Purchased	6 units at 3.38 each
2/27 Purchased	6 units at 4.25 each
2/28 Ending inventory	13 units

Using the five inventory valuation methods, the value of the ending inventory is:

Purchase price method*	$46.78
Weighted average purchase price method	$48.10
FIFO method	$50.05
LIFO method	$41.62
Latest purchase price method	$55.25

*To determine the inventory value using this method, actual purchase price would be used. For this example, 13 unit prices were selected as they may have been in inventory.

As illustrated, the method used makes a big difference in the value of the inventory. For this one product, there is a range of $13.63. With an inventory of several hundred items, the difference would be substantial.

The method of inventory valuation is usually determined by the accounting department, perhaps with input from the dietary department manager. Once the method is determined, it does not change because of its impact on cost for that period. The actual cost would not change, but there would be a change in when those costs were reported. Thus, a valuation change distorts the financial results, which could affect a company's tax obligation. The Internal Revenue Service does not allow companies to change their inventory valuation at will because of the impact the change would have on taxes owed.

Food Cost Records

In addition to accurate inventory records, several other records should be kept in order to determine foodservice costs accurately and to help assign those costs to the appropriate cost center. Several cost centers may be established in a hospital, including patient service, nourishments, cafeteria, restaurant, coffee shop, vending, and catering. Innovation in hospital foodservice has resulted in the addition of new product lines, such as bakery sales, take-out "delis," and frozen dinners. Restaurant operations may establish cost centers for on-premise banquets, off-premise catering, take-out, and dining room. If such cost centers are established, it will be important to maintain an accurate accounting of food costs for these areas so that performance can be evaluated. Each cost should operate within budgetary guidelines specific to the cost center. Therefore, the maintenance of separate performance records will allow corrective action to be taken if the need should arise. Several records can be kept to provide the necessary evaluation data, including meal summaries, food selection forms, food purchase records, and storeroom requisitions.

Meal Summaries. Meal summaries are maintained in most foodservice operations to determine the number of meals served, the types of meals served, and the customer group to whom the meals were served. This information is useful in forecasting and assigning costs to the appropriate user group.

Exhibit 2-1 is a simple summary of a meals served form that might be used in a small hospital or extended care facility. This form necessitates that the foodservice supervisor record the number of patient, staff, and guest meals served each day.

Larger hospitals may need more sophisticated forms to provide additional information for more accurate forecasting. Food costs would be low for some diets, such as clear liquids, and labor costs would be high for blenderized diets. Exhibit 2-2 is an example of a more detailed form for recording meals served daily. Exhibit 2-3 is an example of a monthly summary for patient trays. An annual summary of diet types is provided in Exhibit 2-4.

Food Selection Forms. In order to be effective in controlling costs, using leftovers, and forecasting purchasing and production, it is important to have food selection data. There should be a mechanism in place to record the number of portions of each item selected for the patient area, cafeteria, restaurant, coffee shop, and/or vending operations. Exhibit 2-5 is one form that can be used for recording the usage of the various menu items on the trayline. This form allows recording of the number of items remaining, the

Exhibit 2-1 Summary of Meals Served

SUMMARY OF MEALS SERVED

Month:	Patients	Staff	Guests	Total
Day				
1				
2				
3				
4				
5				
6				
7				
8				
9				
10				
11				
12				
13				
14				
15				
16				
17				
18				
19				
20				
21				
22				
23				
24				
25				
26				
27				
28				

Exhibit 2-1 continued

Month:	Patients	Staff	Guests	Total
29				
30				
31				
Total				

total number of an item served, the run-out time for items, and the substitution used. This information is essential for forecasting production for the next menu cycle. Exhibit 2-6 is a cafeteria breakfast food item tally sheet, and Exhibit 2-7 is a tally sheet to be used for lunch and dinner. An alternate form for recording quantities selected in a cafeteria (or in a restaurant) is shown in Exhibit 2-8.

Monthly Food Purchases. A record of food purchases should be kept in order to determine the monthly food cost. This information should be recorded regularly as orders are delivered. It is useful to break down the food purchases by major food categories so that costs in each category can be monitored and corrective action can be taken where needed. Exhibit 2-9 is an example of a form that could be used for recording monthly food purchases. It has been used in extended care facilities and was developed to provide information on the major food categories of concern. For example, protein foods are the largest expense in foodservice operations and are a controllable expense that could make a big difference in food cost. The food categories can be modified to provide more specific information depending on the needs of the operation. For example, when this form was developed, coffee prices were very high and needed to be monitored. It is best to customize forms to meet the specific needs of the operation. This will eliminate the collection of data that will not be used. Another invoice spreadsheet is presented in Exhibit 2-10. This form records food and supplies.

Requisitions. Many operations provide food to other units. Examples include nourishments and coffee sent to offices or lounges. Costs of these foods need to be recorded separately and not charged to the food cost. Exhibit 2-11 is a form that could be used to record nourishment costs. Records of costs allow costs to be assigned to the appropriate area, provide information to monitor changes in costs over time, and sensitize the user to the cost of these items.

Exhibit 2-2 Summary of Meals Served

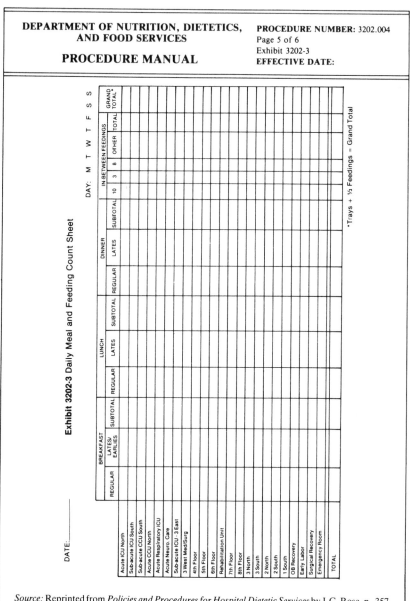

Source: Reprinted from *Policies and Procedures for Hospital Dietetic Services* by J.C. Rose, p. 357, Aspen Publishers, Inc., © 1983.

Exhibit 2-3 Monthly Summary for Patient Trays

DEPARTMENT OF NUTRITION, DIETETICS, AND FOOD SERVICES	PROCEDURE NUMBER: 3202.004
	Page 6 of 6
	Exhibit 3202-4
PROCEDURE MANUAL	EFFECTIVE DATE:

Exhibit 3202-4 Patient Trays Monthly Summary Form

MONTH		1	2	3	4	5	6	7	8	9	10	11	12	13	14	15	16	17	18	19	20	21	22	23	24	25	26	27	28	29	30	31	TOTAL
Acute ICU North	(6502)																																
Sub-acute ICU South	(6504)																																
Sub-acute CCU South	(6506)																																
Acute CCU North	(6508)																																
Acute Resp ICU	(6511)																																
Acute Neuro Care	(6513)																																
Sub-acute ICU 3E	(6514)																																
3 West Med /Surg	(6517)																																
4th Floor	(6519)																																
5th Floor	(6549)																																
6th Floor	(6553)																																
Rehabilitation Unit	(6554)																																
7th Floor	(6555)																																
8th Floor	(6559)																																
3 North	(6573)																																
3 South	(6575)																																
2 North	(6568)																																
2 South	(6571)																																
1 South	(6566)																																
OB Recovery	(6625)																																
Early Labor	(6618)																																
Surgical Recovery	(6615)																																
Emergency Room	(6695)																																
T O T A L																																	

Source: Reprinted from *Policies and Procedures for Hospital Dietetic Services* by J.C. Rose, p. 358, Aspen Publishers, Inc., © 1983.

Exhibit 2-4 Annual Summary of Diet Types

DEPARTMENT OF NUTRITION, DIETETICS, AND FOOD SERVICES	PROCEDURE NUMBER: 3202.007
	Page 6 of 6
	Exhibit 3202-7
PROCEDURE MANUAL	EFFECTIVE DATE:

Exhibit 3202-7 Annual Diet Type Monthly Summary Form

YEAR: _____

Rows: GENERAL, SOFT (MECH & CHEM), FULL LIQUID, CLEAR LIQUID, BLAND/LOW RESIDUE, FAT CONTROLLED, CAL. REST./DIAB, SODIUM RESTRICTED, RENAL, COMBINATION, TUBE FEEDING, OTHER, NPO, GRAND TOTAL

Columns (each with TOTAL and % OF TOTAL): JAN, FEB, MARCH*, APRIL, MAY, JUNE*, JULY, AUG, SEPT*, OCT, NOV, DEC, ANNUAL (GRAND TOTAL, GRAND % OF TOTAL)

*ASSIGNED MONTHS TO BE ANALYZED

Source: Reprinted from *Policies and Procedures for Hospital Dietetic Services* by J.C. Rose, p. 364, Aspen Publishers, Inc., © 1983.

Exhibit 2-5 Usage of Menu Items on Trayline

DEPARTMENT OF NUTRITION, DIETETICS, AND FOOD SERVICES	PROCEDURE NUMBER: 3202.011

DEPARTMENT OF NUTRITION, DIETETICS, AND FOOD SERVICES

PROCEDURE MANUAL

PROCEDURE NUMBER: 3202.011
Page 3 of 4
Exhibit 3202-13
EFFECTIVE DATE:

Exhibit 3202-13 Trayline Station Food Item Tally

DAY: M T W T F S S   MEAL: B L D
DATE: _____   FOOD SERVER: _____
STATION: _____   SUPERVISOR: _____

FOOD ITEM	NUMBER PREPARED	NUMBER REMAINING	TOTAL NUMBER SERVED

RUN-OUT ITEMS	RUN-OUT TIME	SUBSTITUTED ITEMS	# OF SERVINGS SUBSTITUTED

Source: Reprinted from *Policies and Procedures for Hospital Dietetic Services* by J.C. Rose, p. 381, Aspen Publishers, Inc., © 1983.

Exhibit 2-6 Cafeteria Breakfast Food Item Tally Sheet

DEPARTMENT OF NUTRITION, DIETETICS AND FOOD SERVICES	PROCEDURE NUMBER: 3104.001
PROCEDURE MANUAL	Page 4 of 6 Exhibit 3104-3 **EFFECTIVE DATE:**

Exhibit 3104-3 Cafeteria Breakfast Food Item Tally Sheet

DATE:_____   DAY: M T W T F S S

FOOD ITEM	BREAKFAST PLACED ON LINE	TOTAL
BREAKFAST ENTREE'S: (PANS)		
BREAKFAST BREADS: (SERVINGS)		

Source: Reprinted from *Policies and Procedures for Hospital Dietetic Services* by J.C. Rose, p. 322, Aspen Publishers, Inc., © 1983.

Exhibit 2-7 Lunch and Dinner Cafeteria Food Item Tally Sheet

DEPARTMENT OF NUTRITION, DIETETICS, AND FOOD SERVICES **PROCEDURE MANUAL**	**PROCEDURE NUMBER:** 3104.001 Page 5 of 6 Exhibit 3104-4 **EFFECTIVE DATE:**

Exhibit 3104-4 Cafeteria Food Item Tally Sheet

LUNCH AND DINNER MEALS

DATE:_____   DAY: M T W T F S S   CYCLE: I II

FOOD ITEM	LUNCH		DINNER	
	PLACED ON LINE	TOTAL	PLACED ON LINE	TOTAL
HOT FOODS: (PANS)				
DESSERTS: (SERVINGS)				

Source: Reprinted from *Policies and Procedures for Hospital Dietetic Services* by J.C. Rose, p. 323, Aspen Publishers, Inc., © 1983.

Exhibit 2-8 Cafeteria Quantities Selected

DEPARTMENT OF NUTRITION, DIETETICS AND FOOD SERVICES

PROCEDURE MANUAL

PROCEDURE NUMBER: 3104.001
Page 6 of 6
Exhibit 3104-5
EFFECTIVE DATE:

Exhibit 3104-5 Cafeteria Quantities Selected

MEAL:	DAY:	CYCLE: I II
FOOD ITEMS	DATES	

Source: Reprinted from *Policies and Procedures for Hospital Dietetic Services* by J.C. Rose, p. 324, Aspen Publishers, Inc., © 1983.

Exhibit 2-9 Monthly Food Purchases

Facility _____

Date: From _____ To _____

Date	Vendor	Invoice No.	Grocery	Meat, Fish, Poultry, Eggs	Dairy, Cheese	Bakery	Coffee, Tea, Sanka
Total monthly food purchases by group							
Amount budgeted by group							
Total over/under budget							

Total Food Purchases _____

Total Food Budget _____

Total Under/Over Budget _____

Exhibit 2-10 Purchases Record

Facility _____

Record Period _____

Prepared by _____

Date	Vendor	Invoice No.	Grocery	Meat, Fish, Poultry	Dairy	Frozen Foods	Bakery	Produce	Total Food	Disposables	China, Flatware, Utensils	Cleaning Supplies	Office Supplies	Other	Total Supply
Total															

Food Costs | Supply Costs

Exhibit 2-11 Nourishment Costs

DEPARTMENT OF NUTRITION, DIETETICS, AND FOOD SERVICES PROCEDURE MANUAL	PROCEDURE NUMBER: 3202.002 Page 3 of 3 Exhibit 3202-1 EFFECTIVE DATE:

Exhibit 3202-1 Nursing Unit Food Stock Request Form

DIVISION_____ DATE_____

COST CENTER_____   FUNCTION_____

REQUESTED BY:_____RECEIVED BY:_____

	AMOUNT	COST
JUICES		
Apple		
Cranberry		
Orange		
Grape		
Grapefruit		
Prune		
Salt-free Crackers		
Saltine Crackers		
Melba Toast		
MILK & ICE CREAM		
Whole Milk - ½ pint		
Skim Milk - ½ pint		
Buttermilk - ½ pint		
Chocolate Milk - ½ pint		
Ice Cream		
Sherbet		
CARBONATED DRINKS		
Coke		
Dr. Pepper		
7-Up		
Diet 7-Up		
Diet Dr. Pepper		
R-C 100		
SOUPS		
Chicken Noodle Canned		
Instant		
Vegetable Canned		
Instant		
Beef Broth		
Chicken Broth		
Low Sodium Chicken Broth		
Low Sodium Beef Broth		
Gelatin		
Diet Gelatin		

Source: Reprinted from *Policies and Procedures for Hospital Dietetic Services* by J.C. Rose, p. 351, Aspen Publishers, Inc., © 1983.

Exhibit 2-12 Transfer Form

		Date: _____
		Department: _____
		Department Code: _____

Transfer to: _____

Department Code: _____

Item	Cost per Unit	Units Ordered	Total Cost
Total			

Received by: _____

Exhibit 2-12 is a sample transfer form. Specific cost information is provided to the user of the goods, and the form provides a record of transfers so that more accurate food costs can be determined for patient and non-patient foodservice or for other cost centers in an operation. For example, in a restaurant that does catering, a transfer might be made to that cost center.

Labor Costs

Labor is the single largest cost in most foodservice operations. Labor costs are semivariable and controllable. Since management has some control over labor costs, it is important to focus attention on monitoring labor costs and implementing control measures to contain them.

Labor costs can be divided into two categories: direct and indirect. Direct labor costs include all costs (wages and salaries, payroll taxes, and benefits) related to the production of the product or service. Indirect labor costs include costs related to the personnel management functions, such as interviewing, selecting, training, and keeping payroll and personnel records.

Productivity

Productivity issues have been in the forefront of industry concerns in the United States for the past decade. Continued pressure exerted from foreign countries with higher productivity levels and lower labor costs has forced industry leaders to examine productivity and identify ways of improving productivity to keep the United States competitive in the world market.

Productivity is no less a concern to the foodservice industry. In fact, in foodservice operations only 40 to 45 percent of employees' time is spent productively. Since foodservice is so labor intensive, this low productivity rate is a major concern for managers.

It is important to understand how productivity is defined and how it is measured. In the systems model discussed in chapter 1, three basic components were identified: input, transformation, and output. Input is the resources brought into the organization, including food and labor. Output is the outcomes (such as food and service) produced by the operation. Transformation includes the processes of the organization that convert inputs into outputs. Based on the systems model, *productivity* is defined as a ratio of inputs to outputs.

Calculating Equivalent Meals. Output is usually defined as either the number of meals served or the number of equivalent meals served, depending on the type of operation. In a cafeteria, using the actual number of customers would be misleading in productivity calculations. Many cafeteria customers may purchase a single item rather than an entire meal. To adjust for this and to improve the accuracy of productivity measures, the number of equivalent meals is calculated.

The first step in determining the number of equivalent meals is calculating an equivalent meal factor. The *equivalent meal factor* is defined as the sum of the selling price of an entree, starch, vegetable, salad, dessert, bread, butter, and beverage at the noon meal. For example, the following are the average selling prices for the meal components:

Entree	$1.15
Starch	.40
Vegetable	.40
Salad	.50
Dessert	.60
Bread	.20
Butter	.05
Beverage	.40
Total	$3.70

The total, $3.70, is the equivalent meal factor for this cafeteria.

The second step is converting sales into equivalent meals:

$$\text{Equivalent meals} = \text{Sales/Equivalent meal factor.}$$

Following through on the example, the cafeteria sales for one month were $111,000. The number of equivalent meals is calculated as follows:

$$\text{Equivalent meals} = \$111,000/\$3.70 = 30,000.$$

The number of equivalent meals is used to calculate productivity measures for the operation.

Productivity Measures. The most common measure of productivity in foodservice is the number of meals (output) per labor hour (input). This relationship can also be expressed as the number of minutes required to prepare each meal or as the number of labor hours per 100 meals. Since any one of these indicators is appropriate, the manager should select one and consistently use it for the department. The selection can be based on past measures used by the department and on the method used by comparison groups. The following formulas are used to calculate each productivity ratio:

$$1.\ \text{Meals per labor hour} = \frac{\text{Number of meals produced}}{\text{Number of labor hours}}.$$

For example, records for a nursing home showed that 7,440 meals were served during one month and 1,353 hours were worked by foodservice employees. To determine the productivity level for the facility, use the following calculation:

$$\text{Meals per labor hour} = \frac{7,440\ \text{meals}}{1,353\ \text{labor hours}} = 5.5\ \text{meals per labor hour.}$$

$$2.\ \text{Labor minutes per meal} = \frac{60\ \text{minutes per hour}}{\text{Meals per labor hour}}.$$

Using the example, the minutes per meal are:

$$\text{Labor minutes per meal} = \frac{60\ \text{minutes}}{5.5\ \text{meals}} = 10.9,\ \text{or 11.}$$

$$3.\ \text{Labor hours per 100 meals} = \frac{\text{Number of paid labor hours}}{\text{Meals served/100}}.$$

Using the example, the labor hours per 100 meals are calculated as follows:

$$\text{Labor hours per 100 meals} = \frac{1,353 \text{ hours}}{7,440 \text{ meals}/100}$$
$$= \frac{1,353 \text{ hours}}{74.4}$$
$$= 18.2.$$

Productivity in foodservice varies depending on a number of factors, including:

- type of food production system (conventional, commissary, ready-prepared, or assembly-serve)
- level of service (full-service vs. self-serve)
- type of tray delivery system (for health care operations)
- menu (number and complexity of items)
- number of special items (i.e., modified diets requiring special preparation, such as pureeing or grinding)
- level of preparation of purchased items
- equipment
- layout and design of production facility
- production planning
- staffing and scheduling
- training and skill level of employees
- motivation of employees
- size of facility (number of customers).

Average productivity levels for various types of foodservice operations are:

Quick service restaurant	9.5 meals per labor hour
Luxury restaurant	1.4 meals per labor hour
Family restaurant	4.8 meals per labor hour
Cafeteria	5.5 meals per labor hour
Acute care facility	3.5 meals per labor hour
Extended care facility	5 meals per labor hour
School foodservice	13–15 meals per labor hour.

These productivity levels reflect industry averages and should serve only as a guide for determining staffing needs and evaluating performance. To control labor costs effectively, the manager should assess employee performance, identify methods for reducing labor costs, and monitor productivity over time. While it is useful to compare productivity levels of an operation with industry averages, it is critical to compare productivity levels for the operation over time. Because there are many factors that influence productivity, comparisons with other operations may mean little because of differences in the operation. Therefore, it may be best to let an operation serve as its own comparison. In that way, deviations in productivity can be determined and improvement identified.

Calculating Full-Time Equivalents (FTE)

An FTE is a calculation based on one employee who works on a full-time basis for a specific period of time, such as a day, week, month, or year. An FTE does not represent the actual employee but rather an equivalent based on the following number of hours:

- 8 hours per day
- 40 hours per week
- 173.33 hours per month
- 2,080 hours per year.

The FTE calculation is used to determine staffing needs for the department. The number of FTEs can also serve as a comparison statistic for evaluating productivity in a foodservice operation.

For example, to determine staffing needs, the number of meals for a given period are projected. For a 250-bed hospital, it is projected that 23,250 patient meals and 31,000 cafeteria meals will be served next month for a total of 54,250 meals. Historical data show that the productivity level for the operation is 3.5 meals per labor hour. To determine the number of labor hours needed for the next month, use the following calculations:

$$\text{Labor hours} = \frac{54,250 \text{ meals}}{3.5 \text{ meals per labor hour}}$$
$$= 15,500 \text{ labor hours.}$$

$$\text{Number of FTEs} = \frac{15,500 \text{ labor hours}}{173.33 \text{ hours per FTE}}$$
$$= 89.5 \text{ FTEs.}$$

The number of FTEs can be calculated for a day, week, month, or year, depending on need. For any FTE calculation, the total number of labor hours required is divided by the number of hours per FTE for that time period. For example:

1. Daily FTEs = Labor hours per day/8 hours per FTE per day.
   Example: Daily FTEs = 60 hours/8 hours = 7.5 FTEs.

2. Weekly FTEs = Labor hours per week/40 hours per FTE per week.
   Example: Weekly FTEs = 400 hours/40 hours = 10 FTEs.
3. Monthly FTEs = Labor hours per month/173.3 hours per FTE per month.
   Example: Monthly FTEs = 1993 hours/173.3 hours = 11.5 FTEs.
4. Yearly FTEs = Labor hours per year/2,080 hours per FTE per year.
   Example: Yearly FTEs = 19,760 hours/2,080 hours = 9.5 FTEs.

Calculating Actual Labor Costs

When calculating labor costs, most managers immediately think of the wages and salaries paid to employees. Actually, labor costs are much higher when the cost of payroll taxes and benefits are taken into account. To reflect actual labor costs accurately, these costs must be included in calculations.

There are three legally required benefits that must be paid to employees: Social Security tax (FICA), unemployment tax, and workers' compensation. Many other benefits may also be provided, such as vacation leave, sick leave, holidays, health insurance, life insurance, retirement plans, uniform allowances, and meals. For each benefit, there is a cost incurred by the organization.

Table 2-1 shows an example of calculations for labor costs in 1988. This example illustrates the difference in the wage rate per hour and the actual cost per hour for the operation. In this example, the cost of benefits is about 24 percent of the base pay per hour. Benefit costs normally range from 15 to 30 percent for foodservice operations. The percentage may be even higher for managerial employees, especially those employed in the private sector.

The important point is that all costs of labor must be considered when determining the actual costs and evaluating the performance of an oper-

Table 2-1 Total Labor Costs at Two Wage Levels

Hourly wage	$3.35	$5.00
Social Security (7.51%)	.25	.38
Unemployment tax	.11	.16
Workers' compensation	.07	.10
Health insurance	.15	.22
Vacation (2 weeks/year)	.15	.22
Sick leave (1 week/year)	.08	.11
Total cost per hour	4.16	6.19
Cost per productive hour[1]	$8.32	$12.38

[1]Assumes a 50% productivity rate, which is typical for foodservice employees.

ation. Labor costs, even when the majority of employees are paid at the minimum wage, are a significant portion of the costs for an operation. To ensure efficiency and profitability, these costs must be controlled.

Several labor cost indicators may be calculated to provide the data necessary to monitor actual costs and labor cost trends over time. Labor cost percentages (labor %) and ratios of labor costs per day and per meal are calculated in many operations.

Labor cost percentages may be calculated in relation to total departmental expenses or in relation to sales, depending on the type and needs of the operation. The formulas for calculating these percentages are:

1. Labor % of expenses $= \dfrac{\text{Total labor cost}}{\text{Total departmental expenses}}$.

   Example: Labor % of expenses $= \dfrac{\$13,500}{\$30,000} = 45\%$.

2. Labor % of sales $= \dfrac{\text{Total labor cost}}{\text{Total \$ sales}}$.

   Example: Labor % of sales $= \dfrac{\$13,500}{\$35,500} = 38\%$.

It may also be useful to know the relationship of labor costs to a certain time period or to the number of meals served. These cost relationships can be calculated using these formulas:

1. Payroll cost per day = sum of (hourly rate for each employee × number hours worked)

2. Payroll cost per meal $= \dfrac{\text{Payroll cost per day}}{\text{Number meals served per day}}$

3. Labor cost per day = Payroll cost per day + Other direct costs (e.g., fringe benefits)

4. Labor cost per meal $= \dfrac{\text{Labor cost per day}}{\text{Number meals served per day}}$.

In addition to payroll costs, there are other labor-related costs for the organization: orientation and training of employees, turnover, and absenteeism. These costs must also be considered.

Calculating Costs of Absenteeism. For some foodservice operations, absenteeism is a major problem. It can also be expensive when extra employees must be hired to do the work of absent employees. Absenteeism should be monitored and the costs determined. The following formula is used to calculate absenteeism:

$$\text{Absentee rate} = \frac{\text{Total absences in period}}{\text{Total FTE} \times \text{Workdays in period}} \times 100.$$

Example: Absentee rate $= \dfrac{32 \text{ absences}}{26.5 \text{ FTE} \times 22 \text{ days}} \times 100 = 5.5\%.$

What is the cost to the department of a 5.5 percent absentee rate? Using the example, the costs can be calculated:

26.5 FTEs × 2,080 hours per year = 55,120 hours per year
55,120 hours × 0.055 = 3,032 absence hours per year
3,032 hours/8 hours per day = 379 absent days
3,032 hours absent/2,080 hours per FTE = 1.5 FTE.

To cover absences, 1.5 FTEs would need to be hired. Using the two wage rates calculated earlier, the actual cost to the department for these absences would be:

$3.35/hour + 24% benefits × 2,080 yearly hours × 1.5 FTE = $12,960
$5.00/hour + 24% benefits × 2,080 hours × 1.5 FTE = $19,344

As shown in the example, absenteeism is a substantial cost and must be controlled. Several actions can be taken by management to control absenteeism:

- Communicate attendance expectations to employees in orientation sessions.
- Establish an attendance criterion for raises, promotions, and other rewards, and communicate it to employees.
- Maintain written documentation on the attendance of each employee.
- Review the cost of absenteeism with employees.
- Provide employees with feedback about their attendance.
- Take corrective action with individual employees when absenteeism is excessive.
- Maintain a high level of employee morale.

Calculating Costs of Turnover. While some turnover has positive benefits for the organization, too much turnover is undesirable and can be expensive for the organization. High levels of turnover can be indicative of problems, such as low wages or poor working conditions. The turnover rate should be calculated and, if it is too high, possible causes for the turnover should be identified.

The following formula is used for determining the turnover rate:

$$\text{Turnover rate } = \frac{\text{Total terminations in period}}{\text{Number employed in period}} \times 100.$$

Example: Turnover rate $= \frac{2}{80} \times 100 = 2.5\%$ turnover.

The optimum turnover rate is such that poor-performing employees leave the organization and high-performing employees remain. When selecting new hires, there will never be a 100 percent success rate for predicting performance. Thus, it is desirable that some employees resign. Too much turnover can be costly to the organization; therefore, it is desirable to keep the yearly turnover rate below 10 percent.

There are several costs related to turnover, including:

- *Orientation:* Paid time is involved in orientation for both supervisors and new employees.
- *Training:* Paid time is involved for supervisors, the new hire, and current employees involved in training.
- *Productivity:* Until new employees learn their jobs, they may not be as productive as experienced employees.
- *Recruitment and selection:* Advertising costs are incurred in this process as well as time of the supervisor to interview and select the new employee.
- *Bookkeeping:* Record keeping is required when an employee is terminated or hired.
- *Unemployment tax:* The tax burden for the organization increases as former employees use the benefit.

Supply Costs

Supply costs, which fit into the category of controllable expenses, are incurred by all foodservice operations. Since management has some impact on supply costs, it is important that these costs be determined and monitored.

To facilitate the monitoring and controlling of supply costs, the following supply cost categories are usually established: disposables, china, flatware and utensils, cleaning supplies, office supplies, and other. Disposables are a variable cost, while cleaning supplies, china, flatware, and utensils are semivariable costs.

Some foodservice operations post the cost of breakables, such as china and glassware, to sensitize employees to the high cost of these items and to encourage careful handling of the items. A weekly or monthly posting of the number of items broken and the total cost of breakage provides good feedback to employees.

Supply costs are usually budgeted as a percentage of sales or in relation to the volume. This depends on the type of operation. For example, for a restaurant, supply costs as a percentage of sales (supply cost %) is almost always used. In a hospital, consideration is given to sales (cafeteria or restaurant) and to patient load (occupancy percentage). In all operations, the breakdown between disposables and china depends on what is used for service. To determine the supply cost %, use the formula:

$$\text{Supply cost \%} = \text{Cost of supplies/Sales (revenue).}$$

Example: Supply cost % = $500/$10,000 = 5%.

The cost of supplies in relation to sales and over time should be monitored. It is important to note any variance between actual supply costs and budgeted (projected) supply costs. It may also be useful to determine the percentage of total supply costs represented by each of the supply categories. Trends in usage of the various supplies should be monitored.

Utility Costs

Utility costs can be a significant expense for most foodservice operations. Utilities include gas, electricity, and water. Energy costs, including gas and electricity, became a critical issue for foodservice in the late 1970s and early 1980s as the price of oil skyrocketed. The watchword in those days was *conservation.* As a result, equipment manufacturers designed equipment that was more energy efficient, and operators adopted energy conservation practices. While energy prices have moderated, they will continue to be cyclical. Since energy costs are controllable, it is important to determine actual energy costs, monitor the costs over time, and implement energy-saving techniques.

The type of food production system has a major impact on energy costs depending on the amount of on-site production. These costs should be evaluated when determining changes in the food production technology.

Tracking utility costs is useful for determining changes in consumption patterns. The NRA provides useful forms in its *Facilities Operations Man-*

Exhibit 2-13 Utility Consumption and Tracking Form

UTILITY CONSUMPTION AND TRACKING
Year _____ 1988

Month	Gas therms			Electricity						Water gallons					
	1987	1988	Percent Change	Use KWH			Demand KW			1987	1988	Percent Change	1987	1988	Percent Change
				1987	1988	Percent Change	1987	1988	Percent Change						
JAN															
FEB															
MAR															
APR															
MAY															
JUN															
JUL															
AUG															
SEP															
OCT															
NOV															
DEC															

Form B

Source: Reprinted from *Facilities Operations Manual*, published by the National Restaurant Association, © 1986.

Exhibit 2-14 Total Utility Consumption, Tracking, and Cost Form

TOTAL UTILITY CONSUMPTION, TRACKING, AND COST

Month	Total MBTU		Total Utility Cost		MBTU per customer		Utility Cost as Percent of Sales	
	———	Percent Change	———	Percent Change	———	Percent Change	———	Percent Change
JAN								
FEB								
MAR								
APR								
MAY								
JUN								
JUL								
AUG								
SEP								
OCT								
NOV								
DEC								

Form C

Source: Reprinted from *Facilities Operations Manual*, published by the National Restaurant Association, © 1986.

ual. The utility consumption and tracking form (Exhibit 2-13) allows a monthly comparison of gas, electricity, and water usage with the same month of the last year. If these usages vary significantly, the manager can pinpoint needed changes.

Another form developed by the NRA provides for tracking of consumption and utility costs (Exhibit 2-14) for the current year as compared with the past year. The right-hand column provides for tracking of utility costs as a percentage of sales. This tracking allows the manager to identify deviations from last year and from the budgeted amount for utility costs. Controlling utility costs, just as controlling other costs, increases the bottom line—profit—for the operation.

Depreciation

Depreciation is defined as the decrease in value of a fixed asset over its useful life. For a foodservice operation, items that depreciate include the building, furniture, equipment, fixtures, automobiles, and trucks. This decrease in value (depreciation) is caused by usage of the asset. There is wear and tear on these fixed assets. For example, equipment in a production unit becomes less valuable over time because it wears out and becomes less efficient.

Including depreciation expenses is a way to recognize the inevitable obsolescence and need to replace fixed assets. Another way of thinking about depreciation is that it is a savings plan to set aside funds for the replacement unit.

The depreciation expense calculation is based on the depreciable portion of the cost of an asset. The depreciable portion is the new cost (the initial cost of the asset) minus the salvage value. Depreciation expense (as shown on the income statement) is the total annual cost. Accumulated depreciation (as shown on the balance sheet) is the cumulative total of depreciation for each asset. Thus, at the end of the last year of the useful life of a fixed asset, its net value on the balance sheet (value of asset minus accumulated depreciation) will be equal to the salvage value.

The three most commonly used methods of calculating depreciation are:

1. straight-line
2. declining balance
3. sum-of-the-years' digits (SOYD).

Straight-Line Method

Straight-line depreciation is based on the theory that the asset will wear out and decline in value evenly over its life. The straight-line depreciation expense for a particular asset is the same amount for every period of the asset's useful life. It is calculated as follows:

$$\text{Annual depreciation expense} = \frac{\text{Cost} - \text{Salvage value}}{\text{Years of useful life}}.$$

The depreciation expense for any particular month is 1/12th of the annual expense. At the end of the accounting year, accumulated depreciation is equal to 1/12th of the annual depreciation expense multiplied by the total number of months the operation has had the asset. Thus, if an operation has had an asset for three years (36 months), the accumulated depreciation would be 36/12ths of the annual depreciation expense (or three times the annual depreciation). Remember, accumulated depreciation is a cumulative total that is offset against the original cost of the asset. The depreciation expense is the expense recognized for the current period (i.e., month, quarter, or year).

For example, a piece of equipment has an original cost of $24,000, a usable life of eight years, and a salvage value of $2,400. The depreciable portion (net cost) is $21,600 ($24,000 minus $2,400). Using the straight-line method the annual depreciation is:

$$\frac{\$24,000 - \$2,400}{8} = \$2,700 \text{ per year.}$$

Thus, each year, a depreciation expense of $2,700 would be claimed for the piece of equipment (assuming the asset was in service for the entire year).

Declining Balance Method

The calculation of depreciation using the *declining balance method* considers the original cost of the asset and ignores the salvage value. Using this method, the first step is to compute the annual percentage rate of depreciation for straight-line depreciation based on the asset's useful life. For example, an asset with a five-year life declines in value by 20 percent each year on a straight-line basis. An asset with an eight-year life declines by 12.5 percent each year (one year is 12.5 percent of eight years).

The declining balance method usually used is known as the "double the declining balance" (DDB) method. The rate used for this method is twice the *percentage* calculated by the straight-line method. To calculate the first year's depreciation, this rate is multiplied by the initial cost of the asset. For subsequent years, depreciation expense is calculated by multiplying the rate by the net value of the asset (cost minus the previous period

Table 2-2 Accelerated Depreciation: Double Declining Balance (DDB) Method

Year	Cost	Beginning Accumulated Depreciation[1]	Beginning Net Value[2]	DDB Rate	Yearly Depreciation Expense[3]	Ending Net Value[4]
1	$24,000	$ 0	$24,000	25%	$6,000	$18,000
2	24,000	6,000	18,000	25%	4,500	13,500
3	24,000	10,500	13,500	25%	3,375	10,125
4	24,000	13,875	10,125	25%	2,531	7,594
5	24,000	16,406	7,594	25%	1,898	5,695
6	24,000	18,304	5,696	25%	1,424	4,272
7	24,000	19,728	4,272	25%	1,068	3,204
8	24,000	20,796	3,204	25%	801	2,403

[1]Beginning accumulated depreciation is the cumulative total of depreciation expenses.
[2]Beginning new value equals the cost minus the beginning accumulated depreciation.
[3]Depreciation expense for the year equals the DDB rate times the beginning net value.
[4]Ending net value equals beginning net value minus depreciation expense for the year.

accumulated depreciation). The monthly depreciation with this method is 1/12th of the annual rate.

Using the same asset used to calculate the straight-line depreciation, the depreciation expenses using the DDB method are shown in Table 2-2. This example shows that the amount of depreciation expense over the life of the asset is about the same with the DDB and the straight-line methods. To verify this, compare the ending net value of the asset for each method. In both cases, the ending net value is about $2,400. This is the salvage value; there is no reason to depreciate the asset below the salvage value. If the declining balance method had indicated depreciation in the last year that would have reduced the value of the asset to below the salvage value, the depreciation expense should be reduced to a level that would make the net value equal to the salvage value.

Although the total depreciation over the life of the asset is about the same using either method, when the expense is recognized differs a great deal. The recognition of the expense is accelerated with the declining balance method. This early expense recognition makes cash flow available sooner and causes the income tax benefits from the depreciation expense to occur sooner. In other words, total expenses are higher at an earlier time because the depreciation expense is higher. This decreases the operating income and, therefore, income taxes. Keep in mind that the manager wants to pay as little as possible in taxes.

Sum-of-the-Years' Digits (SOYD) Method

The *SOYD method of depreciation* is similar to the declining balance method in that each accelerates the depreciation expense. A larger portion of the total depreciation is recognized in the earlier years of the asset's life than with the straight-line method. The calculation of the depreciation expense for every period is based on the depreciable value (cost minus salvage value) of the asset. The depreciable value is multiplied by a different factor each period.

The denominator of the factor remains the same throughout the life of the asset. It is calculated by adding the number of years in the life of the asset. Thus, an asset with a four-year life will have a factor denominator of 10 (4 + 3 + 2 + 1). This accounts for the method's name.

The numerator of the factor decreases each year of the life of the asset and is equal to the remaining life of the asset. The asset with a four-year life has a numerator of 4 the first year, 3 the second year, 2 the third year, and 1 the last year. The easiest way to derive the factor numerator is simply to assign the reverse of the years to each year beginning with the first year. Then, when looking down the list of years, each year should appear (but in reverse order) in the numerator.

Combining the numerator and denominator, for an asset with a four-year life, the manager would use the following factors to calculate the depreciation expense:

Year 1 factor   4/10
Year 2 factor   3/10
Year 3 factor   2/10
Year 4 factor   1/10

Applying this method to the same asset used as an example with the other depreciation methods, the SOYD depreciation method calculations for annual depreciation expenses are shown in Table 2-3.

Table 2-3 Accelerated Depreciation: Sum-of-the-Years' Digits (SOYD) Method

Year	Depreciable Basis[1]	SOYD Factor	Depreciation Expense[2]	Accumulated Depreciation[3]	Cost	Net Year-End Value[4]
1	$21,600	8/36	$4,800	$ 4,800	$24,000	$19,200
2	21,600	7/36	4,200	9,000	24,000	15,000
3	21,600	6/36	3,600	12,600	24,000	11,400
4	21,600	5/36	3,000	15,600	24,000	8,400
5	21,600	4/36	2,400	18,000	24,000	6,000
6	21,600	3/36	1,800	19,800	24,000	4,200
7	21,600	2/36	1,200	21,000	24,000	3,000
8	21,600	1/36	600	21,600	24,000	2,400

[1]Depreciable basis = Cost minus salvage value ($24,000 − $2,400).
[2]Depreciation expense = Depreciable basis times SOYD Factor.
[3]Accumulated depreciation = Current year depreciation plus all previous depreciation.
[4]Net year end value = Cost minus accumulated depreciation.

The SOYD method is an accelerated method, as is the DDB method. The accelerated methods are frequently used for income tax purposes because of the early reduction in income taxes. Operations that are in highly competitive markets or in situations of tight liquidity should consider using an accelerated method of depreciation because of the cash flow benefit. The recognition of depreciation early in the life of an asset also makes the cash available for reinvestment at an accelerated rate. The reasoning is the same as for the tax benefits with accelerated methods.

Other Costs

There are many other costs involved in a foodservice operation that are a small percentage of the total expense. It is nonetheless important to

Table 2-4 The Restaurant Industry Dollar*

	Full-Menu Tableservice	Limited-Menu Tableservice	Limited-Menu No Tableservice	Cafeteria
Where It Came From*				
Food Sales	72.9	80.8	97.9	92.5
Beverage Sales	23.1	17.9	1.7	4.8
Other Income	4.0	1.3	0.4	2.7
Where It Went*				
Cost of Food Sold	30.5	32.0	32.4	39.1
Cost of Beverage Sold	6.7	5.0	0.3	1.5
Payroll	27.5	24.6	25.0	25.7
Employee Benefits	4.5	3.3	1.6	6.2
Direct Operating Expenses	6.8	6.6	4.6	5.9
Music and Entertainment	1.1	0.8	N	N
Advertising and Promotion	2.0	2.1	4.2	1.3
Utilities	2.5	2.5	4.0	2.3
Administrative & General	4.0	3.1	4.8	2.1
Repairs & Maintenance	1.6	1.3	1.5	0.9
Rent	3.6	4.5	4.2	4.0
Property Taxes	0.5	0.5	0.5	0.2
Other Taxes	0.7	0.6	0.2	0.3
Property Insurance	1.2	1.1	1.0	0.4
Interest	1.0	1.2	1.7	1.0
Depreciation	2.7	2.6	3.8	2.1
Other Deductions	0.7	1.9	2.0	0.1
Net Income Before Income Taxes	2.4	6.3	8.2	6.9

*Based on 1986 data.
**All figures are weighted averages.
N—less than 0.1 percent.

Source: Courtesy of National Restaurant Association, © 1987.

Exhibit 2-15 Monthly Food Service Cost Summary

Institution _____

Month _____

Food Cost

    Beginning inventory . . . . . $ _____

    Add total purchases . . . . . $ _____ $ _____

    Subtract closing inventory . . . . $ _____

Total Food Cost . . . . $ _____

Cost of Supplies

    Beginning inventory . . . . . $ _____

    Add total purchases . . . . . $ _____ $ _____

    Subtract closing inventory . . . . $ _____

Total Cost of Supplies . . . . $ _____

Labor and Other Expenses

    Labor . . . . $ _____   _____ labor hours/month

    Nutritional supplements . . . $ _____

    Special activities . . . . . . $ _____

    Other operating expenses . . $ _____

    Misc. expenses . . . . $ _____

Total Labor and Other Expenses . . . . $ _____

Number of Meals Served		**Food Service Cost Summary**	
Patient	_____	Food	$ _____
Staff	_____	Supplies	$ _____
Guests	_____	Labor & other	$ _____
Total Number of Meals/Month	_____	Total cost	$ _____
		Less revenue	$ _____
		Total Cost	$ _____

Food Service Costs per Meal

Cost per meal $ _____ = Total food service cost $ _____ + Total

                     number of meals per month _____

Food Service Costs per Patient Day

Cost per patient day $ _____ = Total food service cost $ _____ + Total

                     number of patient days _____

recognize these costs and to control them. They may include interest, insurance, taxes, repairs and maintenance, rent, music and entertainment, advertising and promotion, office supplies, office equipment, printing, telephone, postage, and data processing.

Equipment can be a large initial investment for foodservice operations. While equipment is not discussed in this book, there are a number of good books about the selection and use of foodservice equipment. Related to equipment, there are initial costs, depreciation costs, and repair and maintenance costs.

Costs for each operation vary, depending on many management decisions. Ultimately, the targeted percentage of each cost in relation to sales depends on many factors. It might be useful, however, to know industry

---

Exhibit 2-16 Food Service Performance Report

Facility _____

Record Period _____

Prepared by _____

Meal Count

	Current Period	Percentage of Total	Year-to-Date Meals Served
Patient meals			
Cafeteria meals			
Complimentary meals			
Catered meals			
Other			
Total meals			

Food Costs

	Grocery	Meat, Fish, Poultry	Dairy	Frozen Foods	Bakery	Produce	Total Food Cost
Beginning inventory							
Plus purchases							
Minus ending inventory							
Total gross cost							
% of total food cost							
Minus nourishments							
Minus transfers							
Net cost of food							
Year-to-date food cost							

Exhibit 2-16 continued

Supply Costs

	Disposables	China, Flatware, Utensils	Cleaning Supplies	Office Supplies	Other	Total Supplies
Beginning inventory						
Plus purchases						
Minus ending inventory						
Total gross cost						
% of total supply cost						
Minus transfers						
Net cost of supplies						
Year-to-date supply cost						

Labor Costs

Patient labor costs _____
Nonpatient labor costs _____
Allocated labor _____
Total labor costs _____
Total labor hours _____
Total FTE _____

Meal Cost Summary

	Patient		Nonpatient	
	Actual	Budgeted	Actual	Budgeted
Total meal equivalents served				
Total food cost				
Total supply cost				
Total labor cost				
Meals per labor hour				
Cost per meal				

averages for costs. The NRA regularly monitors sources of revenues and expenses for the restaurant industry. Table 2-4 presents the restaurant industry dollar for various types of restaurants, including full-menu tableservice, limited-menu tableservice, limited-menu no tableservice, and cafeterias. This Table shows the differences in income and expenses and, thus, net income of the various types of operations and provides guidelines for managers as to how their operation is performing in relation to industry standards.

PERFORMANCE SUMMARY REPORTS

Several individual expense reports have been introduced in this chapter. It is also useful to develop summary reports to consolidate the information and provide an indication of overall performance for the operation. They usually summarize business volume, food costs, supply costs, and labor costs. These reports are usually compiled on a weekly, monthly, and yearly basis.

Exhibit 2-17 Labor Cost Allocation Form

Position	Total Labor Hours	Total Labor Cost	Patient		Nonpatient	
			Hours	Cost	Hours	Cost

The monthly food service cost summary form (Exhibit 2-15) was developed for use in small extended care facilities. It allows the compilation of the number of meals served, food costs, supply costs, labor costs, and other costs. From these data, the cost per meal and the cost per patient day can be calculated. Productivity measures can also be determined from the information available on this form.

A more extensive food service performance report (Exhibit 2-16) may be used to provide the manager with more detailed information about the performance of the operation. This form provides a summary of information related to business volume, food costs, labor costs, and supply costs. It also provides space for a breakdown of food costs into the following categories:

- grocery
- meat, fish, and poultry
- dairy
- frozen foods
- bakery
- produce.

This breakdown by food category helps the manager monitor food costs. If food costs are too high, the breakdown of costs by category will help the manager identify where costs are out of line and where changes can be made to alleviate the problem.

Notice, too, that labor costs are divided into patient and nonpatient services. Earlier, the idea of allocating costs to the appropriate cost center was introduced. Thus, costs can be allocated to patient or nonpatient services, to appropriate cost centers, or to particular product lines, depending on the needs of the foodservice operation. It is important to allocate costs so that the true costs incurred for a particular activity or cost center are known. Only if the actual costs are known can the pricing of services be effective. In addition, the performance of the various cost centers can be accurately evaluated only if the true costs are known. For example, consider the economic feasibility of continuing a bakery sales operation. To make that determination, the manager must have accurate data about revenue in relation to costs.

Exhibit 2-17 is a form for allocating labor costs. Labor costs are usually allocated based on the percentage of the worker's time that is spent in work related to a particular area. Some employees spend all their time working in one area. For example, line servers may work only in the cafeteria, so all the cost involved in employing these workers are charged to nonpatient service. Some employees, such as dishwashers, pot washers, and sanitation workers are involved with both patient and nonpatient services. Periodic time studies should be done to determine the percentage of time these workers devote to activities related to patient and to nonpatient services. Other workers, e.g., cooks, vegetable preparation workers, bakers, and other food production workers, may be involved with production of food that will be used for patients, the cafeteria, and catered events. These employee costs must be divided based on the employee's contribution to the area. For example, a cook prepares soup for patients, the cafeteria, and a catering menu. One hour is spent making 300 portions: 150 for patient service, 75 for the cafeteria, and 75 for a catered event. If the labor cost for making the soup is $6, then $3 (50 percent) of the cost would be charged to patient service, $1.50 (25 percent) charged to cafeteria service, and $1.50 (25 percent) charged to catering.

Exhibit 2-18 Supply and Direct Cost Allocation Form

Cost Description	Total Cost	Patient Cost	Nonpatient Cost	Other

Food cost for the soup can be calculated in a similar manner. Fifty percent of the total food cost for the soup would be charged to patient service, 25 percent to the cafeteria, and 25 percent to catering. Another method for allocating food cost is through storeroom issues. Using this method, food is charged to a cost center as it is issued from the storeroom.

Supplies and other direct costs should also be allocated to the appropriate area or cost center. This may be done using direct costs for the area or using a percentage of the total used by the various areas. Exhibit 2-18 is a form for use in the allocation of supply and direct costs.

NOTE

1. Scott D. Sink, *Productivity Management: Planning, Measurement and Evaluation, Control and Improvement* (New York: John Wiley & Sons, 1985).

Chapter 3

Cost Control in Purchasing

In the systems model for foodservice operations, food and supplies were identified as inputs or resources brought into the system. These are variable costs for the operation, and both are controllable costs. Purchasing is one important point in the product flow through the system at which costs of food and supplies can be controlled. In this chapter, cost control in purchasing is discussed in relation to product specifications, methods of purchasing, vendor selection and evaluation, inventory control and ordering, and receiving orders.

PRODUCT SPECIFICATIONS

An important part of the planning process in a foodservice operation is determining the menu, the standardized recipes, and the quality of products necessary to produce those menu items. To ensure that the appropriate products are purchased for the menu items produced, specifications should be developed for products purchased. *Specifications* are statements about the required qualities of a product. A specification for a product is a detailed list of characteristics the product must have for its intended use. The specification is a communication tool between the buyer and the seller of a product that must be developed so that it is understood by both parties. In developing specifications, it is important to remember that they may determine the availability of the product, the supplier that can provide the product, and the price of the product.

Types of Specifications

Technical, approved-brand, and performance are three types of specifications that might be used for purchasing products for foodservice operations. The specification type used will depend on the product being purchased. Each type of specification indicates the desired quality. *Technical specifications* indicate a quality measure that can be objectively measured. *Approved-brand specifications* indicate quality by designation of a specific brand. *Performance specifications* indicate quality by specifying the functional requirements for a product. Some specifications might combine the types of specifications, including both technical and performance requirements for a product.

Technical Specifications

Technical specifications are developed for products that have a quality dimension that can be measured objectively. They would be developed for products that are graded in relation to specified standards. For example, when ordering beef, the purchaser must specify quality and yield grades. These grade standards are established by the United States Department of Agriculture (USDA).

USDA has established grading standards for meat and dairy products, fruits, vegetables, poultry, and eggs. A technical specification would be developed for any of these products and for equipment and cleaning supplies.

Approved-Brand Specifications

Approved-brand specifications are developed for items for which there is a brand preference. For example, a certain brand of cracker may be preferred to serve with salads. These specifications can be written for food products, cleaning supplies, or disposables.

Performance Specifications

Performance specifications are developed to indicate the functional capabilities of a product. For example, a restaurant doing catering might write specifications for insulated food carriers that can keep food at or above 145° for one hour.

Guidelines for Developing Specifications

Specifications can be effective communication tools in purchasing and can ensure that the appropriate product is purchased at the best price. Several guidelines should be followed in developing effective specifications:

1. Be clear and concise in writing the specifications. Include only the necessary information.

2. Be specific enough to get the desired product but not so specific that only one product from one distributor is acceptable. Limiting the acceptable products decreases the competition and usually results in higher prices.
3. Develop specifications using standard identification codes and industry terminology. For example, the Institutional Meat Purchase Specifications (IMPS) published by the USDA give cut identification numbers and specifications for fresh beef, pork, lamb and mutton, and veal and calf. Purchase specifications are also established for cured, dried, and smoked beef and pork products. These industry standards would be used to develop specifications for meat products.
4. All components of the specification must be measurable. For example, if the specification designated 3/4-in thick T-bone steaks, the thickness could be measured. Or if 6-oz portions of tenderloin steaks were ordered, the weight of the steaks could be verified.
5. Specifications should be fair both to the seller and the buyer.
6. The product specification should be able to be met by several suppliers or vendors. The rationale for this guideline is that the more potential vendors there are for the product, the more competitive pricing will be, resulting in a lower prices for the operation.
7. Be realistic in developing specifications. The time spent developing specifications should ensure that quality is met and that costs are reduced. If cost savings are not being realized, then the time could be spent more effectively in other aspects of managing the operation.

Writing Specifications

When beginning the process of writing specifications, the menu items for which the products are being purchased should be carefully reviewed. The specifications should be developed based on the intended use of the product. This will ensure that the appropriate product is purchased at the lowest possible price. For example, if tomatoes were needed for spaghetti sauce, tomato pieces would be specified rather than whole tomatoes. Tomato pieces are less expensive and produce the desired results for the menu item. If stewed tomatoes were on the menu, whole tomatoes would be purchased.

Specifications should include:

- name of product
- quality level (grade, yield, brand, or other quality specification)
- size of product (weight, number per unit, measurements)
- unit on which price will be based.

Specifications may also contain other information, including:

- test or inspection that will be given to product
- cost or quantity limitations
- services required (such as delivery days and times).

Other information to be included in the specification depends on the type of product being ordered.

Meats. Meat products are a major portion of the food cost for most operations, so it is especially important that specifications be written for them. There is a wide variation in the quality of meat products available, which further necessitates the careful development of specifications to ensure that the desired product is purchased.

Meat is federally inspected and stamped with a round inspection stamp (Figure 3-1). Beef is also graded for quality and yield. The quality and yield grade stamps, placed on the carcass, are illustrated in Figure 3-1.

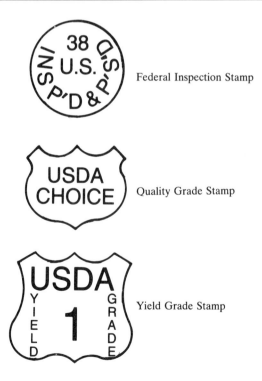

Federal Inspection Stamp

Quality Grade Stamp

Yield Grade Stamp

Figure 3-1 USDA meat stamps. *Source:* United States Department of Agriculture.

Table 3-1 USDA Quality and Yield Grades for Beef

Quality Grades	Yield Grades[1]				
	1	*2*	*3*	*4*	*5*
U.S. Prime			X	X	X
U.S. Choice		X	X	X	
U.S. Select		X	X		
U.S. Standard	X	X	X		
U.S. Commercial		X	X	X	X
U.S. Utility		X	X	X	
U.S. Cutter		X	X		
U.S. Canner		X	X		

[1]The yield grades reflect differences in yields of boneless, closely trimmed, retail cuts. As such, they also reflect differences in the overall fatness of carcasses and cuts. Yield Grade 1 is the highest yield of retail cuts and the least amount of fat trim. Yield Grade 5 is the lowest yield of retail cuts and the highest amount of fat trim.

Source: United States Department of Agricultural, Agricultural Marketing Service, Livestock Division, Washington, D.C., January 1975. *Note:* U.S. Select replaced U.S. Good effective November 23, 1987.

There are eight quality grades and five yield grades for beef (Table 3-1). The grade required should be included in the specification.

Meat specifications may also include:

- weight range
- portion size (weight and thickness)
- fat limitations (including fat content for ground meat and thickness of fat covering for steaks and roasts)
- state of refrigeration (chilled or frozen)
- age
- cutting instructions
- tying instructions.

An example of a meat specification is provided in Table 3-2.

Canned Goods. Canned products may be described by including information about:

- type or style
- pack
- syrup density

Table 3-2 Specification for Beef T-Bone Steak

Product	Beef T-bone steak
IMPS number	1174
Grade	U.S. Choice, Yield Grade 2
Weight range	8 oz ± 1/2 oz
Fat limitations	Not to exceed 1/2 inch
Packaging	20 individual portions, 10-lb box
State of refrigeration	Fresh, ship chilled at temperatures ranging from 33 to 40 degrees

- size (or count)
- specific gravity.

An example of a specification for a canned fruit and for a canned vegetable is given in Table 3-3.

Fresh Fruits and Vegetables. Specifications for fresh fruits and vegetables may include:

- variety (e.g., red delicious apples might be purchased for the vending machine and winesaps for pies)
- geographic origin
- weight
- count
- degree of maturity or ripeness.

Table 3-3 Canned Fruit and Vegetable Specifications

Fruit

Product	Fruit Cocktail
Grade	U.S. Grade A
Syrup density	Heavy (18'-22' Brix)
Minimum drained weight	72 oz per no. 10 can
Contents	Diced peaches, pears, pineapple, whole seedless grapes, red cherries
Purchase unit	6/10

Vegetable

Product	Beans, green
Grade	U.S. Grade A (Fancy)
Style	Whole, cut, stringless
Type	Blue Lake
Size	No. 2 sieve
Minimum drained weight	65 oz per no. 10 can
Purchase unit	6/10

Dairy Products. Dairy product specifications might include:

- temperature upon delivery
- milk fat content
- milk solids
- bacteria count.

What To Avoid in Writing Specifications

To maximize the effectiveness of specifications, several things should be avoided:

- *Establishing unreasonable requirements for vendors:* Be realistic about delivery of products, tolerance limits, quantities purchased, and costs of the products.
- *Establishing quality levels that are too high.*
- *Writing specifications so broadly that everything is acceptable.*
- *Unchanging specifications:* Specifications must be modified to meet the changing needs for the season, menu, customers, and technological changes of the operation.

METHODS OF PURCHASING

Once decisions are made about what products must be purchased and the appropriate specifications are developed, a decision must be made as to how the purchases will be made. Informal and formal purchasing procedures may be used depending on the product, the quantity of product used, the time available, and the organizational guidelines. Steps in the purchasing process, including both formal and informal purchasing methods, are summarized in Figure 3-2.

Informal Purchasing

Informal purchasing occurs when price quotations and purchase orders are made by telephone or through a salesperson who comes to the operation. Most small operations, because of time constraints, the volume of product use, or the lack of a formalized system for purchasing, use informal purchasing. When using informal purchasing, the buyer should obtain price quotes from at least two sources to ensure that competitive prices are charged for purchases.

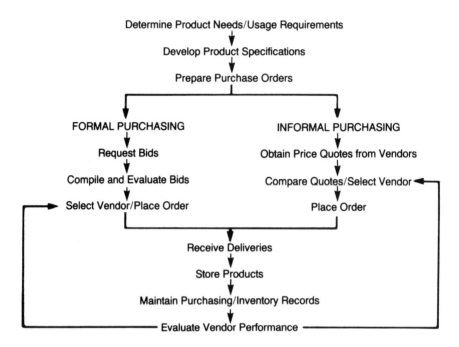

Figure 3-2 Purchasing process

Formal Purchasing

Formal purchasing occurs when competitive bids are obtained for products being purchased. Government agencies, operating with federal, state, or local funding, are usually required to use the competitive bidding process. Commercial foodservices and private institutions may choose the competitive bidding process in an effort to reduce costs. Competitive bidding is especially important for products that are used in large volumes.

Competitive Bidding

Competitive bidding is effective when there are several vendors of food in an area that are willing to bid competitively to provide products and/or services. Product specifications are given to potential vendors, and the vendors give a price quotation. The buyer can then evaluate the bids and select the one that provides the required product at the lowest price. Competitive bids are either daily bids or fixed bids, depending on the product being purchased.

Daily Bids. Daily bids are obtained for items for which prices fluctuate dramatically over the course of the year. For example, produce prices vary according to the season of the year and to production levels. In fact, there is an almost daily fluctuation in produce prices. Since the season for blueberries is May to September, prices for blueberries are lowest during that time. If a natural disaster were to occur, for example, a freeze in Florida that killed orange trees or prolonged flooding in the California lettuce fields, production quantities for those products would be decreased, resulting in higher costs. Because of the limited control over these events, vendors are not willing to commit to prices for the future.

When using the daily bid, the buyer develops a list of potential vendors. Contact is made with these vendors by telephone to obtain price bids. The bids are recorded on a daily bid form (Exhibit 3-1). The form can be individualized to include only the products routinely purchased for an operation. Once bids are obtained, an order is placed with the preferred vendor.

Exhibit 3-1 Daily Bid Form for Produce

Product	Purchase Unit	Amount Needed	Amount on Hand	Amount To Order	Price Quotation Vendor[1]		
					1	2	3
Apples							
Table	113 ct						
Baking	113 ct						
Asparagus	lb crate						
Avocado	lb crate						
Bananas	40-lb box						
Beans, green	bushel						
Blueberries	crate						
Broccoli	crate						
Cabbage	50-lb bag						

continues

Exhibit 3-1 continued

Product	Purchase Unit	Amount Needed	Amount on Hand	Amount To Order	Price Quotation Vendor[1]		
					1	2	3
Cantaloupe	lb						
Carrots	50-lb bag						
Cauliflower	crate						
Celery	crate						
Cucumbers	bushel						
Endive	lb						
Escarole	lb						
Grapefruit	64 ct						
Grapes, Thompson seedless	lb						
Lemons	165 ct						
Lettuce, iceberg	case						
Limes	lb						
Mushrooms	lb						
Onions	50-lb bag						
Oranges	88 ct						
Peppers	lb						
Potatoes, baking	120 ct						
Radishes	lb						
Spinach	bushel						
Strawberries	crate						
Sweet potatoes	bushel						
Tomatoes	5 × 6 lug						
Watermelon	lb						

[1]Vendor 1   Smith's Produce
Vendor 2   Allied Food Distributors
Vendor 3   Big Al's Fresh Produce

Many vendors have established minimum purchase orders because of the high cost of delivery. If small orders are placed, it may be necessary to order all products from the same vendor. If so, it would be necessary to calculate the total order cost for each vendor and select the vendor that provided the lowest overall cost, rather than comparing single items.

Fixed Bids. Fixed bids are obtained essentially for nonperishable products that will be used in large quantities over a long time period. Bid requests are developed and include the specifications for the products open for bidding. Vendors submit price quotations for the products, and the vendor is selected. Government operations must accept the vendor offering the lowest price. Other operations are not required to accept the lowest bid, but if the vendor can meet the product specifications, the lowest bid should be accepted.

Independent, Central, and Group Purchasing

Purchasing may be done by an individual unit or by groups of individual units. Each has advantages and disadvantages for the operations.

Independent Purchasing

Independent purchasing occurs when purchasing is done by the individual unit. For example, in a hospital a dietary department may do all its own purchasing of products. This has the advantage that people trained in foodservice purchase and receive all items, increasing the likelihood that the appropriate products at the appropriate quality level will be available to the operation.

Central Purchasing

Central purchasing occurs when purchasing is done for the entire operation by a central purchasing office. For example, some hospitals have a central purchasing office that orders, receives, and inventories goods for the entire hospital. The advantage is that all purchasing functions are centralized, resulting in centralized control of the bidding process, accounting, computerized systems, and inventory. These functions are usually carried out by individuals with training in the respective area. This results in control of the purchasing function by the hospital.

A major disadvantage of central purchasing is that purchasing may be done by individuals with little or no foodservice experience. Thus, good communication must exist between the foodservice and purchasing units to ensure that the appropriate products are purchased in the appropriate quantities.

Central purchasing is often done by commercial chain foodservice operations. In this case, mass purchasing results in cost savings. It also ensures consistency in products used throughout the nation, one of the advantages of chain foodservice operations. Receiving and inventory control are still handled by the individual foodservice operations.

Group Purchasing

Group purchasing involves independent operations joining together to form a buying group. Participating foodservice managers agree on specifications for products that will be purchased. As cost containment pressures increase, group purchasing will be one way to decrease food costs. Group purchasing will be most useful to small operations that do not purchase food in quantities sufficient to obtain volume discounts.

The major advantage of group purchasing is the increased buying power of the group because of the larger volumes purchased. These larger volumes encourage competition and more competitive bidding among vendors. Other advantages of group purchasing include:

- There is a better opportunity to obtain the desired product quality because there is more choice in suppliers.
- Stockouts may be reduced if central warehousing is done for the purchasing group. A larger inventory can be maintained without a financial strain on any one operation.
- Greater control may be maintained over purchasing.

A major disadvantage may be the need to agree on specifications for the products to be purchased. If each operation uses its own specifications, the advantages of group purchasing will be lost. Therefore, managers must compromise in the development of product specifications to take full advantage of group purchasing. In addition, independent operators may not be able to take advantage of specials from other vendors. Menus may need to be standardized and changes in menus limited.

VENDOR SELECTION AND EVALUATION

In most situations, several vendors are available to supply products. Only in isolated, rural areas are vendors limited to one or two. Because of the availability of numerous vendors, buyers must select vendors that will meet their needs and evaluate the performance of the selected vendors.

Selecting a Vendor

The first step in selecting a vendor is to determine the availability of vendors. Information can be obtained about vendors from a variety of sources, including personal experience, information from the purchasing department, managers at other foodservice operations, members of professional organizations such as the NRA or the American Society of Hospital Food Service Administrators, trade and food shows, sales people, brokers, the Better Business Bureau, and even the Yellow Pages of the telephone directory.

Once the availability of vendors is determined, information can be collected about those vendors. Important information that should be collected includes:

- quality of products
- price
- minimum order quantity
- geographic location
- warranty
- service (may include frequency of delivery; time of delivery; new product information; frequency of outages; follow-up on problems such as damaged merchandise or incorrect product delivered; special services such as menu cost analysis, menu planning, or computer management applications).

There is no hard-and-fast rule about the number of vendors that should be used routinely. The number depends on many factors, such as the quantity of products used, product availability, the number of available vendors, the minimum order requirements of vendors, location, and record keeping and accounting time.

Most small operations have three or four vendors, including bakery, dairy, produce, and general food and supply. In addition to these vendors, larger operations usually have two or more vendors that supply the wide range of food and supply products. A separate meat vendor may also be used. While there is no general rule as to how many vendors to use, the operation should not have so many vendors that it becomes cumbersome to order, keep records, and pay bills. On the other hand, the number of vendors should not be restricted to the point that competition would be eliminated.

Evaluating a Vendor

After selecting a vendor, a procedure for the ongoing evaluation of vendor performance should be implemented. A form similar to the one in Exhibit 3-2 could be used for the evaluation. This form includes criteria for evaluating several important aspects that might affect vendor effectiveness for a foodservice operation, including factors about the products, service, company, and sales personnel. Numerical ratings can be calculated for each vendor and used to make comparisons concerning which vendor to select or retain.

Exhibit 3-2 Vendor Evaluation Form

Vendor: _____   Date: _____

Rating Scale: Excellent   = 2
Good   = 1
Unacceptable = 0

Criterion	Rating
Product Quality	
Consistency	
Price	
Availability	
Service Timely delivery	
Frequency of delivery	
Condition of product upon delivery	
Accuracy of deliveries	
Handling of complaints	
Courtesy of delivery personnel	
Deliveries in emergencies	
Company Size	

Exhibit 3-2 continued

Criterion	Rating
Product selection	
Financial stability	
Location	
Service orientation	
Management policies	
Accuracy of invoices	
Timely handling of credits/invoice adjustments	
Sales Personnel Knowledge of company policies and procedures	
Knowledge of product lines	
Interest in needs of operation	
Willingness to provide information about products	
Provides price quotes in an accurate and timely manner	
Makes sales calls at frequency needed by operation	
Schedules sales calls	
Handles complaints promptly	

Total Score _____

INVENTORY CONTROL AND ORDERING

If the basic function of purchasing is to provide the right product at the right time and price, the relationship between the timing and price must be considered. On the one hand, the manager of a foodservice operation wants to have the products on hand to produce the menu items offered. Telling customers that a menu item they order is unavailable will not create goodwill and could decrease repeat business for the operation. On the other hand, having too large an inventory can be expensive. If the inventory is too large, money is tied up in inventory and is not being used to its best advantage. There are also other costs involved in ordering and maintaining inventory, such as storage costs (more square feet will be needed as inventory quantities increase), insurance on inventory, and personnel costs to maintain the storeroom, take inventory, and calculate the cost of goods on hand. Maintaining too large an inventory may increase spoilage and theft. Thus, it is useful to look at some techniques to determine the appropriate quantities of products to order and when they should be ordered.

INVENTORY TURNOVER

An *inventory turnover rate* can be calculated to determine the frequency at which the inventory is being used. The basic formula is:

$$\text{Inventory turnover rate} = \frac{\text{Annual cost of goods sold}}{\text{Average \$ value of inventory}}.$$

An example of the use of the inventory turnover rate formula is:

$$\text{Inventory turnover rate} = \frac{\$120,000}{\$5,000} = 24.$$

To find the monthly inventory turnover rate, calculate the cost of goods sold for the month using the formula in chapter 2. To determine the average dollar value of the monthly inventory, use the formula:

$$\text{Average dollar value of monthly inventory} = (\text{Beginning of month inventory} + \text{End of month inventory})/2.$$

A restaurant's monthly inventory records included the following data:

Beginning inventory	$ 6,500
Ending inventory	7,900
Purchases	18,050

The monthly inventory turnover rate for the restaurant would be:

$$\begin{aligned} \text{Inventory turnover rate} &= \frac{6,500 + 18,050 - 7,900}{(6,500 + 7,900)/2} \\ &= \frac{16,650}{7,200} \\ &= 2.3. \end{aligned}$$

For food inventories, the average turnover rate ranges from 24 to 48 times annually. For liquor inventories, the average turnover rate is seven to ten times per year.

If the inventory turnover rate is much higher than the average, it may indicate that the operation cannot afford to purchase in sufficient quantities, which may result in higher costs of products. A high rate may also indicate that the operation cannot obtain credit from vendors, which lowers the competitive buying power of the operation, resulting in higher costs.

An inventory turnover rate that is much lower than the average suggests that too much of the operation's money is tied up in inventory. This inadequate utilization of the operation's assets results in decreased profitability. Low turnover may also indicate that merchandise is old and not of the best quality when it is sold, which could have negative impacts on customer satisfaction with the product.

The inventory turnover rate should be calculated on an ongoing basis (usually monthly) in foodservice operations. The inventory turnover rate varies, depending on the type of operation (e.g., quick-service restaurants with daily deliveries have high inventory turnover rates). It is important for each operation to establish what its usual inventory turnover rate is and monitor deviations from its own baseline (or standard). This rate is an indicator of how effectively assets are managed and can be indicative of operational success.

Inventory Control Methods

The goal of purchasing is to have adequate products available for production and service while maintaining the minimum inventory investment possible. Three methods are available to the foodservice operator to determine when products should be purchased and what quantity should be purchased. These three methods include the economic order quantity (EOQ) method, the ABC method, and the minimum-maximum method.

Economic Order Quantity

The *EOQ formula* can be used to minimize the costs of purchasing and maintaining inventories:

$$EOQ = 2FU/PC$$

where F = fixed cost of ordering; U = usage of product annually; P = purchase price per unit; and C = carrying costs as a percentage of inventory. The fixed cost of ordering includes costs related to ordering, bookkeeping, paying invoices, and data processing. The carrying costs include costs such as the cost of keeping capital invested in inventory, storage costs, insurance, handling, deterioration, and breakage.

As an example of calculating the EOQ, a school serves 750 tacos 18 times during the school year. The taco shells cost $5 for a case of 200 shells. It is calculated that the fixed cost of ordering is $6 and the carrying costs are 15 percent. The EOQ for this product is:

$$EOQ = \sqrt{\frac{2 \times \$6 \times 68}{\$5 \times .15}}$$

$$= \sqrt{\frac{816}{0.75}}$$

$$= \sqrt{1088}$$

= 33 cases (rounded up to the nearest whole number).

If 33 cases should be ordered each time, the next question is how often should orders be placed. To calculate the number of orders each year for the taco shells, the annual usage is divided by the EOQ (number of units to order each time). In the example, the formula is:

Number of orders annually = 68/33

= 2.06, or 2 times (rounded to nearest whole number).

A margin of safety could be added if desired.

The EOQ formula is not commonly used in foodservice operations but may be beneficial in operations using large quantities. Unless inventory control is computerized, the procedure is cumbersome to calculate and may not be a good use of management resources.

Several conditions may exist that are not taken into account in the EOQ, such as variations in demand, seasonal changes, discounts for quantity purchases, shipping costs, and the risk of obsolescence.[1] The presence of these conditions will limit the usefulness of the EOQ formula for determining order quantities.

ABC Method

The basis for the *ABC method* is that a small number of products account for the major value of the inventory and that those products should be monitored most closely. Using this method, products are divided into three categories: *A* items have a high cost and are a high percentage of the value of the inventory; *B* items have moderate cost; and *C* items are a low percentage of the value of the inventory.

A items usually represent only 15 to 20 percent of the total number of inventory items but account for 75 to 80 percent of the value of the inventory. Items such as meats and liquor are examples of *A* items. These items should be monitored closely to determine how much and when to order. The inventory of *A* items should be kept to a minimum. Careful control of these items should be maintained in the operation. These items may be locked in separate storage rooms, refrigerators, or cages for which there are a limited number of keys. Usage of these items should be monitored and should match purchases.

B items usually represent 20 to 25 percent of the total number of items in the inventory and account for 10 to 15 percent of the value of the inventory. While these items should be ordered with care and monitored routinely, they do not require the close scrutiny and control that the *A* items require.

C items represent the majority of the inventory items (60 to 65 percent) yet account for a small portion of the overall value of the inventory (5 to 10 percent). Items such as flour, baking powder, yeast, breakfast cereal, and paper supplies are examples of *C* items. While it is important to control all costs, the emphasis on cost control is not placed on these items.

The ABC method sets priorities for control of inventory items by category and helps the manager determine which products cost the most and, therefore, require the most careful monitoring and control.

Minimum-Maximum Method

This method of inventory control requires the establishment of minimum and maximum levels of each product that should be kept in inventory. This provides guidelines for when to order and how much to order.

The order quantity for each product is established based on the quantity of the product that is normally used according to past records. A margin of safety for the item is determined based on how long it would take to receive a delivery and on anticipated fluctuations in demand for the product. The minimum level for each product, then, is the *margin of safety*. When this minimum level is reached, it is time to reorder. This minimum level, or reorder point, is the lowest stock order that can be maintained without stockouts.

The maximum level for each item is the order quantity plus the margin of safety. Stock levels for each item should not exceed the maximum. Sometimes the maximum level is referred to as "par stock."

RECEIVING ORDERS

The receiving of deliveries is a critical control point for the foodservice operation. Receiving procedures can have an impact on the receipt of the proper quantity of products that meet the specifications at the quoted prices. The receiving procedures (of which storage is a component) can also affect food quality and pilferage. Each of these factors can have a significant cost impact on the operation. Because of the importance of receiving as a control mechanism, policies and procedures should be developed and implemented.

The following guidelines should be followed in receiving orders:

1. Check all products listed on the invoice against the product received.
   - Count items that can be counted (i.e., number of cases).
   - Weigh all products that are ordered by weight.
2. Verify invoices with the purchase order. This ensures that only products ordered were delivered.
3. Check prices on the invoice against the prices on the purchase order or bid forms (daily price quotations).
4. Check that items delivered are of the quality desired. Make sure that all products meet the specifications for the products ordered.
   - Check all produce items for freshness. If the produce is *not* fresh, *do not* accept it.
   - Check the count on produce items that are ordered by count (i.e., baking potatoes, apples, oranges).
5. Check cans for dents or bulges. Dented cans may have a seal weakened to the point that allows contamination by microorganisms. Use of these products could lead to foodborne illness. Bulging cans indicate that microorganisms have penetrated the container and are forming gas; thus, food from these containers would *not* be safe for use.
6. Spot check cases to ensure that they are full and that all products in the case are of the same quality.
7. Store all perishable items promptly. This ensures that the appropriate temperatures are maintained to retain quality.
8. Store all items in their proper location, changing appropriate records (i.e., perpetual inventory records).
9. Record all purchases on a monthly food purchases form (Exhibit 2-9) or on an invoice spreadsheet (Exhibit 2-10).
10. Send all invoices and credit memos to the departmental secretary/ accounting office promptly.

A rubber invoice stamp may be used when receiving products to verify the date, person, price and extension verification, and readiness for payment of invoices (see Exhibit 3-3). Depending on the procedures of the operation, the manager initials the final "OK" for payment. This communicates to the manager that the product was received, who was responsible for checking the order, and that the invoice was verified for accuracy.

Exhibit 3-3 Invoice Stamp

Invoice Stamp	
Date _____	Prices Verified _____
Received by _____	Extensions Verified _____
OK for Payment _____	

One or two employees should be designated to perform receiving duties. The manager should never allow "just any worker" to receive deliveries. Training should be provided to employees performing the receiving function. They should be very familiar with the receiving procedures and with the specifications used by the operation and should be trained to evaluate product conformance to specifications. They should also be trained to evaluate the quality of products, such as produce.

Limiting the number of employees receiving orders assigns responsibility and helps control losses. Maintaining locked storage with limited access to employees is another control mechanism that can help reduce pilferage.

An ingredient room may also be established to control the use and quality of products. An ingredient room is a central area, usually in the storeroom or adjacent to it, where ingredients are weighed or measured for production. Only one or two trained people should have access to the ingredients and should assemble ingredients for production based on production sheets. Not only does this limit pilferage, it helps ensure that standardized recipes and production sheets are followed, resulting in a consistent product prepared in the appropriate quantities.

NOTE

1. Marian C. Spears and Allene G. Vaden, *Foodservice Organizations: A Managerial and Systems Approach* (New York: John Wiley & Sons, 1985), p. 217.

Chapter 4

Cashiering Systems: Control Mechanism and Marketing Tool

The cashiering system is an integral part of any foodservice operation in which cash and credit card transactions are made. The cashiering system is the major control mechanism in the sales exchange. An effective cashiering system provides sales data needed for evaluating the composition of sales, monitoring product use in relation to sales, and forecasting sales so that appropriate purchasing and production decisions can be made for the operation. These data may also be valuable for evaluating menus to determine high and low sales volume items that would indicate modifications to make on future menus. This chapter focuses on computerized cashiering systems, cashier records, the role of the cashier, management's responsibility, the control function of the system, and decisions related to data generated by the system.

COMPUTERIZED CASHIERING SYSTEMS

There are a wide variety of cashiering systems available and in use in today's foodservice operations, ranging in sophistication from the simple cash box to the electronic point-of-sale (POS) cash register system. The cashiering system to select depends on many factors, such as the sales volume, the money available for investment in the system, the level of control required, and the information that must be generated by the system.

Electronic Point-of-Sale Cash Register Systems

Electronic POS cash register systems are accurate and provide a wealth of information about the sales of an operation. They can be preprogrammed with the items for sale, including item descriptions and sale prices. If special calculations, such as employee discounts, are needed, they can also be programmed. POS cash registers produce a number of records that are used to track sales.

The first record produced is the customer's receipt, or check. Figure 4-1 is an example of a customer's cash register receipt generated from a cash register in a hospital cafeteria. The receipt provides the customer with a detailed description of purchases, including a description of each item, its selling price, the subtotal of the purchase, tax, and total purchase. In this particular operation, employees are given a 50 percent discount on some items. The discount is programmed into the system and appears on the receipt.

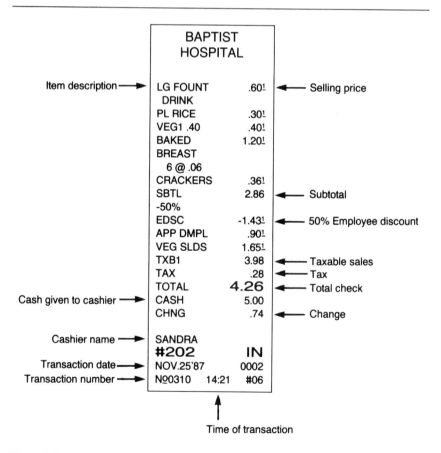

Figure 4-1 Customer's cash register receipt. *Source:* Courtesy of East Tennessee Baptist Hospital, Knoxville, Tennessee, 1987.

The training mode of the system can be used for training new cashiers. A sample of a receipt generated during a training session is shown in Figure 4-2. Note that the sales receipt indicates that the training mode is being used and that the receipt is invalid.

Another record that can be produced with the POS system is a meal sales summary, as shown in Figure 4-3. Intermittent readings may be taken at specific times or after each meal to determine sales. In this example, information is given about the total gross sales, the sales tax, the number of transactions, the net sales, the number of employees discounted, the total amount of employee discounts given, and the average check total. The bottom of the printout shows the date, the time the reading was taken, and the cashier. These data are useful in monitoring sales, preparing the various records for taxation and reporting employee discounts, calculating productivity ratios, determining staffing patterns, and determining hours when the operation might be closed because of a low volume of sales.

Summaries can also be made of sales by product category. The categories can be defined by the individual operation, depending on how the data will be used. Figure 4-4 shows sales summary information for a hospital cafeteria. The category is beverages and breads. This record gives information about the number of each item sold, the total dollar sales for each

---

```
            BAPTIST
            HOSPITAL


HONEYDW                 .80!
SBTL                    .80
-50.00%
EDSC                   -.40!
TRAINING MODE
TXB1                    .40
TAX                     .03
TOTL                    .43
CASH                    .43

 INVALID RECEIPT
 MARY M.
 #225                    IN
 NOV.25'87              0002
 N⁰TRNG      15:57      #12
```

Figure 4-2 Cash register tape in training mode

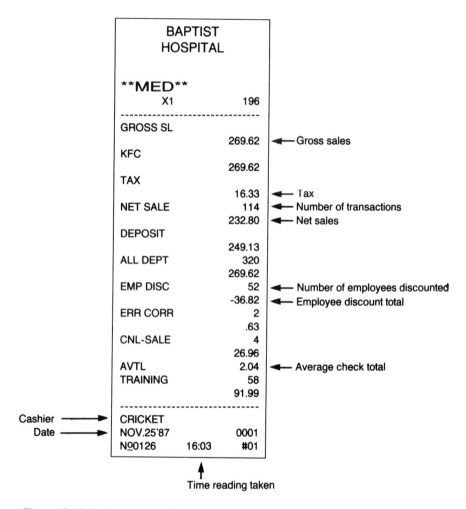

Figure 4-3 Meal sales summary. *Source:* Courtesy of East Tennessee Baptist Hospital, Knoxville, Tennessee, 1987.

item, the total dollar sales for the category, the total number of items sold in the category, and the percentage of total dollar sales for the category each item represents. Using the example, the second item is milk and the following data are provided for the item:

MILK
#000022   2.9%
733.60
1834

```
      BAPTIST              SM  MM   LEMONADE            441
      HOSPITAL             #000040          .0%      CRN BRD
                                           8.50      #000072          .6%
  **PLU**                     17                                   143.20
           X1      123     MED  MM  LEMONADE             716
  --------------------     #000048          .1%      LG BISC
  SM TEA                                   14.00      #000079          .0%
  #000020          .2%        20                                       .50
                  52.50     LG MM  LEMONADE              1
     175                   #000049          .1%      ROLL
  MILK                                     18.00      #000080          .3%
  #000022         2.9%        20                                     87.40
                 733.60     SM COFF                      437
                   (4)     #000050         1.7%      WW ROLL
    1834                                  432.60      #000082          .0%
  CRT JUIC                    1442                                      .60
  #000023          .1%      MUFFIN                        2
                  16.60     #000052          .5%      HRD ROLL
     54                                   137.90      #000083          .0%
  MED TEA                      394                                    5.20
  #000028          .1%      FR BREAD                                   (1)
                  15.50     #000053          .1%         26
     31                                    14.40      SAUS  BISCUIT
  LG TEA                       96                       #000090          .0%
  #000029          .3%      LG COFF                                   9.35
                  85.80     #000059         2.5%         11
    143                                   624.00      H M  DANISH
  SM MM   JUICE               1248                      #000100          .0%
  #000030          .2%      CIN RSN BISCUIT                            5.60
                  48.60     #000060          .0%         7
     81                                     4.00      TOTL            44651
  MFLD TEA                      8                                  25359.42
  #000032          .0%      CRACKERS                  --------------------
                    .80     #000062          .3%      MARY M.
      2                                    66.42      NOV.25'87         0002
  MFLD LEM                    1107                     №0009    16:37    #12
  #000033          .0%      BISCUIT
                   2.40     #000063          .0%
      6                                    10.40
  MED MM   JUICE               52
  #000038          .2%      HM BISCUIT
                  50.40     #000070          .9%
     56                                   220.50
  LG MM   JUICE
  #000039          .1%
                  22.80
     19
```

Figure 4-4 Cash register summary of items sold in one category

This means that 1,834 servings of milk (item #00022) were sold, generating $733.60 in revenue. For the beverage and bread category, the total sales was $25,359.42. Milk sales were 2.9 percent of the total dollar sales for the category. This percentage is calculated by dividing milk dollar sales by the total dollar sales for the category.

These data can be used to monitor sales over time. It is useful to determine whether there is seasonal variation in sales so that purchasing and production levels can be adjusted accordingly. Also, it is useful to know the number of units of products sold in order to forecast business volume for a future time period, which is needed for preparing budgets, purchasing, determining production quantities, and staffing.

These records can also provide important information for the control systems. A comparison should be made between the number of items purchased and the number of items sold. For example, if an operation had a beginning-of-the-month inventory of 30 steaks, purchased 50 steaks, and had an end-of-month inventory of 5 steaks, sales records should reflect that 75 steaks were sold. If these numbers matched, the operation would be well controlled. If only 70 steaks had been sold, there would be 5 steaks that could not be accounted for. This would mean that food costs were higher than they should be. The foodservice manager should determine the cause of the deviation and take corrective action to prevent recurrence. Theft, not receiving steaks paid for, customers returning overcooked steaks, or an employee dropping a steak on the floor could be reasons the numbers did not reconcile.

Debit-Card Systems

Debit-card systems that have been used in college and university operations for a number of years are now being used in hospitals.[1] These systems rely on the use of an identification card with a magnetically coded strip that is placed in a cash register terminal. The magnetic strip allows the account status to be determined, e.g., what meal plan the individual is on and whether the individual is eligible to eat. The system provides accuracy in recording meals; in fact, one operation using the system found it to be about 99.9 percent accurate.[2] In addition, the operation greatly reduced the employee time spent on record keeping, from 80 hours a month to about 5 hours.

Another advantage to the debit-card system is that money does not exchange hands at the cash register for people on meal plans. This provides an effective cash control mechanism, which is important in light of the national statistic that the cash-skimming rate is $30 per 100 beds.[3]

Exhibit 4-1 Cashier's Summary Form for a Hospital

CASHIER'S SUMMARY

Date __10/15/88__

Shift __1__

Cashier __Sally Jones__

Customer Group	Cash Sales	Charge Sales	Total Sales
Patient meals	0	0	0
Cash meals	1085	0	1085
Employee meals	300	0	300
Doctor/intern meals	0	175	175
Administration meals	0	0	0
Other	0	0	0
Total sales	1385	175	1560

Ending transaction number	1235
Minus beginning transaction number	715
Total number of transactions	520
Cash in drawer	1482.50
Minus bank	100.00
Net cash colllected	1382.50
Minus cash sales	1385.50
Cash over (short)	(2.50)
Voids	1

Verified by __J. Smith__

Exhibit 4-2 Cashier's Summary Form for a Restaurant

Cashier's Summary

DATE _____ DAY _____ PREPARED BY _____

	(A)	(B)	(C)	(D)	(E)
	Bar Register		Service Register		Total
1. **Bank Deposit** Part I	Day	Night	Day	Night	All Shifts
2. Currency					
3. Silver					
4. Checks					
5. Subtotal					
6. Credit Cards:					
7. MasterCard/Visa					
8. American Express					
9. Diners Club					
10. Others					
11. Other Receipts					
12. Total Bank Deposit					
13. **Cash Summary** Part II					
14. Sales per Register					
15. Tax per Register					
16. Adjustments:					
Over/Under Rings					
18. Transfers					
19. Other					
20. Total Adjustments					
21. Sales to Be Accounted for					
22. Tax to Be Accounted for					
23. Accounts Collected					
24.					
25. Other Receipts					
26.					
27. Tips Charges:					
28. MasterCard/Visa					
29. American Express					
30. Diners Club					
31. Other					
32. House Accounts—Tips					
33. Total Receipts					
34. Deduct: Paidouts					
35. House Charges					
36. Total Deductions					
37. Net Cash Receiipts					
38. Bank Deposit (Line 12)					
39. (Over) or Short					

Source: Reprinted from *Uniform System of Accounts for Restaurants,* p. 93, with permission of National Restaurant Association, © 1986.

CASHIER RECORDS

At the end of each shift, each cashier should prepare a record of transactions for the shift. The information to be included depends on the type of operation. At a minimum, the record should include the total dollar sales and total number of customers served. The cash register tapes provide data for the summary. The cashier's report, or summary, provides data used to develop a daily report of the operation's activity.

Exhibit 4-1 is an example of a cashier's report developed for use in a hospital. It includes information on the number of clients served by category. It also includes information about the number of transactions and the amount of cash received during the shift. The form requires the cashier to reconcile the sales with the amount of cash in the drawer and to record whether the cash is over or short. In this example, the cashier was $2.50 short. The amount the cashier is over or short and the number of times this occurs should be monitored. Ideally, neither of these cases should occur with great frequency. If they do, corrective action should be taken.

Exhibit 4-2 is a cashier's summary form for a restaurant. Notice that it separates sales by cash, check, and credit card. A record is also kept of

---

Exhibit 4-3 Summary of Items Sold

Date _____

Day _____

Meal _____

Item	Number Sold	Total Sold
Total		

tips charged so that the wait staff can be paid that amount. Like the cashier's report for the hospital, tax and over and short amounts are recorded.

When POS cash registers are not available, the cashier may also be responsible for recording the number of particular items sold. These data can be summarized from guest checks. Exhibit 4-3 is an example of an item summary recorded by a cashier.

ROLE OF THE CASHIER

The cashier has an important role in the foodservice operation. The cashier must have technical skills, human relations skills, and sales skills. Each skill is important for the effective functioning of the cashier. Standards of performance should be set for each of these areas and training must be done to ensure that cashiers have the knowledge and skills necessary to perform their job well.

Technical Skills

Technical skills are basic to the role of the cashier and must be mastered before other skills.[4] The cashier must be proficient in the use of the cash register used in the operation. In using the cash register, the cashier must be able to:

- open the register (this includes counting the opening bank to verify that the appropriate amount of cash is there to begin the shift)
- take intermittent cash register readings at the designated times
- close the register (this includes taking final readings from the cash register, counting money, preparing the cashier's report, preparing the bank for the next shift, and possibly preparing the bank deposit)
- handle sales activities efficiently (this includes knowing the prices or the appropriate keys for the items sold, how to count change, and how to give change to customers)
- handle voids
- give refunds
- handle charge sales
- pay out cash when appropriate (e.g., for a cash on delivery [COD] item).

Human Relations Skills

The cashier must have excellent human relations skills because of the constant contact with customers. In *Service America! Doing Business in the New Economy,*[5] Albrecht and Zemke emphasized the importance of each "moment of truth," or each contact point between the customer and the organization. They also stressed that, to the customer, employees *are* the company. Thus, as a representative of the foodservice operation and as, perhaps, the last "moment of truth" in the operation, the interaction between the cashier and the customer is critical to the success of any foodservice operation.

Martin[6] identified two major dimensions of service: procedural and convivial. For cashiers, procedural service relates more to technical aspects such as timeliness, accommodation, communication, and feedback. The convivial dimension relates to human relations skills and is affected by the employee's attitude, behavior, and verbal skills. An employee's words and body language communicate important messages to customers.

Indicators of good human relations skills that a cashier must demonstrate include:

- a friendly smile
- a pleasant greeting
- calling return (or regular) customers by name
- diplomatic handling of problems (such as a drink being knocked over, a tray being dropped, or someone feeling he or she has been mischarged for an item)
- diplomatic handling of angry customers.

Sales Skills

Cashiers can be a positive influence on sales in a foodservice operation, particularly in cafeterias. Suggestive selling can be done by cashiers to increase the sales volume. Cashiers can mention specials to customers and recommend additional items that might go with the customer's selections. They might also point out items that have been overlooked by the customer, such as butter to go with bread or ice cream to top off the hot apple cobbler. These helpful suggestions will usually be appreciated by the customer and can serve to increase the average check for the operation.

MANAGEMENT'S RESPONSIBILITY

Managers in a foodservice operation set the stage for whether the cashiers are effective in doing their jobs and in relating well to the public. Managers are responsible for developing policies and procedures, developing performance standards, training cashiers, and evaluating the performance of cashiers. The effective performance of these functions has a major impact on the quality of service in a foodservice operation.

Developing Policies and Procedures

Policies and procedures related to the cashiering systems should be developed by the manager of the foodservice operation. Policies and procedures are clearly written statements of what is to be done and the step-by-step method for accomplishment. Policies and procedures might be developed for opening the cash register, taking intermittent cash register readings, closing the cash register, and handling sales activities with customers.

These policies and procedures must be communicated to the cashiers if implementation is to occur. They should be used as the basis for training programs in the operation. Written copies of the policies and procedures may be given to cashiers during training sessions so that they may read and refer to them. A written copy of the policies and procedures should be available at all times as a reference for employees.

Developing Standards of Performance

Standards of performance should be developed for the cashier. Standards of performance are objective, observable, and measurable statements of behaviors or results expected from a task or job. The acceptable deviation from those standards should also be identified.

For example, a standard of performance might be that cashiers smile at all customers. The observable behavior is a smile. There is no acceptable deviation from the standard as it is designated that the cashier should smile at *all* customers. Another standard might be that cashiers must always be within plus or minus $2 of the amount of cash taken in during a shift. The accepted deviation in this case is $2 short or $2 over the daily cash transactions. Amounts that exceeded $2 would be brought to the attention of the manager, who would seek explanations and, perhaps, take corrective action.

Standards of performance provide the basis for control in the foodservice operation. Any time the actual performance deviates too much from the desired performance defined by the standard of performance a "red flag" should go up. This red flag signals that the manager needs to determine why the deviation occurred and make changes so it does not continue. For example, a new cashier is short $5 three days in a row. The manager needs to determine if the cashier does not make change properly, if the cashier is stealing $5 each day, or if some other cause exists. A change must be made because an operation cannot afford to keep a cashier who is consistently short in the cash bank.

Standards of performance are also important when training new cashiers. The standards must be communicated to the cashier and should form the basis for training. They are also the cornerstone for evaluating the performance of cashiers because they identify the expected behavior and the desired performance level.

Training Cashiers

Training is an important function of the manager of a foodservice operation. During the initial training session, the policies and procedures and the standards of performance for cashiers should be communicated to new employees. It is important to let employees know what the expectations are for the job.

Training methods should be developed to allow the cashier some hands-on opportunities to practice the skills they will be required to perform on the job. Most cash registers have a training mode, which allows practice without the data being entered into the actual business of the operation. The cashier should sit in front of the register when the different parts of the register and their use are discussed.

Scenarios should be developed that estimate real life events to give the new cashier an opportunity to practice skills. Scenarios could include:

- sample trays to ring up
- a sample charge tray
- a tray for which the customer decides not to take an item, resulting in a void
- a tray with an unusual item (one for which there is no cash register key) that must be rung up by hand

- a customer who lost money in the vending machine
- an irate customer who found a hair in his food
- a COD item for which the cashier must pay
- a customer who says that she was overcharged
- a customer who says that he was given the wrong change.

These scenarios give the cashier an opportunity to develop both technical and human relations skills. The manager or trainer should observe how the new cashier handles the scenarios. Feedback should be given on both the strengths and weaknesses of the cashier's performance. Remember, the training phase is the time to develop the skills and confidence of the new employee.

It is also important to keep in mind that training is an ongoing process, not one that is completed after the first week on the job. As performance is being monitored, areas of improvement can be identified for future training sessions. Employee development is a major responsibility of foodservice managers.

Evaluating Performance of Cashiers

Employee performance evaluation should be an ongoing process in the foodservice operation. In the daily operation, informal feedback should be given to employees regarding their performance. If a manager sees an employee doing something very well, the manager should let him or her know. If an employee is performing in a manner that is inappropriate, immediate, specific feedback will help correct the inappropriate performance.

For example, if a cashier deals with an angry customer in a very diplomatic manner, let that person know what a good job he or she did. Pat the cashier on the back and let him or her know that you appreciate the performance. Likewise, if you see that a cashier did not ring up an item on the tray of a friend, call the cashier into your office and let him or her know that the performance is unacceptable.

Remember that the basis for evaluation is the policies and procedures, the standards of performance, and the job description. Communicate these to employees so they will know the expectations of the job. Then give timely, specific feedback on performance related to the job expectations. Research has shown that goal setting along with feedback about performance in relation to goals is very effective in improving performance. Thus, jointly set goals may help the cashier meet the objectives of the operation.

In addition to informal evaluation and feedback, a formal performance appraisal system should be established for an operation. *Performance appraisal* is a formal procedure that occurs in most operations at the end of the probationary period and at 6- or 12-month intervals thereafter. Performance appraisal forms, which are often standardized for the entire operation, are used to evaluate the performance of individual employees. A session is scheduled for the immediate supervisor to discuss performance with the individual employee.

While formal performance appraisal is useful, it should be combined with the informal feedback system discussed earlier. Research has shown that feedback is more effective if it is immediate and specific. Performance appraisals given on a six-month or yearly basis are certainly not timely. Too much time lapses when changes in employee behavior could be made. Thus, special efforts should be made to make evaluation and feedback an ongoing process in the organization.

CONTROL FUNCTION OF CASHIERING SYSTEMS

The cashiering system serves as an important control mechanism in the foodservice operation. A properly planned and implemented cashiering system will control cash and theft in the foodservice operation.

Cash Control

To run profitably, the foodservice operation must sell all products produced at the established selling price. The cashiering system helps ensure that all items ordered are paid for and that the appropriate price is charged. Several features of the cashiering system ensure cash control, including:

- automatic change dispensers to speed the payment process and increase accuracy
- a paper tape receipt that summarizes transactions
- the presetting of cash registers with product prices
- the breakdown of sales into categories, such as food and liquor
- sales records
- automatic sales tax and discount calculations
- separate cash drawers for each cashier

- intermittant readings of cash registers
- the review of cashiers' reports by management
- guest check numbering.

Theft Control

Theft can be a major problem in many foodservice operations. When the theft rate is high, food and liquor costs increase, resulting in decreased profits for the foodservice operation. Management must establish control mechanisms to eliminate theft and, thus, control costs. Theft can occur in the operation both in the back of the house and in the front of the house by employees and customers.

Employee Theft

Back-of-the-house theft can be monitored by comparing the sales data with purchase records. For this reason, it is important to keep records of the number of each item sold (as illustrated in Exhibits 4-3 and 4-4). If sales and purchases do not match, the manager will have to determine the reason and take the appropriate corrective action.

In the front of the house, several fraudulent acts may be done by employees, including:

- serving an item and not charging for it
- overcharging the customer and pocketing the amount overcharged
- reusing a guest check or using an unauthorized (unnumbered) guest check
- giving incorrect change.

Each of these types of fraud can be controlled by using and monitoring the appropriate cashiering system. Control mechanisms that might be incorporated into the cashiering system include:

- Use a computerized prechecking system with remote workstation printers. The wait staff is required to enter each item ordered into a computer. The items are printed out at the appropriate remote workstation, such as the bar or the grill area. All items prepared and sent out from these workstations are recorded on the computer. Only those items printed out would be sent out from the production area.

- Use a food-checker system where the food trays are inspected by the food checker who rings up all items on the tray.
- Use a computerized cash register system to calculate all guest checks.
- Number guest checks and allocate them to the wait staff by numbers.
- Use duplicate guest checks.
- Require that all checks be rung up separately.
- Pay guest checks directly to the cashier, thus separating responsibility for service and collection of payment.
- Clearly post prices on menus and menu boards.
- Check sales records.

Customer Theft

In foodservice operations, there are several ways that customers might not pay their checks. Customers might walk out without paying their bill, pay the bill with a bad check or credit card, manipulate the guest check, or complain about the food so they will not have to pay. Managers, cashiers, and wait staff should be trained on ways to watch for these occurrences and how to handle them if they occur.

Several control mechanisms can be used to avoid nonpayment by customers. Examples of control mechanisms to eliminate customer theft include:

- Locate the cashier at the exit.
- Train staff to watch for customers who "disappear," to return promptly for payment of check, and to "keep an eye" on the exits.
- Require proper identification on all check and credit card transactions. Such identification would include current address and telephone number, photo identification such as a driver's license, driver's license number and state, and an additional credit card number. The cashier would make sure that the same name was on all three records.
- Require that all checks be written to the foodservice operation (no two-party checks).
- Use clearly legible machine-stamped prices on all guest checks. If cash registers are not available to do this, use ball point pens to write all guest checks; never use pencil that could be erased.
- Indicate the number served on each check.
- Investigate all customer complaints to determine whether they are justified. The manager or supervisor on duty should take care of the problem.

DECISIONS BASED ON CASHIER SYSTEM DATA

Sales data generated by the cashiering system are important for decision making in the foodservice operation. Decisions related to purchasing, production, and menu depend on accurate sales data. Forecasting based on sales is an essential element of effective purchasing and production decisions.

Forecasting

Forecasting is the estimation of future events based on historical and statistical data. Forecasts are used as the basis for decision making and planning in the foodservice operation.

Historical data are obtained from the records of purchases, sales, and volume kept by the foodservice operation. These data provide insight into the past performance of the operation, which can be indicative of future performance.

Statistical data include economic trends, demographic data, government regulations, and other external factors that may affect business volume and costs. Internal factors can also affect business volume and costs. For example, an operation is expanded in size and the kitchen renovated with state-of-the-art equipment. These factors could affect volume and must be factored into any forecasts of future business activity. These statistical data are discussed in more detail in chapter 6.

Several methods of forecasting can be used in the foodservice operation. The two methods used most frequently are the popularity index and the time series model.

Popularity Index

The *popularity index* can be used in forecasting sales. To derive a popularity index, the sales of each item in a category is compared with the total sales for the category. For example, in a restaurant, five entrees are on the menu (Exhibit 4-4). To calculate a popularity index for these items, divide the number of each item sold by the total number of entrees sold. The calculations are:

Cajun chicken	18	15%
Filet mignon	39	33%
Grilled salmon	22	19%
Prime rib	35	29%
Shrimp alfredo	5	4%
	119	100%

Exhibit 4-4 Summary of Items Sold

Date ___November 12, 1988___

Day ___Saturday___

Meal ___Dinner___

Item	Number Sold	Total Sold
Cajun chicken	𝍷𝍷𝍷 𝍷𝍷𝍷 𝍷𝍷𝍷 III	18
Filet mignon	𝍷𝍷𝍷 𝍷𝍷𝍷 𝍷𝍷𝍷 𝍷𝍷𝍷 𝍷𝍷𝍷 𝍷𝍷𝍷 𝍷𝍷𝍷 IIII	39
Grilled salmon	𝍷𝍷𝍷 𝍷𝍷𝍷 𝍷𝍷𝍷 𝍷𝍷𝍷 II	22
Prime rib	𝍷𝍷𝍷 𝍷𝍷𝍷 𝍷𝍷𝍷 𝍷𝍷𝍷 𝍷𝍷𝍷 𝍷𝍷𝍷 𝍷𝍷𝍷	35
Shrimp alfredo	𝍷𝍷𝍷	5
TOTAL		119

To use these data for sales forecasts, multiply the percentage by the total volume forecasted. For example, this restaurant anticipates having 150 covers next Saturday. To determine how many of each item to purchase and produce, multiply the total number anticipated by the popularity index. For example, for cajun chicken the calculations are:

$$\text{Number orders cajun chicken} = 150 \text{ covers} \times .15$$
$$= 22.5, \text{ or } 23.$$

This calculation would be used for the remaining items on the menu.

Time Series Model

The *time series model* is based on patterns of occurrences over time on the assumption that past activity is the best predictor of future activity. For example, sales volume on Saturday nights can best be predicted by the sales volume on past Saturday nights.

A *moving average time series model* is often used. This method calculates the average of a predetermined number of observations, using the most recent occurrences. For example, sales records for entrees in a hospital cafeteria show the following volume for lasagna at noon on Friday:

February 1	56 portions
February 8	82 portions
February 15	62 portions
February 22	49 portions

The forecast for lasagna sales (and, thus, purchasing and production) for March 1 is the average of those four days. For March 1, the manager would expect to sell 62 portions [(56 + 82 + 62 + 49)/4] of lasagna.

On March 1, the actual sale of lasagna was 60 portions. The forecast for March 8 is the sales volume for February 8, 15, 22, and March 1. Notice that the oldest date is eliminated and the newest date added. Thus, the forecast for March 8 is 63 portions [(82 + 62 + 49 + 60)/4]. Notice that this method smooths out high and low volume days to get an average number of portions.

Purchasing

Purchasing decisions are based on the forecast for usage of items. Keeping accurate data ensures that the correct quantities are purchased, thus controlling the food costs of the operation. Also, as discussed in chapter 3, purchasing based on forecasts can prevent excess inventory investment.

Production

Forecasts of sales based on previous sales is instrumental in determining production quantities. Overproduction is a common cause of food costs that are too high. Accurate forecasts help control food costs while ensuring that the needed quantity is produced to meet the demand of customers.

Menu

Sales records should be used to evaluate the effectiveness of the menu and the contribution of each item to the profit objective. Menu analysis is one method for evaluating the sales volume of menu items in relation to the contribution margin. This analysis helps the manager determine what changes might be made in the menu to improve profitability.

Menu Analysis

In addition to considering the popularity of menu items, it is important to consider the contribution margin of each of the menu items. The *contribution margin* is the selling price of the item minus the variable cost or, in other words, the portion of the selling price that can be applied to paying the fixed costs of the operation and to profit. The combination of the sales and the contribution margin for each menu item helps the foodservice operator determine which items to retain on the menu and which to replace.

Figure 4-5 shows a two by two table that can be used to classify menu items. The vertical axis is *sales volume,* divided into high and low categories. The horizontal axis is the *contribution margin,* divided into high and low categories. The high category includes items higher than the average and the low category includes items lower than the average. Each of the four categories has a label, e.g., items that have a low sales volume and a low contribution margin are referred to as *dogs.* These items do not contribute to either the sales volume or the contribution margin, so they would be prime candidates for replacement by items that will either sell in larger volumes or provide a higher contribution margin.

Old standbys are the items that sell in large volume but have a low contribution margin. The selling price for these items may need to be increased to improve their contribution margins. Increasing the contribution margin will result in more profit for the operation. Because they are

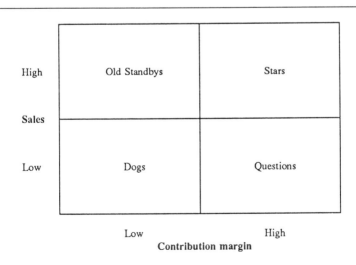

Figure 4-5 Menu analysis classification

already popular, the sales volume probably could not be significantly increased.

Stars are the menu items the foodservice manager really wants. These items are very popular and have a high contribution margin. Stars need special consideration, too. The manager should study their price elasticity. What effect will raising the price have on the number sold? What effect will lowering the price have on the volume sold? If a slight price decrease would result in a significantly larger quantity being sold, that might be a wise strategy. Special attention should also be given to the quality of these items. Quality assurance is imperative to continuing the high sales volume.

Items that have a high contribution margin but a low sales volume are called *questions*. Although these items are profitable, something must be done to increase their sales volume. Several factors may be affecting their sales, such as:

- *Product quality:* Perhaps the item is of poor quality. Are standardized recipes used so that the product is consistently of high quality?
- *Price/value relationship:* Perhaps customers perceive that the item is overpriced for what they get.
- *Product popularity:* Perhaps the item is not popular in a particular area. Market research may provide answers to why customers are not selecting the item. Some changes in these menu items should be initiated, either making changes that will result in increased sales or replacing them.

The earlier example can be analyzed to determine where the items would be classified. Table 4-1 shows a work sheet that might be used to evaluate the menu items. The cajun chicken and the shrimp alfredo are low in sales and have a low contribution margin, so they would fit into the *dogs* cat-

Table 4-1 Menu Analysis Worksheet

Menu Item	No.	%	Food Cost	Selling Price	CM[1]	CM Category	Sales Category
Cajun chicken	18	15	2.50	7.95	5.45	Low	Low
Filet mignon	39	33	5.15	14.95	9.80	High	High
Grilled salmon	22	19	4.85	13.95	9.10	High	Low
Prime rib	35	29	5.75	15.95	10.20	High	High
Shrimp alfredo	5	4	4.00	12.50	8.50	Low	Low

[1]CM = contribution margin.

egory. The filet mignon and the prime rib are *stars* in that they have a high popularity and a high contribution margin. Salmon has a high contribution margin but a low popularity and fits into the *questions* category.

NOTES

1. "Who's On First? And Who Gets Seconds?," *Restaurants & Institutions,* April 29, 1987, pp. 160–161.

2. Ibid.

3. Ibid.

4. James C. Rose, "Cashiers: Profit and Promotion," *Food Management,* October 1987, p. 44.

5. Karl Albrecht and Ronald Zemke, *Service America! Doing Business in the New Economy* (Homewood, Ill.: Dow Jones-Irwin, 1985).

6. William Martin, *Quality Service: The Restaurant Manager's Bible* (Ithaca, N.Y.: Cornell School of Hotel Administration, 1986).

Chapter 5

Cost and Price Determination

COST DETERMINATION

To meet the financial objectives of an operation, the foodservice manager must know the costs involved in the operation. In chapter 2, fixed, variable, and semivariable costs were discussed. While each of these cost categories is important, most pricing decisions for foodservice operations are based on the variable cost of the product. Therefore, in this chapter, the focus is on determining these variable costs (food costs) for products sold.

Standardized Recipes

Standardized recipes provide the foundation for determining variable costs. A *standardized recipe* is a formula for combining measured ingredients using a specific procedure to produce a predetermined product. A standardized recipe is one that has been accepted by management and serves as a quality/quantity control mechanism for the foodservice operation.

A standardized recipe must include several components to be an effective control tool for management, including:

- product name
- list of ingredients
- amount of each ingredient by weight, volume, or count
- procedures
- yield
- portion size
- equipment and utensils needed

- cooking time and temperature
- serving and garnishing suggestions.

A standardized recipe form, such as the one shown in Exhibit 5-1, should be used in each operation. This form will become familiar and easy to use by the production employees.

Each standardized recipe should be costed on a routine basis to determine the current food cost. The *standard cost* for a product is the cost of all ingredients required to make one portion. The standard cost for all items on the menu should be determined and used as the basis for determining the selling price for the item. Since food costs fluctuate, someone should be responsible for keeping the standard costs updated. When food prices increase, the standard cost of an item will increase. If the selling price is not adjusted accordingly, the contribution margin will decrease. The *contribution margin* is the selling price minus the variable costs. In other words, the contribution margin is that portion of sales that can be

---

Exhibit 5-1 Standardized Recipe Form

Baking Powder Biscuits

Oven Temperature: 425° F   Yield: 100 2 1/2" biscuits

Baking Time: 15 minutes   Portion: 1 biscuit

Ingredients	Weight	Volume	Procedure
Flour, all purpose Baking powder Salt Shortening, hydrogenated Milk	5 lb 5 oz 1 lb 4 oz	 2 T 1 3/4 qt	1. Combine dry ingredients in mixer bowl. Blend on low speed for 10 sec using pastry knife. 2. Add shortening. Mix on low speed for 1 min. Stop and scrape sides and bottom of bowl. Mix 1 min. Mixture will be crumbly. 3. Add milk. Mix on low speed to form a soft dough, about 30 sec. *Do not* overmix. 4. Place half of dough on lightly floured board. Knead lightly, 15–20 times. 5. Roll to 3/4" thickness. Cut. 6. Place on baking sheets 1/2" apart. 7. Bake.

Exhibit 5-2 Back of Standardized Recipe Form

Ingredients	100-Unit Quantity	Unit Cost	Cost	Unit Cost	Cost	Unit Cost	Cost
Flour, all purpose	5 lb	.105/lb	.525				
Baking powder	5 oz	.647/lb	.202				
Salt	2 T	.084/lb	.007				
Shortening	1 lb 4 oz	.720/lb	.900				
Milk	1 3/4 qt	1.87/gal	3.273				
Total cost			4.907				
Cost per portion			.049				
Date			5/9/87				
Costed by			JS				

used for fixed costs and profit. If the contribution margin decreases, the profitability of the item will decrease. To make the task of costing recipes easier, each standardized recipe form should have a place for costing, as depicted in Exhibit 5-2.

To be an effective control mechanism, standardized recipes must be followed. The manager must ensure that standardized recipes are followed by carefully training and supervising food production personnel. If standardized recipes are not followed, there will be no way to determine the standard costs for the products sold. For example, a standardized recipe for meat loaf calls for 12 lb of ground beef and has a standard cost of $.40. The cook does not weigh the ground beef and puts 14 lb in the recipe instead of 12. This increases the standard cost to $.455. For 50 servings, the variable cost would increase $2.75, reducing the contribution margin by the same amount. If this occurred with a number of food products over time, the cost increases would be substantial. Thus, the foodservice manager must control variable costs to meet the financial goals of the operation.

Yields

When costing recipes, it is important to calculate the yield of some products in order to determine an accurate food cost. For most foods, losses occur in cooking and handling. These losses must be taken into account in determining the amount of product to purchase, determining production quantities, and costing the products for recipes.

Two important terms related to yield are *as purchased* (sometimes noted as AP) and *edible portion* (EP). The first refers to the weight of the product as it is purchased. The EP refers to the usable weight. For example, potatoes have an 81 percent yield. Ten pounds of potatoes AP would yield 8.1 lb EP. If a recipe called for 10 lb of potatoes, 12.35 lb would need to be purchased. Yields for products can be determined in three ways: table values, butcher test, or cooking loss test.

Table Values

Tables providing yield data for a variety of products, including fresh fruits and vegetables and meats, are available from a number of sources. The USDA publishes two good yield guides: *Food Yields Summarized by Different Stages of Preparation* and *Food Buying Guide for School Food Service. Food for Fifty,* a commonly used reference in foodservice, also provides food yield information that is helpful for purchasing and costing. To determine the EP or AP for a product, use the yield value provided in one of the published tables.

Determining EP. To determine the EP for a product, use the formula:

$$EP = AP \text{ weight} \times \text{Yield from Table (as a decimal)}.$$

For example, 100 4-oz portions (25 lb) of cabbage are needed. The receiving clerk weighs the cabbage in stock and reports that there is 30 lb. Will that be enough cabbage? Using the formula, determine the EP as follows:

$$EP = 30 \text{ lb} \times .87 = 26.1 \text{ lb}.$$

The conclusion: There is enough cabbage in stock to meet the needs.

Determining AP. To determine the AP for a product, use the following formula:

$$AP = EP \text{ weight}/\text{Yield from Table (as a decimal)}.$$

For example, 50 4-oz portions (12.5 lb) of cauliflower are needed for a catered dinner. How much cauliflower should the purchasing agent order?

Using the formula, determine the AP as follows:

$$AP = 12.5 \text{ lb}/.62 \text{ (or } 62\% \text{ yield)} = 20.16.$$

Thus, the purchasing agent would need to order 21 lb of cauliflower to have an adequate amount for the dinner.

Butcher Test

The *butcher test* is another method of determining yield for meats. With the meat industry trend toward boxed meat and the increased availability of preportioned and even precooked meat, the need for the butcher test is diminishing. Some operations, however, still buy wholesale cuts and do some fabrication of meat. For the butcher test, the meat is weighed as purchased and after it has been cut for use. The usable meat is weighed and provides the information for determining the yield percentage (yield %) for the meat. This yield can be used to determine quantities to purchase and the cost per usable pound.

Exhibit 5-3 shows an example of a butcher test for sirloin prepared for making beef stroganoff. In doing a butcher test, each byproduct (such as fat, bone, and usable meat) of the breakdown is recorded by weight. The percentage of the total (or the yield %) for each of these can be determined by dividing the weight of the byproduct by the total weight of the product. In this example, the usable meat weighs 8 lb 2 oz and the total weight of the sirloin is 12 lb 8 oz. It is easier to calculate if only one unit is used (either pound or ounce). It is easy to see that 12 lb 8 oz is 12.5 (or 12.5 lb). To convert ounces to pounds, simply divide the number of ounces by 16 (number of ounces in a pound). For example, 2/16 equals 0.125 lb. To find the yield % for the usable meat, use the formula:

$$
\begin{aligned}
\text{Yield \%} &= \text{Weight of usable meat/Total weight AP} \\
&= 8.125/12.5 \\
&= 65\%.
\end{aligned}
$$

To determine the cost per usable pound, divide the total cost of the meat by the weight of the usable meat. Using the example, the cost per usable pound is:

$$\text{Cost per usable lb} = \$26.88/8.125 \text{ lb} = \$3.31.$$

To determine the cost per usable ounce, divide the cost per usable pound by 16. In the example, $3.31/16 equals $.21 per ounce. It is useful to know the cost per ounce to determine the standard cost for a portion. For example, if the sirloin had been cut into 6-oz steak portions, the standard cost per portion would have been $1.26 (6 oz × $.21).

Exhibit 5-3 Butcher Test Form

Butcher Test

Item __Sirloin__   Date __3/15/88__

Grade __U.S. CHOICE__   Cost/lb __$2.15__

Weight __12__ lb __8__ oz   Total cost __$26.88__

Supplier __Red's Meats__

Breakdown	Weight		% Total	Cost/Usable	
	lb	oz		lb	oz
Fat trim	1	6	11%		
Bone	2	8	20%		
Loss in cutting		8	4%		
Usable meat	8	2	65%	$3.31	$.21
TOTAL	12	8	100%		

The butcher test can be used for any meat. This method is useful for comparing meat from different suppliers and for determining yield for pricing and purchasing.

Cooking Loss Test

A portion of the total product weight is lost in cooking and is of special concern for meat products. Meat loses weight in the cooking process because of drip loss and evaporative loss. Cooking techniques, such as temperature, time, and puncturing the meat tissue (which might occur, for example, when the cook pierces the meat when turning it with a meat fork), all influence the amount of loss. For some products, especially roasted meats, the amount of cooking loss is an important factor to consider in determining the portion cost.

For example, a boneless round of beef is roasted for the cafeteria line. The standard serving size for the noon meal is 3 oz. The purchase price for the meat is $3.15 per pound. A 10-lb roast was purchased. In Exhibit 5-4, an example of a cooking loss test is given for this piece of meat.

Exhibit 5-4 Cooking Loss Test Form

Item __Boneless Beef Round__   Date __3/18/88__

Grade __U.S. Choice__   Cost/lb __$3.30__

Cooking Temperature __300°__   Total Cost __$34.24__

Cooking Time __3½ hrs.__   Supplier __Red's Meats__

Breakdown	Weight		Ratio to Total Weight[1]
	lb	oz	
1. Original weight	10	6	100%
2. Weight after trimming	10	0	96.4%
3. Trim loss (1—2)		6	3.6%
4. Cooked weight	6	12	65.1%
5. Cooking loss (2—4)	3	4	31.4%
6. Bones and trim		6	3.6%
7. Product to sale	6	6	61.4%

$$\text{Yield \%} = \frac{\text{Weight of product to sale (7)}}{\text{Original weight (1)}} = 61.4\%$$

Once the yields are known, the results can be used to determine standard costs. The following formulas, applied to the example presented in Exhibit 5-4, are used for costing:

$$\text{Cost per salable pound} = \frac{\text{Original total cost}}{\text{Weight of product to sale}}$$
$$= \$34.24/6.375 \text{ lb}$$
$$= \$5.37.$$
$$\text{Cost per salable ounce} = \frac{\text{Cost per salable pound}}{16}$$
$$= \$5.37/16$$
$$= \$.336.$$
$$\text{Cost per portion} = \text{Cost per salable ounce} \times \text{ounces per portion.}$$

For a 6-oz portion the cost per portion would be $2.02.

The amount of cooking loss provides the most accurate cost determination per portion and should be the value used to determine the selling price. Periodic cooking loss tests should be done to determine costs. The cooking test may also reveal whether recommended cooking techniques are being followed. If cooking losses are too high, it may be indicative of poor cooking techniques, such as oven temperatures that are too high or cooking times that are too long.

PRICE DETERMINATION

Pricing is an important aspect of any business and is critical for achieving the targeted return on investment, maintaining or improving market share, meeting or preventing competition, and maximizing profits. Once the cost of a product is known, several methods can be used to determine the selling price.

Markup Factors

An easy method of product pricing is using markup factors. A *markup factor* is a multiplier based on the desired food cost percentage (food cost %) of a product. The selling price is determined by multiplying the food cost for a product by the markup factor.

The formula for the markup factor is:

$$\text{Markup factor} = 100/\text{Desired food cost \%}.$$

For example, a manager wants an entree to be priced so that there is a 25 percent food cost. The following formula would be used:

$$\text{Markup factor} = 100/25 = 4.$$

Suppose a portion of spaghetti had a food cost of $.90. To find the selling price for the portion of spaghetti, use the formula:

$$\text{Selling price} = \$.90 \times 4 = \$3.60.$$

Some foodservice operations use a single factor representing the same food cost % for all products. For example, products might be priced so that all items have a 32 percent food cost. In this case, a cost factor of 3.1 would be used for all products. Others may price items using different food cost percentages for different products. Table 5-1 provides markup factors for many commonly used food cost percentages.

Table 5-1 Markup Factors for Menu Pricing Desired

Desired Food Cost %	Factor	Desired Food Cost %	Factor
25	4.00	38	2.63
26	3.85	39	2.56
27	3.70	40	2.50
28	3.57	41	2.44
29	3.45	42	2.38
30	3.33	43	2.33
31	3.23	44	2.27
32	3.13	45	2.22
33	3.03	46	2.17
34	2.94	47	2.13
35	2.86	48	2.08
36	2.78	49	2.04
37	2.70	50	2.00

Food Cost Percentage Method

Another method for determining selling prices for products is the *food cost percentage method*. The resulting selling price using this method will be identical with the markup factor method, but the formula used for calculation is a little different:

$$\text{Selling price} = \frac{\text{Total food cost}}{\text{Desired food cost (as a decimal)}}.$$

For example, the food cost for a product is $1.25 and the manager wants to sell it at a price that will result in a 35 percent food cost. Using this method, the formula is:

$$\text{Selling price} = \$1.25/.35 = \$3.57.$$

To avoid pricing items using odd numbers, this number can be rounded to a number that fits into the desired pricing strategy, such as $3.60.

Cost-of-Profit Pricing

Some foodservice managers may want to price their products to ensure a predetermined percentage of profit from each item. In this case, profit is established as a cost and is included in determining the selling price along with food cost, labor cost, and fixed costs. For example, a manager determines that a 10 percent profit must be made on all items sold in the cafeteria. In calculating costs, the following are identified:

Fixed cost	25%
Labor cost	35%
Profit cost	10%
Total cost	70%

Fixed and labor cost percentages can be taken from the monthly or yearly income statements prepared for the dietary department. When profit is considered a cost, the total of all costs is 100 percent. Therefore, to find the targeted food cost %, subtract the total cost from 100 percent.

$$\text{Food cost \%} = 100\% - 70\% = 30\%.$$

Now the selling price can be determined by using the same formula illustrated earlier with the food cost percentage method.

$$\text{Selling price} = \frac{\text{Total food cost}}{\text{Desired food cost (as a decimal)}}.$$

For example:

$$\text{Selling price} = \$.78/.30 = \$2.60.$$

Pricing Considerations

While commercial foodservice operators have long recognized the importance of marketing, institutional operators have only recently become sensitized to marketing strategies. The current cost pressures in health care have necessitated that the foodservice manager develop a marketing approach for the foodservice department. In many operations, the cafeteria, restaurant, and/or coffee shop have become important profit centers. As a result, pricing of products for these areas has become an important function for the manager.

The primary objective in pricing is to establish prices such that the foodservice operation can meet its profit objective. In meeting this objective, prices for products must be high enough to be profitable for the operation and low enough so that customers will purchase them. In establishing the pricing strategy for a foodservice operation, consideration must be given to the customer, the competition, and the product.

Customer

Information about current and prospective customers is vital in making pricing decisions for any foodservice operation. In a hospital cafeteria, restaurant, or coffee shop, customers may be grouped into the following categories (market segments):

- physicians
- administrators
- medical staff
- clerical staff
- family of patients
- visitors.

While it may be extremely convenient for these customers to eat in the hospital, they certainly do not represent a captive market. As a result, the foodservice manager must determine what these customers perceive as value and how much they are willing and able to pay for food. Customer identification is useful in determining the appropriate product/pricing combination for each foodservice operation.

Foodservice operators in other settings identify the market segments they wish to serve. Examples of market segments are young families, double income no kids (DINKS), well-off older people, children, working people, or any number of potential segments. Identification of the market segment served is important in any foodservice setting.

To understand customers better, several questions should be answered:

- How many customers currently eat in the facility?
- What percentage of customers is represented by each market segment?
- How many potential customers are there in each of the market segments?
- How much are customers willing to spend for breakfast, lunch, dinner, and/or coffee breaks?
- What products do customers want?
- When do customers have meal and coffee breaks?
- If customers do not eat in the facility, where do they eat?
- Why do customers eat in the facility?
- What are customers' perceptions of advantages and disadvantages of eating in the facility?

Data needed to answer these questions can be collected in a variety of ways, including customer comment cards, written surveys distributed to target groups, and observations. In addition, records kept by the foodservice operation staff can be examined to determine the total number of customers, the number of customers during specific time periods, the number of each type of menu item sold, and the average check price. If records providing these data are not available, they should be developed and implemented as an integral process of the operation.

Competition

Astute foodservice managers always know their competitors, the products they offer, and the prices they charge. Just like the restaurateur, the manager in institutional foodservice operations should conduct market research to identify and describe the competition. Suggestions for the types of information the manager must know about the competition are given in Exhibit 5-5.

Once managers know their competition, they can make decisions about pricing. If products are very similar to those of competitors, they will usually be priced at the level of the competition.

An analysis of the competition is also useful for decision making in areas other than pricing: the product mix for the menu, advertising, public relations opportunities, and other marketing-related activities.

Exhibit 5-5 Tracking Competitors: Information to Know

Location
Size
   Number of seats
   Business volume
Products
   Product mix
   Service mix
   Distinguishing features
   Special advantages, benefits, and/or image
   Quality and consistency
Pricing
   Objectives
   Method
   Product prices
   Sensitivity to customers/competitors
Promotions

Product

The product itself will influence the pricing strategy. The customers' perceptions of value are of utmost concern. People consider the cost/value relationship when making purchasing decisions; therefore, the foodservice manager must keep that relationship in mind when pricing products.

Several characteristics of the product affect the selling price: volume, shelf-life, popularity, probability of change in popularity, food cost, labor cost, and competition among items.

Foods with a low food cost generally have a higher markup than items with a high food cost. For example, soup has a higher markup (lower food cost–to-sales ratio) than does roast beef. Soup might be priced at a 15 to 20 percent food cost, and the entree might be priced at a 40 to 60 percent food cost.

Foods that have a high demand (or ones that everyone selects) are priced such that the food cost % is low. Beverages are a good example. Items, such as desserts, that might be considered an impulse buy or an add-on item used to increase check totals might be priced at a higher food cost %.

Products that have higher labor costs can have a higher markup (lower food cost %) than products that require little labor. Homemade bear claws are an example of a product that might have a low food cost %. When considering customers' perceptions of value, products that are difficult to make or that customers are not likely to prepare at home can usually have a higher markup. Convenience items, on the other hand, require little labor and can be priced with a relatively high food cost % because of the low labor costs.

Product differentiation is another strategy that can be developed. If the food products produced in an operation are significantly different from competitors' products, pricing will be more independent of the competition. To avoid competitive pricing, a manager may consciously make the menu and food products different from those of the competition. For example, if the menu in the cafeteria included a quarter-pound hamburger, the price should be similar to that charged at the local McDonald's. On the other hand, it would not be so necessary to consider competitor's prices for unique products such as shrimp creole or pork tenderloin sandwiches.

There are advantages to having products similar to those of competitors and may be a strategy employed by the foodservice manager: customer familiarity and product popularity are two advantages. This is the reason for the increase in the number of salad bars, delis, baked potato bars, and similar products in foodservice operations such as hospital cafeterias, school cafeterias, and restaurants. Another advantage to having products similar to those of competitors is the impact of their marketing efforts. Competitors' marketing efforts, such as television commercials and newspaper advertisements, may actually increase the demand for a product offered.

Odd-Even Pricing

When pricing products, it is important to consider the value perceived by the customer. Some people think that odd-number prices such as $3.95 or $4.95 are perceived to be a better value and will result in a higher volume of sales than the comparable even-number prices of $4 or $5. As a result, many products are priced using the *odd-number pricing strategy*. Market research studies have not provided conclusive evidence to support the value of odd-number prices.

Percentages vs. Contribution: The Reality

In the discussion about pricing in relation to food cost %, it is easy to focus on the desirable (or targeted) food cost % and forget about the dollars of sales revenue. This must be kept in perspective since it is dollars, not food cost %, that are deposited in the bank, paid to employees, and used to purchase food and equipment.

While these percentages are often used for pricing, attention must be given to the contribution margin. The working definition of *contribution margin* is the dollars available for fixed expenses and profit and is calculated using the formula:

$$\text{Contribution margin} = \text{Sales} - \text{Variable costs}.$$

The goal of the foodservice manager is to obtain a contribution margin that pays all fixed costs and that provides the targeted operational profit.

The importance of the contribution margin in relation to the food cost % can best be illustrated with an example. Two of the a la carte entrees on a restaurant lunch menu are spaghetti and rib eye steak. A comparison of these products shows the following:

	Spaghetti	Rib Eye Steak
Food cost	$ .85	$1.50
Selling price	$2.60	$3.75
Food cost %	33%	40%
Contribution margin	$1.75	$2.25

Which of these entrees would the manager want to sell in the highest volume? The spaghetti has a lower food cost–to-sales ratio (food cost %) than does the steak. However, the contribution margin is $.50 higher for each steak, so more dollar sales could be made with the steaks, providing more money for fixed costs and profits. Thus, the wise manager would want to sell the rib eye steaks! The contribution margin should always be taken into consideration when pricing products, determining what products to sell, and determining how the products will be placed on the menu (layout and design of the menu).

MAKE/BUY ANALYSIS

Today the foodservice manager has many choices of forms in which foods can be purchased. Many products can be purchased fully prepared, requiring only re-thermalization before serving. Most foods can be purchased all along the food processing continuum from the basic ingredients for producing the product to the complete product.

For example, if apple pies were on the menu, there would be many choices in the form to purchase. The manager could purchase flour, shortening, salt, raw apples, sugar, and cinnamon and have the baker produce the pies using a standardized recipe. Another option would be to purchase ingredients for the crust and canned apple pie filling and require the baker to make the crusts from a standardized recipe and fill them with the commercially prepared filling. A third option would be to purchase ready-prepared frozen apple pies that would require the baker only to bake and portion the pies. Another option would be to purchase fully-cooked pre-portioned slices of applie pie that would require no work on the part of the baker.

Similar examples of purchasing choices could be given for most products, including breads, entrees, sauces, soups, vegetables, and desserts. The foodservice manager is faced with the decision of whether to make or buy many products. What should be the basis for the make/buy decision? Several factors must be considered, including cost, quality, skill level of employees, availability of employees, equipment, availability of product, and storage facilities. Another important consideration is the impact the product may have on sales volume and, consequently, profit.

Cost will always be a major consideration when making the make/buy decision. Usually, the more preparation done by the manufacturer, the higher the food cost. In addition to the basic food cost, other costs that must be considered include the cost of any extra ingredients added by the operation to "customize" the product, the cost of garnishes, labor costs (wages and fringe benefits), and energy costs. Each of these costs must be calculated for products made in the operation and for those purchased with some or all of the preparation completed.

If the food cost is higher for a convenience item, the cost differential must be offset by lower costs elsewhere (e.g., labor costs) or with an increased selling price in order to maintain the desired profit level. If using convenience items would enable the manager to eliminate a position or decrease the total number of labor hours, the use of convenience items might be cost-effective. If, however, the increased food costs were not offset by decreased costs in other areas (labor or operational), then profits would decrease. In most foodservice operations, productivity could be improved. It is important to consider labor cost and productivity when making make/buy decisions.

Cost cannot serve as the only criterion for the make/buy decision. Quality considerations must be given high priority. The first step in assuring quality products in an operation is to develop quality standards for the food products served. These quality standards can be used for evaluating products made in the operation or may serve as the basis for developing specifications and evaluating products to be purchased. The second step

Exhibit 5-6 Product Rating Form

Instructions: *Please taste the products one at a time. For each product, indicate your rating of the appearance, taste, and texture using the following rating scale:*

$$\text{Rating Scale} \quad 4 = \textbf{Excellent}$$
$$3 = \textbf{Good}$$
$$2 = \textbf{Fair}$$
$$1 = \textbf{Poor}$$

Then indicate your opinion of the overall acceptability of the product: excellent, acceptable, unacceptable. Please write down any specific comments you have about each product.

Attribute	Product	Product	Product
Appearance			
Taste			
Texture			
Overall acceptability E = Excellent A = Acceptable U = Unacceptable			

Comments:

is to establish a menu committee to evaluate food products that might be included on the menu. This committee should be composed of a variety of people, including the manager, purchasing agent (if applicable), chef, food servers, and cooks from different areas (salads, baker, etc.). It is also beneficial to have consumer groups (such as residents, patients, or cafeteria/restaurant customers) taste test products to provide important feedback on acceptability.

To get specific feedback on important qualities for a new product, the manager may want to develop a product evaluation form. This form, developed for a specific product, should include such descriptors as flavor, odor, color, shape, consistency, texture, moistness, tenderness, and size.

More often, the menu committee is asked to participate in taste tests of a new recipe being considered for the menu or of new products introduced by a vendor. In these cases, the manager may want general information on quality attributes, such as appearance, taste, and texture, along with an overall acceptability measure for a single food item. A sample product rating form designed to provide general information about product quality is shown in Exhibit 5-6.

Or, the manager may want the committee to rank order products by preference. For example, you want to evaluate three clam chowder products: one prepared from scratch, one canned product, and one frozen product. The menu committee and a consumer panel might be asked to taste each of the three products and rank order them, giving the product they liked best a *1* and the product they liked least a *3*. For taste panels, the sample products are coded in such a way that the panelists do not know which product is which, in an attempt to avoid bias. Codes such as letters

---

Exhibit 5-7 Product Rank-Ordered Comparison Form

Taste each of the food samples. Consider the appearance, taste, and texture of each product. Rank order the products by writing a 1, 2, or 3 in the blank beside the product letter. Use the following codes:

1	**I like this product best.**
2	**I like this product second best.**
3	**I like this product least.**

Product	Ranking
M	_____
P	_____
O	_____

(*N, M, O, P*), random numbers (*056, 698, 543*), symbols (∗, #, @, ○), or colors may be used. A sample form for a rank-ordered comparison is shown in Exhibit 5-7.

If a product does not meet the quality standards for an operation, it should not be considered for implementation despite its cost or convenience. Quality must always be considered.

Employee considerations must also be taken into account, especially the skill level of the employees and the number of labor hours. If the operation does not have a baker with the skill to make a quality cake from scratch, then the manager would opt to purchase mixes or ready-prepared cakes. It might not be realistic to use the time of a baker for labor-intensive products, such as croissants, so you would opt to purchase frozen croissant dough that requires only shaping and baking or ready-baked croissants.

Exhibit 5-8 Criteria for Make/Buy Analysis

	Standardized Recipe	Product A	Product B
Recipe cost	_____		
Product cost		_____	_____
Cost of added ingredients		_____	_____
Yield	_____	_____	_____
Food cost per portion	_____	_____	_____
Labor time/100 servings	_____	_____	_____
Hourly wage for cook/chef	_____		
Hourly fringe benefits	_____	_____	_____
Labor cost/100 servings	_____	_____	_____
Labor cost per portion	_____	_____	_____
Energy cost	_____	_____	_____
Energy cost per portion	_____	_____	_____
Quality	_____	_____	_____

The criteria for conducting a make/buy analysis are given in Exhibit 5-8. This format for comparing a standardized recipe with other product alternatives will ensure that the make/buy decision is based on multiple factors rather than on food cost or labor cost alone.

Accurate cost determination and effective pricing strategies are essential in achieving the profit objective of any foodservice operation. The process is challenging because of the many dimensions that must be considered. The successful manager will establish and maintain an ongoing process for monitoring costs, determining when pricing changes must be made, and evaluating the performance of the foodservice operation.

Chapter 6

Developing and Using a Budget

As discussed in chapter 1, planning is an important managerial function. Just as there should be written plans of strategy for reaching the goals and objectives of the operation, there should be specific plans for reaching the profit objective. A budget is a numerical forecast of the income, expenses, and profit (loss or break-even) of an operation for a specified time period. A budget represents management's goals and objectives in financial terms and provides a comparison standard for the financial performance of the unit. As an analogy, a budget is to a business (or department) what a road map is to a vacationer because it provides guidance (or direction) on the best way to get to the intended destination.

Several objectives are achieved through the budgeting process. The effective budget:

- provides a written plan of the financial goals and objectives for a specified time period
- identifies how resources are to be allocated in accordance with the overall financial plan of the operation
- establishes a basis or standard for comparing the financial performance of the operation
- provides a tool for controlling expenses
- communicates financial goals and objectives to individuals at the organizational and departmental levels
- sensitizes management to the relationship between expenses and revenue and to the necessity of controlling costs.

If these objectives are met, the financial goals and profitability are more likely to be achieved.

The budget process is not, however, without disadvantages. Major disadvantages include:

- Effective budgets are time-consuming to prepare, which means that they are expensive.
- Effective budgeting requires the involvement of many individuals on the staff, requiring them to cooperate and be committed to the process.
- Forecasting the future is difficult, so budgets will not accurately predict the operation's revenues and expenses.
- Extensive, accurate records of past performance of the operation must be available to develop an effective budget since past performance provides the basis for forecasting future performance.

Although disadvantages exist, budgeting should be done. Yet managers should be aware of these problems and work toward their alleviation. A well-developed budget is vital to the successful management of any business.

COMPONENTS OF A BUDGET PROGRAM

The budget program for an operation can range from the very simple to the very complex. Individual managers can select the components of the total budget program they want to implement in their particular foodservice operation. This decision should be based on the following factors:

- objectives of the budget
- resources (mainly time) that can be allocated to the budget process
- level of accuracy and sophistication needed.

A total budget consists of four basic components:

1. operating budget
2. cash budget
3. capital budget
4. master budget.

Each component serves a specific function for the operation and is discussed individually.

Operating Budget

The *operating budget* is the forecast of revenue (sales), expenses, and profit for a specified time period for an operation. This is the budget that guides the day-to-day operations of the department and serves as an important component of the control process. All foodservice operations, regardless of size and complexity, should have an operating budget to guide decision making and control mechanisms. The operating budget has three important components: the statistics budget, the expense budget, and the revenue budget.

Statistics Budget

The *statistics budget* is an estimate, or forecast, of the volume of sales or services for the next specified period. It may be developed monthly and/or yearly.

The accuracy and relevancy of the statistics budget depend on the availability of a number of statistical tools. Historical data provide a beginning for the development of the statistics budget. Records of past performance that provide important data for budgeting include:

- sales volume
- number of covers
- number of patients
- number of equivalent meals
- expenses, such as the costs of food, supplies, labor, energy, and other operating expenses.

These performance data provide a reasonable basis for the projection of volume and costs in the near future. Ratios of costs to sales volume (or revenue) are usually determined and used in the budgeting process for determining projected expenses in relation to the projected sales volume.

As discussed in chapter 1, the environment can have a significant impact on the foodservice system. Because of this influence, external factors must be considered. Statistical data should be collected in relation to:

- demographic trends
- the economy
- the Consumer Price Index
- federal and state commodity reports
- unemployment rates

- area wage and salary rates
- current legislation
- trends in the industry (may be related to restaurant, health care, catering, business and industry, airline, travel, or other appropriate industry).

Internal decisions related to price structure changes and cost-of-living and merit increases should also be considered. These data should be gathered and evaluated. By taking these factors into account, a more accurate forecast can be made for making budget projections.

Revenue Budget

The *revenue budget* is a projection of expected income for the budget period. These projections are based on the data gathered for the statistical budget, taking into consideration any changes in products or services that might be made during the next budget period. For example, a goal of the department is to increase revenue from catered events by 30 percent. An advertising campaign will be used to introduce catering services to prospective clients. As a result of this active advertising posture for catering, an estimated 30 percent increase in catering revenue is included in the budget. To measure performance and control costs, revenue projections should be made for appropriate departments or cost centers for the food service operation.

Expense Budget

The *expense budget* consists of a projection of the food, labor, supply, and other operating costs for the next time period. Expenses are usually estimated based on a ratio of cost to sales volume. These ratios may be based on past performance or desired relations. For example, if the desired food cost for catered events is 35 percent, then the revenue projection for catering multiplied by 0.35 would yield the food cost in dollars for catering. For example, if catering sales are projected to be $200,000 for the year with an average food cost of 35 percent, the projected food cost would be calculated as follows:

$$
\begin{aligned}
\text{Projected food cost} &= \text{Projected revenue} \times \text{Food cost \% (as a decimal)} \\
&= \$200,000 \times 0.35 \\
&= \$70,000.
\end{aligned}
$$

Cash Budget

A *cash budget* is developed to project the receipt of revenue and the expenditure of funds. The cash budget is a projection of an operation's cash flow. The purpose of the cash budget is to determine if funds will be available when needed to meet the financial obligations of the operation.

The cash budget is usually divided into monthly intervals. An example of a cash budget for a small coffee shop is shown in Table 6-1. This budget helps in planning for cash availability. Having too little cash to meet financial obligations results in slowness to pay debts, which could lead to problems in obtaining credit. Having too much cash on hand means that the cash is not being used to its full advantage. Notice in the example that insurance and interest expense both come due in January. To cover these expenses, the manager of the coffee shop must have $2,450 in cash available to pay these costs. In the example, there is adequate cash available to pay for these costs. The cash budget helps project the amount of cash needed during each time interval.

Capital Budget

A *capital budget* is prepared to estimate the cost of capital expenditures. Capital expenditures include improving, expanding, or replacing equipment, buildings, or land and would include purchasing a new piece of

Table 6-1 S & K Coffee Shop: Cash Budget for 1st Quarter, 1988

	Jan.	Feb.	Mar.	Apr.
Cash				
Beginning bank balance	$ 9,000	$11,932	$15,106	$23,929
Sales	37,200	33,600	46,500	
Total cash available	$46,200	$45,532	$61,606	
Expenditures				
Food	$11,160	$10,080	$13,950	
Labor	12,462	12,462	12,462	
Operating expense	6,696	6,384	9,765	
Lease	1,500	1,500	1,500	
Insurance	2,000			
Interest	450			
Total expenditures	$34,268	$30,426	$37,677	
Ending Balance	$11,932	$15,106	$23,929	

equipment, replacing an existing piece of equipment, renovating facilities, and purchasing a new facility. Capital expenditures must meet criteria established by administration, which might include:

- cost level (i.e., cost of $300 or more)
- usable time period (i.e., item must be capable of being used for a period of at least three years)
- item not sold or consumed by patients or clients.

In meeting these criteria, capital expenditure items become fixed assets for the operation. These items are usually depreciated over time because they will wear out and/or the technology will become outdated. These capital investments will also be used to provide services to customers (patients or clients) or to generate revenue.

Capital budgets are prepared for at least a three-year period with a yearly estimate of expenditures. The capital decision-making process is directly influenced by a number of external and internal constituencies. For hospitals, external influence is exerted by third-party payers, financing sources, and rate setting and rate control agencies. Because of provisions in Public Laws 92-603 and 93-641, health systems agencies affect capital expenditure decisions for hospitals receiving federal monies from Medicare (Title XVIII), Medicaid (Title XIX of the Social Security Act), or Maternal and Child Health (Title V).[1] Internal constituencies may include the board of trustees or board of directors, the planning committee, the finance committee, administrators, department managers, the medical staff, the controller, and the treasurer.

In preparing the capital budget, managers should prepare a schedule of need for each request, which would include:

- a description of the item requested
- whether the item is new, a replacement, or an improvement
- unit costs
- total costs
- justification for the expenditure, including alternatives
- salvage value of item, if applicable.

The foodservice manager may also be asked to prioritize capital expense requests or to categorize them as to whether they are urgent, essential, economically desirable, or generally desirable.[2]

The decision concerning which capital expenditures will be made can be based on a number of evaluation techniques, some qualitative and some quantitative. These techniques include:

- cost-benefit analysis
- payback period
- net present value
- internal rate of return.

A more thorough discussion of these techniques is presented in chapter 9. You may also refer to *Essentials of Hospital Finance.*[3]

Master Budget

The *master budget* is a compilation of the operating budget, the cash budget, and the capital budget. The master budget, in turn, provides the basis for projecting financial statements, specifically the income statement and the balance sheet. These "pro formas" are the capstone of the master budget.

STEPS IN THE BUDGET PROCESS

The budget planning process will be facilitated if the steps in the process are taken in a logical, sequential manner.

- *Step 1: Review the mission statement for the foodservice operation.* All decisions made for the department should be congruent with the mission and should support accomplishment of the mission. An example of a general mission statement for a dietary department in a for-profit hospital might be:

The mission of the dietary department is threefold:

1. to provide high quality food and service for patients, guests, and employees and to provide nutrition services for inpatients and out-patients
2. to provide stockholders with a return on investment equivalent to that of other hospitals
3. to contribute to the professional and personal development of employees.

- *Step 2: Review the goals and objectives established for the operation.* If specific, measurable financial objectives have not been established, this should be done before the budget process continues. All subsequent budgetary decisions should be made so that the operation's financial objectives can be achieved. Examples of specific measurable objectives include:

  - Achieve a 15 percent return on investment.
  - Maintain an average food cost of 35 percent.
  - Provide cost-of-living raises (projected to be 4 percent for the next fiscal year) for all employees.
  - Provide dietary instructions for all patients released from the hospital on a special diet.

- *Step 3: Collect statistical data to use in making budget decisions.* Many sources should be tapped for information about trends that could affect the revenue and expenses of the foodservice operation. These provide the basis for the statistics budget.

- *Step 4: Prepare the revenue budget.* This budget should take into account the statistical data collected in step 3, especially any changes in pricing structure for the operation. Separate revenue projections should be made for each department or cost center. For a hospital, revenue should be projected for the cafeteria, the coffee shop, vending, catering, and/or take-out, depending on the cost centers used. For a hotel food and beverage department, revenue would be projected for the restaurant, the coffee shop, room service, and banquets and catering. It is important to project revenue for each cost center or department because each has a different cost structure. Separating these data will also help in evaluating the performance effectiveness and efficiency of the various units or departments.

- *Step 5: Prepare the expense budget.* This budget will depend on the revenue projections made in step 4. The statistics budget will also provide important data for projecting expenses.

- *Step 6: Develop the cash budget.*

- *Step 7: Develop the capital budget.*

- *Step 8: Prepare pro forma financial statements, including projected income statement and balance sheet.* The *income statement* presents the income, expenses, and profit (loss or break-even) that is projected over the course of the budget period. The *balance sheet* presents the assets, liabilities, and equity for the operation. These financial statements indicate the financial condition of the operation at the end of the budget period and can be analyzed to determine if the projected performance of the organization will meet the financial goals established in step 2. The methods for developing and analyzing financial statements are presented in chapters 7 and 8.

• *Step 9: Revise budgets as necessary to ensure achievement of financial goals.* The budget must be revised as trends change or as management recognizes that forecasts are unrealistic. For example, a new health maintenance organization opens in the city, causing a 10 percent decrease in hospital occupancy, or a new restaurant opens next door, causing a 15 percent decrease in sales. Income and expenses must be modified for the next budget period to take this decrease into account.

• *Step 10: Review and approve budget.* The process for review and approval of the budget depends on the type of operation. For hospitals, budget hearings may be held with final approval coming from the hospital budget committee. A board of directors may approve budgets for foodservice operations such as private clubs. The corporate office staff may approve budgets for chain operations.

Managers of a department or operation must be astute about how the budget process works in their operation. In order to get an adequate budget approved, foodservice managers must develop a realistic budget based on the objectives of their operation. In order to "sell" the budget to administrators, managers must:

• develop the budget in relation to the overall goals and objectives of the organization
• justify how each expenditure contributes to the achievement of the goals and objectives of the operation
• identify the impact of varying budget levels on the level and the quality of service
• project the pay-back time for expenditures
• project the revenue generated by the expense incurred.

For example, the hospital is establishing a new fitness center. The director of the dietary department would like to add a clinical dietitian to consult in the new fitness center. Several questions should be asked: Does this fit with the departmental goals and objectives? What benefits will result from the new position? How much cost will be incurred? How much revenue will be generated by the service?

TYPES OF OPERATING BUDGETS

There are several types of operating budgets, each with advantages and disadvantages. The type of budget used will depend on the needs of the foodservice operation and, perhaps, the policies of the larger organization.

Fixed Budget

A *fixed budget* is developed for a specific, predetermined level of annual volume (number of patient days, cafeteria sales, catering sales, and/or vending sales for hospitals; number of customers and sales volume for restaurants). It is based on past sales and costs and predicted trends.

The first step is to prepare the statistics budget. Statistical data, which will be used to develop a sample budget, are shown in Exhibit 6-1. The example will be for a 300-bed hospital with a cafeteria.

The next step is to determine the volume of activity for the coming year. The estimated number of patient days and the estimated revenues for the cafeteria should be determined. Based on the data available, patient days will remain stable at 88,221. A 10 percent increase in the number of cafeteria meals is expected. The total number of meals for the next budget period will be:

Patient meals = 88,221 patient days × 3.11 meals per patient day
= 274,367 patient meals
Cafeteria meals = 384,450 × 1.1 (110%) = 422,895 meals
Patient meals = 274,367 (39%)
Cafeteria meals = 422,895 (61%)
Total meals = 697,262 (100%).

The revenue from the cafeteria is projected to increase 10 percent and will be:

Cafeteria revenue = $3.20 per equivalent meal × 1.1 increase × 422,895 meals
= $1,488,590.

The next step is to determine the expenses that will be incurred with this level of activity. These expenses will be based on last year's expenses taking into consideration projected increases for the next year attributable to price increases and salary increases. These expenses can be estimated as follows:

Expense	Current Cost		Projected % Increase		Total Meals		Total Expense
Food	$ .925	×	4	×	697,262	=	$ 670,766
Labor	1.16	×	5	×	697,262	=	849,265
Supply	.185	×	7	×	697,262	=	138,023
Operating	.37	×	6	×	697,262	=	273,466
					Total		$1,931,520

Exhibit 6-1 Sunnyvale Hospital (300 Bed): Performance Data for 1987

Patient meals per patient day		3.11
Direct expense per patient day		$10.72
Direct expense per 100 meals		$264.27
Salary expense per 100 meals		$115.07
Paid hours per 100 meals		24.5
Nonpatient meal equivalent factor		$3.20

	Patient Days		Cafeteria Meals	
January	8,370	9.5%	37,200	9.7%
February	7,644	8.7%	30,800	8.0%
March	8,277	9.4%	34,100	8.9%
April	7,200	8.2%	31,200	8.1%
May	7,440	8.4%	32,650	8.5%
June	6,750	7.7%	30,500	7.9%
July	6,510	7.4%	30,200	7.8%
August	6,500	7.4%	29,875	7.8%
September	7,200	8.2%	32,175	8.4%
October	7,626	8.6%	31,250	8.1%
November	7,450	8.4%	33,000	8.6%
December	7,254	8.2%	31,500	8.2%
Total	88,221		384,450	

The number of patient days is projected to remain stable, while cafeteria meals and revenues are expected to increase 10%. Estimated cost increases for the coming year: labor 5%, food 4%, supply cost 7%, operating costs 6%.

The completed annual operating budget for this foodservice department is shown in Exhibit 6-2. The operating expenses can be broken down further, depending on the needs of the operation.

Monthly budgets can be developed from the yearly budget in one of two ways. The first, and easiest, method is simply to divide the yearly budget by 12. This method does not take into account the seasonal fluctuations that will occur in almost every type of foodservice operation.

The second method relies on historical data on volume trends. For example, in Exhibit 6-1, data are provided on the number of patient days and the number of cafeteria meals served each month of the last year. The percentage of meals served each month could be determined and used for estimating volume and costs for each month. This method is recommended since it is likely to be a much more reliable forecast of the volume and the costs.

Exhibit 6-2 Sunnyvale Hospital: 1988 Annual Operating Budget

Estimated Revenue		
Cafeteria	$1,488,590	
Total estimated revenue		$1,488,590
Estimated Expenses		
Food	$ 670,766	
Salaries and wages	679,500	
FICA taxes	48,584	
Employee benefits	121,181	
Supplies	138,023	
Operating expenses	273,466	
Total estimated expenses		$1,931,520
Estimated Net Loss		$ (442,930)

The developed budgets serve as the basis for the development of pro forma financial statements. The pro forma income statement projects the sales, expenses, and net income or loss for the year. Table 6-2 provides a pro forma income statement for the hospital used in Exhibits 6-1 and 6-2. Notice that the data for developing the pro forma income statement are in the operating budget. The pro forma balance sheet projects the assets, liabilities, and owner's equity for the next year's end. To develop the pro forma balance sheet, projected activity from the operating and capital budgets are combined with the figures on the balance sheet for the current year.

The pro forma balance sheet shows what changes are expected in the three areas of the balance sheet: assets, liabilities, and owner's equity. For example, the purchase of a piece of equipment for $15,000 is included in the capital budget. On the pro forma balance sheet there would be an increase in fixed assets of $15,000 and an increase in either liabilities or owner's equity, depending on how the purchase was made. An example of a pro forma balance sheet is shown in Exhibit 6-3.

Flexible Budget

A *flexible budget* is developed to reflect various levels of volume (patient census or sales volume). In the fixed budget developed earlier, all expenses were based on 697,262 meals. The actual volume could be higher or lower, so expenses associated with higher and lower volumes should be calculated.

A flexible budget could be prepared for volume levels of 90 and 110 percent of the original estimation. In calculating the expenses associated

Table 6-2 Sunnyvale Hospital: Income Statement

	Amounts	%
Food Sales	$1,488,590	100
Cost of Food Consumed	670,766	45.1
Gross Profit	$ 817,824	54.9
Other Income	—0—	
Total Income	$ 817,824	54.9
Controllable Expenses		
Salaries and wages	$ 679,500	45.6
Employee benefits	169,768	11.4
Direct operating expenses		
Uniforms	15,000	1.0
Laundry	18,252	1.2
China, glassware, and flatware	42,600	2.9
Cleaning supplies	49,423	3.3
Paper supplies	46,000	3.1
Energy and utility expense	47,214	3.2
Repairs and maintenance	20,000	1.3
Administrative and general	93,000	6.2
Total controllable expenses	$1,180,754	79.3
Income Before Occupation Costs	$ (362,930)	24.4
Occupation Costs	$ 50,000	3.4
Income Before Depreciation	$ (412,930)	27.7
Depreciation	$ 30,000	2.0
Income Before Income Taxes	$ (442,930)	29.8

with that volume, the cost percentages may vary. For example, in the fixed budget, food cost was 35 percent, labor cost was 44 percent, supply cost was 7 percent, and other operating cost was 14 percent of the total costs. A decrease in volume by 10 percent would not automatically lower costs by 10 percent nor would a 10 percent increase in volume necessarily increase costs by 10 percent. Some costs, such as food, vary directly with volume, while other costs, such as labor, do not. Thus, in the flexible budget, cost percentages may vary in relation to the volume of business. An example of a flexible budget is presented in Table 6-3. Although the flexible budget is more time-consuming to prepare, it is a more useful management tool than the fixed budget. It is more realistic to recognize the ranges of volume that are likely to occur in most foodservice operations.

Zero-Base Budget

Zero-base budgeting (ZBB) was popularized in the 1970s as a budgeting technique that would ensure fiscal responsibility in allocating resources and

Exhibit 6-3 Sunnyvale Hospital: Balance Sheet for Year Ended December 31, 1988

Assets			
Current assets			
Cash		$20,000	
Accounts receivable		—0—	
Inventories			
Food	$18,700		
Beverage	1,000		
Other	6,200	25,900	
Prepaid expenses		15,000	
Total current assets			$60,900
Fixed assets			
Equipment	$200,000		
Less accumulated depreciation	100,000	$100,000	
Furniture and fixtures	50,000		
Less accumulated depreciation	10,000	40,000	140,000
Total assets			$200,900
Liabilities and Owner's Equity			
Current liabilities			
Accounts payable		$30,000	
Current portion long-term debt		2,500	
Accrued expenses		15,000	
Total current liabilities			$47,500
Long-term liabilities			37,500
Total liabilities			$85,000
Owner's equity			115,900
Total liabilities and owner's equity			$200,900

controlling costs. ZBB requires that a budget be prepared for each departmental activity and that each activity be fully justified. Other types of budgets begin with the last year's budget to which a percentage is added to account for inflation or other factors that are projected to change. The ZBB technique, on the other hand, requires the manager to begin budget preparation with a blank piece of paper.

Steps in the ZBB Process

The process of ZBB is different from the other types of budgets. The four basic steps in the ZBB process are:

1. *Determine the decision packages (decision units, programs, or activities) for the department.* In other words, what activities or programs are currently being carried out by the department and what activities or programs might be implemented to improve departmental effectiveness?

Table 6-3 Sunnyvale Hospital: 1988 Annual Operating Budget

	Level of Sales Volume		
	90%	*100%*	*110%*
Estimated Revenue			
Cafeteria	$1,339,731	$1,488,590	$1,637,449
Total estimated revenue	$1,339,731	$1,488,590	$1,637,449
Estimated Expenses			
Food	$ 603,689	$ 670,766	$ 737,843
Salaries and wages	645,525	679,500	682,000
FICA taxes	48,479	51,030	51,218
Employee benefits	112,967	118,735	119,350
Supplies	124,220	138,023	151,825
Operating expenses	259,774	273,466	287,139
Total estimated expenses	$1,794,654	$1,931,520	$2,029,375
Estimated Net Loss	$ (454,923)	$ (442,930)	$ (391,926)

Kaud[4] presented a priority ranking for a number of activities, including management service, purchasing and storage, food production service, patient meal service, nutrition service, and nonpatient feeding. These are basic services for a hospital dietary department. Other activities can be added. For example, hospital dietary departments are becoming involved with activities such as wellness centers, supplemental feedings for homebound patients, counseling, bakery outlets, production of meals for other groups (such as Meals-on-Wheels, Headstart, and nursing homes), and other revenue generating activities for which decision packages would be developed. The decision packages vary with the individual foodservice operation.

2. *Develop an analysis for the decision package.* The analysis provides in-depth information about the activity and requires the manager developing the analysis to weigh the advantages and disadvantages of the activity for the overall operation of the department or operation. In the analysis process the manager must also justify the activity in relation to the goals and objectives of the department. The analysis should include:

- *The purpose of the activity*
- *The feasibility of the activity*
- *The costs of the activity:* This section includes both the income (revenue) generated by the activity and the costs (expenses) associated

with the activity. From these data, an estimated net profit/loss can be determined for the activity.

- *The benefits of the activity*
- *Consequences of **not** having the activity:* If the activity were not funded, what impact would that have on the operation? For some activities that are necessary to the operation, a minimum budget level may be established.
- *Alternatives to the activity.*

A hypothetical decision package was developed for a food and nutrition services department proposing to add a dietitian to work with a newly formed health and fitness center (Exhibit 6-4). This example shows how each component of an analysis can be developed.

3. *Rank the decision packages from highest to lowest priority.* If every request cannot be funded, which activities are most critical to the department? Which activities would be "nice to have" but would not have a significant impact on the quality of the basic product and/or services offered by the department? This ranking requires management staff to evaluate critically each activity in which they are involved and consider the necessity of those activities for goal attainment.

4. *Allocate resources.*

Advantages and Disadvantages of ZBB

ZBB has both advantages and disadvantages. Advantages include:

- *Increased attention to fiscal responsibility:* The process requires managers to plan carefully for desired outcomes and evaluate the current operation. Attention must be given to the cost-benefit analysis and to prioritizing activities according to their importance to the department.
- *Focused analysis of alternative courses of actions and activities for the department*
- *Improved communication among departments within the organization:* The process may facilitate a better understanding of the contributions made by the various departments.
- *Improved documentation upon which to make decisions and documentation of the rationale for the decisions made.*

Disadvantages of ZBB include:

- *Requires a substantial amount of resources, especially the time of management staff*

Exhibit 6-4 Decision Package for Zero-Base Budget

Department: Food and Nutrition Services
Activity: Dietitian for Health and Fitness Center
Purpose of Activity: To employ a full-time clinical dietitian with expertise
in counseling to be involved with the hospital's new health and fitness center.
Feasibility of Activity: The hospital will institute the new center at the beginning
of the new fiscal year. Having a registered dietitian on the staff is essential to
providing consumers with complete health information and, thus, to the success of
the center. Registered dietitians are available in the area, and one could easily be
recruited by the department. A fee for service could be developed for consultation
time. The dietitian could also develop nutrition programs such as weight
management that would fit the overall mission of the center. Individual fee
structures would be developed for each program.
Cost-Benefit Analysis: The following costs and benefits have been identified for the
first year of the program:

Revenues			
Individual consultation	$18,000	$18,750	$22,500
Weight management	8,000	9,000	12,000
Costs			
Salaries	$25,000	$25,000	$25,000
Wages (hourly)			4,000
Administrative	500	500	500
Office supplies	200	300	400
Printing	100	300	500
Net Income	$200	$1,650	$4,100

Potential Benefits:
1. Increased revenue for the department
2. A comprehensive approach to health and fitness provided to clients, resulting in
   a product that has a higher value to clients.
3. Improved nutrition knowledge and behavior for citizens of the community,
   thereby improving the health of those citizens.
4. Establishment of the hospital and the department as leaders in nutrition related
   to health and fitness, creating feelings of trust and goodwill in the community.

Consequences of Not Approving Decision Package:
1. No nutrition services will be provided to clients of the Health and Fitness
   Center.
2. Other hospitals will develop such a program and gain a competitive edge.
3. Fewer dollars will be generated by the department.

Alternatives to Activity:
1. A part-time position could be created for the center; however, limited dollars
   would be generated because of limited time of staff.
2. An existing clinical position could be split to provide some time for the center.
   This would have a negative impact on patient services.
3. The department could not participate in the Health and Fitness Center.

- *Requires extensive paper work*
- *May create hard feelings both within and among departments because of justification requirements for activities*
- *May be difficult to implement as the process was designed:* Resource allocation may still be based on the power bases of individuals and departments rather than on documented needs and contributions of the activities and departments.

Even if ZBB is not implemented in its purest sense, a modified approach could be useful to any operation. The approach would encourage decision makers to evaluate carefully the current state of the operation and justify the costs and benefits of existing as well as new programs and activities.

NOTES

1. William O. Cleverley, *Essentials of Hospital Finance* (Rockville, Md.: Aspen Publishers, Inc., 1978).

2. F.A. Kaud, "Budgeting: A Comparative Analysis of Techniques and Systems," in J.C. Rose, ed., *Handbook for Health Care Food Service Management* (Rockville, Md.: Aspen Publishers, Inc., 1984), pp. 115–130.

3. Cleverley, *Essentials of Hospital Finance.*

4. Kaud, "Budgeting."

Chapter 7

Financial Statements: Development and Use

After the foodservice manager prepares the budgets for the foodservice operation, it is essential to use this baseline information as a guideline for monitoring the operational performance throughout the budget period. Effective financial management of the foodservice operation is as important as the menu planning and nutritional standards functions. Although the chief financial officer (or hospital administrator) usually has the primary responsibility for managing financial resources, the foodservice manager is in the best position to control, monitor, and report the costs of the foodservice operation. Even if the foodservice manager is not responsible for compiling financial statements for the operation, it is still important that the manager understand the financial condition of the operation. Therefore, financial statements should be compiled, whether or not the manager is assigned the task.

In light of the excess capacity in the health care field, cost control and containment are becoming increasingly important to the success and survival of the foodservice operation, the foodservice director, and the institution. Generally speaking, the operational objective of the institution is to provide a socially desirable service without regard for financial gain (if it is a nonprofit institution).

In today's highly competitive markets, an important institutional objective should be the continued financial viability of the institution. Financial efficiency and effectiveness have become imperative; therefore it is essential to design and maintain an accounting system that will provide the information necessary for the foodservice manager to manage the financial aspects of the operation. The accounting procedures used by the institutional manager should be logically consistent with the operational objectives of the organization and should provide accurate, useful information for interested user groups on a timely basis. User groups typically include the foodservice staff, the administrative services department, large suppliers, banks, corporate management, and the board of directors; and they use the financial information in various ways. Groups and departments within the organization use the information to analyze performance and plan for future operations. External user groups frequently use operational reports to make decisions to extend credit to the department or to recommend the organization to possible customers, clients, or employees.

ACCOUNTING PRINCIPLES

In the practice of accounting, the American Institute of Certified Public Accountants (AICPA) has promulgated generally accepted accounting principles to guide both the accountant and the management team in tracking, recording, and reporting the financial activities of the organization. These accounting principles consist of a framework that includes:

- basic concepts
- definitions
- three bases of reporting.

Basic Concepts

The *basic concepts* are the rules of thumb that form the basis of operation for all organizations and include:

- the matching concept
- the consistency concept
- the full disclosure concept.

The Matching Concept

The *matching concept* means that the revenue from a transaction should be reported with the associated expense. Transactions should be reported in the accounting period in which they occur, regardless of when the associated monies flow into or out of the foodservice operation.

The Consistency Concept

The *consistency concept* means that management should use the same methods for reporting from period to period so that the financial statements can be compared and the operational changes determined without distortion of results by changes in accounting methods. For example, there are several inventory valuation methods: LIFO, FIFO, and weighted average are three examples. These valuation methods were explained in chapter 2. The selected inventory valuation method should remain constant from one accounting period to the next in order to satisfy the consistency requirement.

Financial statements are frequently compared to monitor the trends of the organization's financial condition. Thus a change in the bookkeeping methods (e.g., inventory valuation or depreciation method) could affect the financial picture dramatically and mislead the user of the information (unless the financial statements contained a footnote detailing both the change and the related impact). The consistency requirement provides users of financial statements further assurance that the statements accurately report operational results and provide a valid basis for comparison with prior operational results.

The Full Disclosure Concept

The *full disclosure concept* means that pertinent information must be explained in the financial statements. These explanations, or disclosures, are usually found in the footnotes of the financial statements. Typically, inventory valuation methods, depreciation methods, and other changes in methodology are described in the footnotes.

Definitions

Certain terms are used in the accounting field and are defined for the following specific items:

- asset
- depreciation
- liability
- capital
- revenue
- expense
- retained earnings.

Asset

An *asset* is anything owned by the organization (tangible or intangible) that has a monetary value. Assets are broken into two categories: current assets and fixed assets.

Current assets are liquid assets. *Liquid assets* are cash, marketable securities, accounts receivable expected to be collected within one year, and inventory the operation expects to sell within one year.

Fixed assets consist of furniture, fixtures, the plant, the building, equipment, and land. Except for land, these assets decrease in value over time and will eventually require replacement. Fixed assets are reported at their original cost.

Depreciation

Depreciation is the decrease in value of a fixed asset over the useful life of that asset. The specific depreciation methods include straight-line depreciation and various accelerated methods. (These methods were discussed in chapter 2.) The selection of the depreciation method for a particular asset depends on tax laws, the estimated life of the asset, and the cash flow requirements of the operation.

Operations are required to report the depreciation of fixed assets in two ways. *Depreciation expense* is the depreciation for a specific asset for the *current* accounting period and is always reported on the income statement. *Accumulated depreciation* is the *cumulative* total of an asset's periodic depreciation expenses over the life of the asset. This cumulative total is reported on the balance sheet.

Liability

A *liability* is any obligation, or debt, the organization has incurred. Liabilities decrease the value of the organization because they represent claims on the operation's assets. Liabilities are categorized as either current or long-term.

Current liabilities are those the operation expects to pay within one year, using current assets. Examples of current liabilities are:

- accounts payable
- wages payable
- taxes payable
- the current portion of long-term debt

Long-term liabilities are liabilities that typically are not paid within the current year using current assets. Liabilities such as debentures, the noncurrent portion of a note or mortgage, and similar debt instruments are the most common examples of long-term liabilities. Long-term liabilities are often used by an operation to provide the funding for major capital purchases or improvements such as the plant, equipment, land, furniture, and fixtures.

Capital

The *capital* is the *net worth,* or the value, of the operation. The net worth, or capital, is calculated by subtracting total liabilities from total assets. Table 7-1 provides an example of the calculation of an operation's net worth. The operation's net worth of $9,000 indicates that there will be assets remaining for future use even after all the present liabilities are paid. If the total liabilities had been more than the total assets, it would have indicated that the operation is in debt and probably requires emergency loans.

Revenue

Revenue is all income to the operation that is a result of providing goods and/or services to customers. In a hospital foodservice operation, these goods and services usually consist of patient meals, cafeteria meals, and catering.

Expense

An *expense* is any cost that is incurred in order to produce revenue. The specific expenses incurred vary with the complexity of the organization. Virtually all foodservice operations have labor expense. Some operations separately track cafeteria labor and patient meals labor.

Table 7-1 Harriet Hospital: Balance Sheet

Cash	$ 1,000		
Accounts receivable	14,350		
Inventory	6,650		
Total current assets		$22,000	
Equipment	$28,000		
Accumulated depreciation	(20,000)		
Net equipment		$ 8,000	
Furniture and fixtures	$14,000		
Accumulated depreciation	(4,000)		
Net furniture and fixtures		$10,000	
Total fixed assets		$18,000	
Total assets			$40,000
Accounts payable	$12,000		
Wages payable	4,500		
Total current liabilities		$16,500	
Long-term debt	$14,500	$14,500	
Total liabilities			$31,000
			$ 9,000[1]

[1]Net worth (capital) = Total assets − Total liabilities.

Retained Earnings

Retained earnings is income that is retained for use in the business after all expenses are paid.

Bases of Reporting

There are three bases of reporting operational results, which are actually methods of reporting:

1. fund accounting
2. accrual basis accounting
3. cash basis accounting.

Fund Accounting

Fund accounting is usually used by municipalities, government departments, universities, and many hospitals. It involves the separation of resources into either restricted or unrestricted categories. The separation of these resources is based on whether the resources carry external restrictions or designations. In other words, if internal management or the board of directors restricts previously unrestricted funds, the accounts will still be categorized within the unrestricted or general fund. Therefore, restricted funds or revenues are frequently classified as:

- endowment funds
- plant replacement and expansion funds
- other earmarked funds.

Accrual Basis Accounting

Accrual basis accounting means that revenue is reported in the period in which the service (or sale) occurs regardless of when the payment is received. Liabilities are also reported in the period in which they are incurred regardless of when the payment is made. This basis is in keeping with generally accepted accounting principles, particularly the matching concept. An operation that uses fund accounting can simultaneously report activities on an accrual basis.

Cash Basis Accounting

Cash basis accounting means recording income and expenses only when the cash changes hands. This means that a sale is recorded only when the money is received for it, and a purchase is recorded only when payment is made for it. Although this is the way individuals keep track of their own funds, firms usually do not use this method. The reason is that in any particular accounting period revenue or expenses can end up being severely overstated or understated because of the difference between the transaction and the actual movement of cash. Since the cash basis method violates the matching concept, it is usually used only by sole proprietors or very small businesses.

DESIGNING THE ACCOUNTING/RECORD KEEPING SYSTEM

The department's *accounting system* is the routine employed to keep track of all transactions that occur as a result of departmental operations. By having predetermined procedures, the manager and the foodservice department employees will know the appropriate sequence of record keeping events under most operational circumstances.

This chapter addresses the setting up and maintaining of a manual accounting system. Countless software packages are available for accounting and record keeping systems. It is essential, however, to understand the inner workings of the accounting and record keeping system before relying on an automated system.

Flowcharting Departmental Activities

The first step in designing the appropriate record keeping system for an operation is to prepare a flowchart of operational activities. A *flowchart* is a chart that outlines the logical progression of events from inception to completion so as to clarify the sequence of events. After each step is identified and laid out in the order of performance, the corresponding record keeping/accounting systems can be designed. Figure 7-1 is an example of a flowchart for a foodservice operation.

In order to design an accounting system that is appropriate for an individual operation, it is critical to keep this operational flowchart in mind. It is especially significant to note the iterative nature of the flowchart. In other words, the cycle of operations repeats each accounting period. Flowcharting also highlights problem areas and provides a logical approach for systemizing the operation as well as the record keeping.

The identification of appropriate record keeping systems is accomplished by adapting the operational flowchart. Figure 7-2 provides a logical approach to establishing, creating, and maintaining a record keeping system

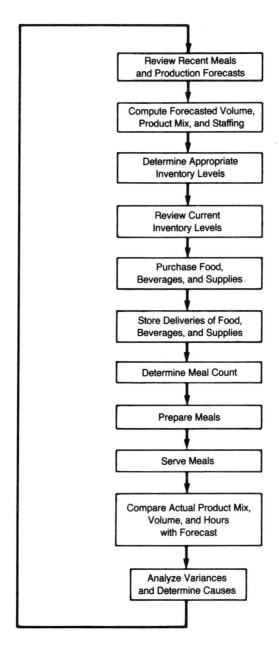

Figure 7-1 Foodservice department flowchart of departmental procedures

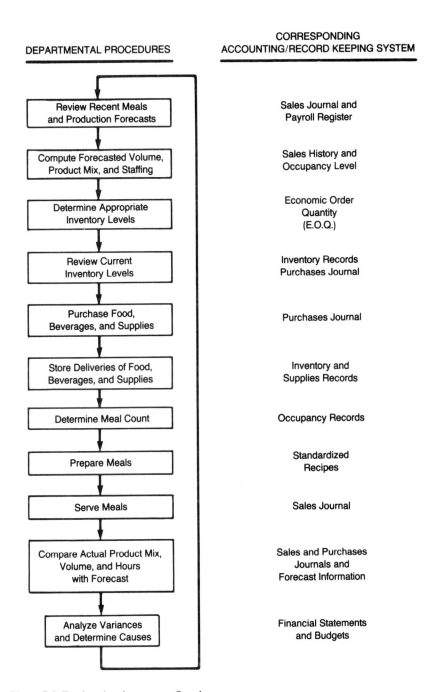

DEPARTMENTAL PROCEDURES	CORRESPONDING ACCOUNTING/RECORD KEEPING SYSTEM
Review Recent Meals and Production Forecasts	Sales Journal and Payroll Register
Compute Forecasted Volume, Product Mix, and Staffing	Sales History and Occupancy Level
Determine Appropriate Inventory Levels	Economic Order Quantity (E.O.Q.)
Review Current Inventory Levels	Inventory Records Purchases Journal
Purchase Food, Beverages, and Supplies	Purchases Journal
Store Deliveries of Food, Beverages, and Supplies	Inventory and Supplies Records
Determine Meal Count	Occupancy Records
Prepare Meals	Standardized Recipes
Serve Meals	Sales Journal
Compare Actual Product Mix, Volume, and Hours with Forecast	Sales and Purchases Journals and Forecast Information
Analyze Variances and Determine Causes	Financial Statements and Budgets

Figure 7-2 Foodservice department flowchart

that matches the flow of activities with the flow of transactional data and the existing performance and expense reports.

For example, food items are ordered on account from the wholesaler. An order form is prepared, and the delivery is received. The invoice is recorded in the purchases journal. The total monthly purchases are posted to the general ledger at the end of the month. Financial statements are compiled based on the general ledger account balances and other entries made to adjust account balances to match revenues and expenses.

Chart of Accounts

The *chart of accounts* categorizes the transactions of an operation. Operational events and transactions affect asset, liability, capital, revenue, and expense accounts. A chart of accounts may already be established, or one may need to be developed. In designing the chart of accounts, each transaction category is assigned a general series number. For example, all asset accounts could be from 100 to 199, liabilities from 200 to 299, capital from 300 to 399, revenue from 400 to 499, and expenses from 500 to 599. Each individual account would then be assigned an account number within the appropriate account series. An example of a chart of accounts is provided in Table 7-2.

Table 7-2 Chart of Accounts

Balance Sheet Accounts	Income Statement Accounts
100 Assets	400 Revenue
110 Cash–Cafeteria	410 Sales–Cafeteria
111 Cash–Patient pymt. allocation	411 Sales–Patient meals
120 Accounts receivable	412 Sales–Catering
130 Supply inventory	413 Sales–Other
140 Food inventory	500 Expenses
150 Prepaid utilities	510 Purchases–Inventory
160 Kitchen equipment	520 Purchases–Supplies
165 Accumulated depre.–Equip.	530 Salary expense
170 Building	540 Utility expense
175 Accumulated depre.–Bldg.	550 Depreciation expense
200 Liabilities	(kitchen equipment)
210 Accounts payable	560 Depreciation expense
220 Salaries payable	(building)
230 Long-term note payable	570 Misc. expense
300 Capital	
310 Retained earnings	
320 Income summary	

Restaurants usually use a standardized chart of accounts. The widely accepted standardized chart of accounts for restaurants is Laventhol and Horwath's *Uniform System of Accounts for Restaurants.* Most hospitals, universities, and governmental units have an established chart of accounts the foodservice director should use.

Posting Rules

Posting a transaction to a specific journal or ledger means to record it in the appropriate place. The determination of the appropriate place and way to record the item is based on basic debit and credit rules. These rules define whether increases and decreases in a particular account that are caused by a specific transaction are recorded as debits or credits. Table 7-3 gives guidelines for analyzing transactions.

The accounting system the manager establishes should incorporate the use of a dual-entry accounting system. A *dual-entry system* means that each entry made to the books must increase one account and decrease another; that is, each entry must contain a debit and a credit.

OVERVIEW OF ACCOUNTING SYSTEM DESIGN

An operation's accounting procedure and system should be designed in accordance with the flow of activities and be based on the generally accepted accounting principles already discussed. Although each manager will customize the accounting system to fit the operation, certain accounting procedures are universal to all operations. These procedures are:

- Post to transaction journals.
- Post transaction journals to general ledger.

Table 7-3 Posting Guide

Account Title	How To Record Increases	How To Record Decreases	Account Balance Usually Is a
Revenue	Credit	Debit	Credit
Expense	Debit	Credit	Debit
Asset	Debit	Credit	Debit
Accumulated depreciation	Credit	Debit	Credit
Liability	Credit	Debit	Credit
Capital	Credit	Debit	Credit

- Prepare the trial balance and make adjustments.
- Prepare financial statements.
- Make closing and reversing entries.

Before presenting these procedures, however, the following components of the accounting system must be defined:

- source documents
- transaction journals
- general ledger
- general journal.

Source Documents

Source documents are the proof of the transaction and include:

- cash register tapes
- invoices
- bills of lading
- packing lists
- time cards
- meal and headcount reports
- deposit slips.

Transaction Journals

Transaction journals are spreadsheets, or worksheets, that are organized by type of transaction. These journals are used to record chronologically every transaction occurring during the accounting period. At the end of the accounting period, the transaction journal totals are transferred to the general ledger.

General Ledger

The *general ledger* is used to record and report summary transaction and adjustment information. The information is categorized by account number, as dictated by the chart of accounts. There should be a separate section, or page, allocated to every account number in the chart of accounts.

General Journal

The *general journal* is used to record adjusting entries for the accounting period. These adjusting entry totals are ultimately transferred to the general ledger.

POST TO TRANSACTION JOURNALS

Each activity or transaction that occurs in an operation during the course of an accounting period is recorded in chronological order in the appropriate journal. This is done to indicate the impact the transaction has on the profitability of the operation. Whenever a transaction occurs, the manager should ensure that both sides of the transaction are posted. For example, if food is received, the inventory level will be affected but so will either accounts payable or cash, depending on whether the food was charged on account or paid for upon delivery.

There is a transaction journal for each specific transaction category. Each of the journals provides a multicolumn spreadsheet approach to the transaction category. The following transaction journals are discussed:

- sales journal
- cash receipts journal
- purchases journal
- cash disbursements journal
- payroll register.

Sales Journal

Institutional foodservice operations often bill a client or customer on a periodic basis rather than deal in cash at the time the service is provided. This is also the case with allocations and third-party payments. When this is the case, the transaction that occurs at the time the foodservice is provided is called a "sale on account." All sales on account are recorded in the *sales journal*. Each sale on account increases the operation's accounts receivable (which will at some point in the future be collected, and cash will flow into the operation). Of course, each sale on account also increases total sales. Therefore, these sales are posted in the sales journal as follows:

- debit to accounts receivable
- credit to sales.

If the operation will regularly estimate sales for payment by allocation or third-party payments, there should be a column set up in the sales journal especially for this. The basis of estimation should be defined in the journal and should be reviewed on a regular basis for reasonableness so as to ascertain the appropriateness of the estimation.

Whenever a sale on account is cancelled, the following entry is made in the sales journal:

- debit to sales
- credit to accounts receivable.

Table 7-4 is an example of a sales journal with entries for sales on account and a cancellation of a sale on account.

Source documents could consist of charge records, cover counts for the period, running counts of cafeteria meals, catered meal counts, or patient meal counts. The various reports for capturing this information were presented in chapter 2.

Cash Receipts Journal

The *cash receipts journal* is used to track, report, and account for all cash flowing into the operation during the course of the accounting period. The operation's total cash activity consists of more than just the cash in the cash drawer. All cash must be reported. This includes cash allocated to the operation by administrative services or accounting. Allocations can occur when an institution receives third-party payments. When this happens, a portion of the total payments received over the period is usually allocated to the operation. The manager should pay particular attention to this activity and the basis of the allocation so that the appropriate amount is allocated to the operation. Cost, expense, and performance reports should be used to prove how much the meals served in-house really cost the operation. Managers should ensure that cash allocations cover costs (including labor, overhead, and depreciation in addition to food and beverage costs) so that the operation can remain viable. Specific cost and expense controls should be in place to safeguard cash once it is received and to ensure that the right amount of it comes in.

Regular cash receipts are posted to the cash receipts journal as follows:

- debit to cash
- credit to accounts receivable.

Table 7-4 Sales Journal (Sales on Account)

Date	Account Debited	Caf. or Patient ID No.	Accounts Receivable Dr.	Sales Cr.
4/1	Patient meals		$3,200	$3,200
4/2	Cafeteria charges		$85	$85
4/3	Patient meals		$2,650	$2,650
4/4	Patient meals		$2,175	$2,175
4/5	Patient meals		$2,085	$2,085
4/6	Patient meals		$2,216	$2,216
4/7	Patient meals		$2,150	$2,150
4/8	Patient meals		$1,875	$1,875
4/9	Patient meals		$2,260	$2,260
4/10	Patient meals		$1,720	$1,720
4/11	Patient meals		$4,980	$4,980
4/12	Overcharge		($1,000)	($1,000)
4/14	Patient meals		$1,190	$1,190
4/15	Patient meals		$1,150	$1,150
4/16	Patient meals		$1,450	$1,450
4/17	Patient meals		$1,460	$1,460
4/18	Patient meals		$1,520	$1,520
4/19	Patient meals		$1,560	$1,560
4/20	Patient meals		$1,560	$1,560
4/21	Patient meals		$1,540	$1,540
4/22	Patient meals		$1,460	$1,460
4/23	Patient meals		$1,490	$1,490
4/24	Patient meals		$1,440	$1,440
4/25	Patient meals		$1,510	$1,510
4/26	Patient meals		$1,620	$1,620
4/27	Patient meals		$1,550	$1,550
4/28	Patient meals		$1,680	$1,680
4/29	Patient meals		$1,590	$1,590
4/30	Patient meals		$1,820	$1,820
Totals			$49,986	$49,986

Cash receipts from allocations are posted to the same journal as follows:

- debit to cash
- credit to accounts receivable (sales).

Table 7-5 is an example of cash receipts journal and depicts both kinds of cash receipts transactions. Deposit tickets, lock box deposits, and cash register tapes comprise the typical source documents for the postings.

Table 7-5 Cash Receipts Journal

Date	Account Credited	Other Accounts Cr.	Cafeteria Sales Cr.	A/R Cr.	Cash Dr.
4/1	Patient accts. Pymt. allocation			$5,860	$5,860
4/5	Cafeteria pymt.		$165		$165
4/8	Patient accts. Pymt. allocation			$6,250	$6,250
4/15	Patient accts. Pymt. allocation			$3,470	$3,470
4/22	Patient accts. Pymt. allocation			$1,620	$1,620
4/29	Patient accts. Pymt. allocation			$865	$865
Totals		$0	$165	$18,065	$18,230

If the operation must issue a cash refund, e.g., in the case of an over-allocation or overcharge on a credit sale, the cash refund is *not* posted to the cash receipts journal. Rather, it is posted to the cash disbursements journal, which is presented in a later section.

Purchases Journal

The purpose of the *purchases journal* is to keep track of all purchases on account. The theory is similar to that for the sales journal. Any item an operation receives (over the course of the accounting period) and does not pay cash for is posted to the purchases journal.

Typical foodservice purchases include food, beverages, and supplies. The posting should reference the invoice or purchase order number to facilitate tracking and provide an additional audit trail. In the institutional setting, purchases frequently require an approved purchase order in advance from the accounting or administrative services department. In this case, the purchases journal should reference the internally authorized purchase order number when the purchase is posted. The purchase order number should be referenced even if the purchase order system is self-contained within the foodservice department.

The posting source documents consist of invoices, packing slips, and bills of lading. Specific columns should be set up in the journal to categorize inventory purchases (i.e., meat, produce, and beverages).

The purchases on account are posted to the purchases journal as follows:

- debit the specific inventory column
- credit accounts payable.

At times, after inspecting a shipment, it may be necessary to return food, beverage, or supply items to the supplier. If this occurs, the transaction should be posted to (and the invoice number referenced) the purchases journal as follows:

- debit to accounts payable
- credit to inventory (or supplies).

An example of a purchases journal that shows purchases on account, and some returns as well, is provided in Table 7-6.

Cash Disbursements Journal

All transactions involving an outflow of cash (or checks) from the operation are recorded in the *cash disbursements journal*. Many transactions involve cash outflows, including:

- payroll
- payroll taxes
- payments for equipment
- payments for services
- utilities
- refunds
- payments to vendors for purchases on account.

In the cash disbursements journal, the manager should provide a column for accounts payable and a column for miscellaneous payments as well.

The payments for purchases previously made on account are posted as follows:

- debit to accounts payable
- credit to cash.

Cash disbursements for utilities, salaries, and other miscellaneous items do not initially go through the purchases journal as an increase to accounts

Table 7-6 Purchases Journal

Date	Vendor	Accounts Payable Cr.	Purchases (of Invty.) Dr.	Supplies Dr.	Other Accounts Dr.
4/1	Am. Hosp. Supply	$188		$188	
4/1	Food Wholesalers	$11,730	$11,730		
4/1	Main Office Equip.	$82			$82
4/12	Dairy Products Co.	$675	$675		
4/13	Food Wholesalers	$13,265	$13,265		
4/15	MW Food Distrib.	$816	$596	$220	
4/15	Simek's Meats	$723	$723		
4/18	Dairy Products Co.	$10,675	$10,675		
4/20	Irv's Catering Sply.	$136		$136	
4/21	TX Kitchen Equip. Co.	$63			$63
4/22	Midwest Food Distrib.	$279	$279		
4/25	Food Wholesalers	$337	$337		
4/29	Cub Foods	$19		$19	
4/30	Dairy Products Co.	$675	$675		
Totals		$39,663	$38,955	$563	$145

payable. Therefore, when disbursement is made for these items, the disbursement is posted to the disbursements journal as follows:

- debit to the miscellaneous payments column
- credit to cash.

An example of a cash disbursements journal is provided in Table 7-7.

Payroll Register

The *payroll register* is used to calculate and track the details concerning the payroll checks issued to employees. In other words, the payroll register functions as a payroll journal and provides data for paying employees as well as paying the various taxing authorities.

The salary expense amount that is transferred from the payroll register to the cash disbursements journal should be the gross pay amount. At first glance, this may seem incorrect since the employee receives only the net pay amount. The difference between gross and net pay, however, is still the employee's pay. The operation serves only as an intermediary and ultimately passes this money along to the appropriate taxing authority.

Table 7-7 Cash Disbursements Journal

Date	Account Debited	Other Accounts Dr.	Accounts Payable Dr.	Cash Cr.
4/1	Am. Hosp. Supply		$225	$225
4/1	Food Wholesalers		$1,500	$1,500
4/1	Dairy Products Co.		$715	$715
4/8	Simek's Meats		$916	$916
4/8	Main Office Equip.	$71		$71
4/15	Salaries	$2,860		$2,860
4/22	Utilities	$165		$165
4/22	Midwest Food Dist.		$1,266	$1,266
4/30	Salaries	$2,785		$2,785
Totals		$5,881	$4,622	$10,503

The payroll register should include all pertinent information for each employee, including:

- rate of pay
- hours worked
- tax rate
- tax withholdings
- net pay.

The manager is, of course, required both to supply this information and to disburse the withheld taxes to the government. The payroll register functions as a spreadsheet, as can be seen in Table 7-8, which shows a sample register, complete with tax calculations.

General Journal

The *general journal* is used to record some of the adjusting, closing, and reversing entries at the end of each accounting period. The entries are discussed later in this chapter.

POST TRANSACTION JOURNALS TO THE GENERAL LEDGER

At the end of each accounting period, every transaction journal is posted to the general ledger. Before posting the transaction journals to the general ledger, however, each journal must be totaled and the balances verified.

Table 7-8 Payroll Register

			Gross Pay			Tax Deductions			
Date	Name	Total Hours	O.T.	Reg.	Gross Total[1]	Fed.	FICA	State	Net Pay
4/15	P. Barry	48	$0	$240	$240	$53	$17	$19	$151
4/15	T. Kerley	90	$90	$480	$570	$125	$41	$46	$358
4/15	K. Riley	80	$0	$400	$400	$88	$29	$32	$251
4/15	K. Rink	90	$90	$480	$570	$125	$41	$46	$358
4/15	R. Sittley	100	$180	$480	$660	$145	$47	$53	$415
4/15	M. Zwitt	70	$0	$420	$420	$92	$30	$34	$264
Subtotals		478	$360	$2,500	$2,860	$629	$204	$229	$1,798
4/30	P. Barry	33	$0	$165	$165	$36	$12	$13	$104
4/30	T. Kerley	90	$90	$480	$570	$125	$41	$46	$358
4/30	K. Riley	80	$0	$400	$400	$88	$29	$32	$251
4/30	K. Rink	90	$90	$480	$570	$125	$41	$46	$358
4/30	R. Sittley	100	$180	$480	$660	$145	$47	$53	$415
4/30	M. Zwitt	70	$0	$420	$420	$92	$30	$34	$264
Subtotals		463	$360	$2,425	$2,785	$613	$199	$223	$1,750
Totals		941	$720	$4,925	$5,645	$1,242	$404	$452	$3,548

[1]Gross pay is posted to the cash payments journal.

This means to ensure that within each transaction journal, the total of all the debit columns equals the total of all the credit columns.

In closing each transaction journal to the general ledger, two entries are recorded:

- transferring entry
- clearing entry.

Transferring Entry

The first step in closing transaction journals to the general ledger is to post a transferring entry. The *transferring entry* is composed of the totals that were initially calculated when summarizing the journals. The figures are from the transaction journals, but the transferring entry is posted to the general ledger.

Table 7-6 provides data to derive the purchases journal transferring entry. The entry in the general ledger is posted as follows:

Debit inventory	$38,955
Debit supplies	$ 563
Debit other accounts	$ 145
Credit accounts payable	$39,663.

When posting journal totals to the general ledger, the transaction journal title should be referenced in the entry.

Examples of general ledger accounts after posting the transferring entries are provided in Table 7-9.

Clearing Entry

Once the transferring entries have been posted, the transaction journals can be "closed out." This means that the totals for each account (column) in each journal must be made to equal zero. The *clearing entry* is the entry made within the transaction journal of the amount that will "zero out" the column totals. For example, refer again to the purchases journal in Table 7-6. The clearing entry for the purchases journal is as follows:

> Debit to accounts payable for $39,663
> Credit to inventory   for $38,955
> Credit to supplies   for $ 563
> Credit to other accounts   for $ 145.

After the clearing entries are posted to the transaction journals, every column total for every journal should be recalculated. Each column should then be equal to zero. Table 7-10 shows the impact of the purchases journal clearing entry on the purchases journal. (Refer to Table 7-6 to compare this with the purchases journal before the clearing entry).

Table 7-9 General Ledger Postings From Transaction Journals

AC#:111 Title: Cash

Date	Source Journal	Dr.	Cr.	Balance
3/31	Balance forward			$36,350
4/30	Cash payments		$10,503	$25,847
4/30	Cash receipts	$18,230		$44,077

AC#:120 Title: Accts. Receivable

Date	Source Journal	Dr.	Cr.	Balance
3/31	Balance forward			$112,960
4/30	Sales	$49,986		$162,946
4/30	Cash receipts		$18,065	$144,881

continues

Table 7-9 continued

AC#:130 Title: Supplies

Date	Source Journal	Dr.	Cr.	Balance
3/31	Balance forward			$629
4/30	Purchase	$563		$1,192

AC#:140 Title: Inventory

Date	Source Journal	Dr.	Cr.	Balance
3/31	Balance forward			$6,950
4/30				
4/30				

AC#:160 Title: Kitchen Equipment

Date	Source Journal	Dr.	Cr.	Balance
3/31	Balance forward			$48,000
4/30	Purchase	$145		$48,145
4/30	Cash payments	$71		$48,216

AC#:165 Title: Accum. Depre–Equip.

Date	Source Journal	Dr.	Cr.	Balance
3/31	Balance forward			($18,000)

AC#:170 Title: Building

Date	Source Journal	Dr.	Cr.	Balance
3/31	Balance forward			$90,000

AC#:175 Title: Accum. Depre.–Bldg.

Date	Source Journal	Dr.	Cr.	Balance
3/31	Balance forward			($48,000)

AC#:210 Title: Accounts Payable

Date	Source Journal	Dr.	Cr.	Balance
3/31	Balance forward			($102,589)
4/30	Cash payments	$4,622		($97,967)
4/30	Purchases		($39,663)	($137,630)

Table 7-9 continued

AC#:220 Title: Salaries Payable

Date	Source Journal	Dr.	Cr.	Balance
3/31	Balance forward			$0

AC#:310 Title: Retained Earnings

Date	Source Journal	Dr.	Cr.	Balance
3/31	Balance forward			($126,300)

AC#:411 Title: Sales

Date	Source Journal	Dr.	Cr.	Balance
3/31	Balance forward			$0
4/30	Sales		($49,986)	($49,986)

AC#:510 Title: Purchases–Invty.

Date	Source Journal	Dr.	Cr.	Balance
3/31	Balance forward			$0
4/30	Purchases	$38,955		$38,955

AC#:530 Title: Salaries Expense

Date	Source Journal	Dr.	Cr.	Balance
3/31	Balance forward			$0
4/30	Cash payments	$5,645		$5,645

AC#:540 Title: Utility Expense

Date	Source Journal	Dr.	Cr.	Balance
3/31	Balance forward			$0
4/30	Cash payments	$165		$165

AC#:550 Title: Depre. Exp.–Equip.

Date	Source Journal	Dr.	Cr.	Balance
3/31	Balance forward			$0

AC#:560 Title: Depre. Exp.–Bldg.

Date	Source Journal	Dr.	Cr.	Balance
3/31	Balance forward			$0

Table 7-10 Purchases Journal and Adjusting Entries

Date	Vendor	Accounts Payable Cr.	Purchases (of invty.) Dr.	Supplies Dr.	Other Accounts Dr.
4/1	Am. Hosp. Supply	$188		$188	
4/1	Food Wholesalers	$11,730	$11,730		
4/1	Main Office Equip.	$82			$82
4/12	Dairy Products Co.	$675	$675		
4/13	Food Wholesalers	$13,265	$13,265		
4/15	MW Food Distrib.	$816	$596	$220	
4/15	Simek's Meats	$723	$723		
4/18	Dairy Products Co.	$10,675	$10,675		
4/20	Irv's Catering Sply.	$136		$136	
4/21	TX Kitchen Equip. Co.	$63			$63
4/22	Midwest Food Distrib.	$279	$279		
4/25	Food Wholesalers	$337	$337		
4/29	Cub Foods	$19		$19	
4/30	Dairy Products Co.	$675	$675		
Totals		$39,663	$38,955	$563	$145
4/30	Clearing entry (brackets indicate opposite of column headings)	($39,663)	($38,955)	($563)	($145)
4/30	Ending balance	$0	$0	$0	$0

PREPARE THE TRIAL BALANCE

The *trial balance* is the process that takes the manager from the end-of-period general ledger totals, through any necessary adjustments, up to the financial statement preparation stage. The trial balance is usually prepared on a trial balance worksheet, which is a multicolumn spreadsheet. The first column of the worksheet should contain every account that appears in the general ledger, in the same order. This first column is followed by four pairs of columns.

The first pair of columns is used to duplicate the debit or credit totals for each account in the general ledger immediately after transferring the journal totals to the general ledger. The second pair of columns is for the debit or credits that will be adjusting entries. (These adjusting entries are discussed later in this chapter.) The third and fourth pairs of columns are for extending the adjusted worksheet totals to the appropriate pair of financial statement columns. (These columns and extensions are discussed later in this chapter.)

The first pair of columns can be completed immediately after the journals' totals are posted to the general ledger. The manager should simply copy the new total for each account directly onto the worksheet. An example of a trial balance worksheet with general ledger totals is provided in Table 7-11.

Adjusting Entries

Generally speaking, *adjusting entries* are made because of accrual basis accounting. This ensures the reporting of revenues and expenses when they occur, regardless of when the cash flow occurs. The adjusting entries are recorded in the general journal, referencing the account number from the chart of accounts. All of the adjustments are then copied from the general journal onto the trial balance worksheet in the pair of adjustment columns. These adjusting entries are handled separately from the other transaction journal entries because the entries are not caused by a transaction but are made so that revenue and expenses will match. There are specific types of adjusting entries that will probably be required almost every accounting period:

- supplies adjustments
- inventory adjustments
- depreciation adjustments
- salary adjustments.

Supplies

Supplies expense for the period means the change in total supplies on hand. The period's supplies expense is calculated as follows:

Supplies cost of sales = Beginning supplies inventory
+ Supplies purchases − Ending supplies inventory.

The adjusting entry to post this supplies cost of sales to the general journal is:

- debit to supplies expense
- credit to supplies inventory.

Inventory

The *inventory adjustment* is similar to the supplies adjustment in that the adjustment is made so that the final inventory total will be equal to

Table 7-11 Trial Balance Worksheet

Acct. No.	Account Title	Trial Balance Dr.	Trial Balance Cr.	Adjustments Dr.	Adjustments Cr.	Income Statement Dr.	Income Statement Cr.	Balance Sheet Dr.	Balance Sheet Cr.
111	Cash	$44,077	$0						
120	Accounts receivable	$144,881	$0						
130	Supplies	$1,192	$0						
140	Inventory	$6,950	$0						
150	Prepaid expenses	$0	$0						
160	Equipment	$48,216	$0						
165	Accum. depre.–Equipment	$0	$18,000						
170	Building	$90,000	$0						
175	Accum. depre.–Building	$0	$48,000						
210	Accounts payable	$0	$137,630						
220	Salaries payable	$0	$0						
230	Long-term notes payable	$0	$0						
310	Retained earnings	$0	$126,300						
320	Income summary	$0	$0						
410	Sales–Cafeteria	$0	$165						
411	Sales–Patient meals	$0	$49,986						
510	Purchases	$38,955	$0						
520	Supplies expense	$0	$0						
530	Salary expense	$5,645	$0						
540	Utility expense	$165	$0						
550	Deprec. exp.–Equipment	$0	$0						
560	Deprec. exp.–Building	$0	$0						
570	Misc. general expenses	$0	$0						
		$380,081	$380,081						

Net income
Final verification

the ending inventory and the cost of sales account will be equal to the inventory used during the period. The cost of sales is calculated as follows:

Cost of sales = Beginning inventory + Purchases − Ending inventory.

The general ledger already reflects the beginning inventory and purchases figure. To post the cost of sales through the general journal, the following steps are required:

- debit income summary account for beginning inventory
- credit inventory account for beginning inventory.

The purpose of this step is to include beginning inventory in the total cost of sales. The second step is:

- debit inventory account for ending inventory
- credit income summary account for ending inventory.

The purpose of this step is to exclude the ending inventory from the total cost of sales.

Depreciation

The decreased value of a fixed asset over time is a cost. This cost, called "depreciation," must be recorded in the operational records and on the financial statements. Since the source of this cost is not a transaction, the only way to capture the cost is to make an adjusting entry to the accounting system. The recognition of depreciation enables the manager to determine which assets are approaching obsolescence and will need replacing. An adjusting entry is recorded each accounting period to recognize this depreciation expense. The adjusting entry to the general journal for each period is:

- debit depreciation expense
- credit accumulated depreciation.

The specific amount of the entry depends on the specific asset the manager is depreciating and on the depreciation method, useful life, and original cost of that asset.

Salaries

Frequently, the end of the accounting period does not coincide with the end of all employees' pay periods. For example: assume that pay dates are the 15th and last day of the month, but the paychecks on the 31st include only the hours worked through the 24th. Then the salaries for hours worked from the 25th through the 31st will be paid the next month, although the work was performed this month. The salary expense from the 25th through the 31st must be reflected in the current month's salary expense.

The adjusting entry to recognize this accrued liability in the general journal is:

- debit salary expense
- credit salaries payable.

Posting Adjusting Entries

All adjusting entries must be posted to the general journal. Table 7-12 is an example of a general journal reflecting the adjustments discussed.

The adjustments must then be recorded in the appropriate adjustment columns on the trial balance worksheet. An example of this is provided in Table 7-13.

Extending the Worksheet Balances

In order to determine whether an account should be extended to the balance sheet or income statement columns, compare the account number with the chart of accounts. Asset, liability, and capital accounts are balance

Table 7-12 General Journal

Date	Description	Acct. No.	Debit	Credit
Adjusting Entries				
4/30	Income summary account		$6,950	
	Inventory (beginning balance)	140		$6,950
4/30	Inventory (ending balance)	140	$8,675	
	Income summary account			$8,675
4/30	Supplies expense	520	$740	
	Supplies	130		$740
4/30	Depreciation expense–Equipment	550	$506	
	Accumulated deprec.–Equipment	165		$506
4/30	Depreciation expense–Building	560	$250	
	Accumulated deprec.–Building	175		$250
4/30	Salaries expense	530	$1,415	
	Salaries payable	220		$1,415

sheet accounts. Revenue and expense accounts are income statement accounts.

The manager should determine the adjusted balance for each account line by combining the original balances in the first pair of columns with the adjustments from the second pair of columns. The adjusted balance of each account line should then be recorded in either the debit or the credit column, depending on whether the adjusted balance is a debit or a credit balance. The only exception to this is for the income summary account. For this line, record both the debit and the credit adjustments in the income statement columns.

After extending each line item to the appropriate financial statement column, the manager should calculate the sum of each column on the trial balance worksheet. The manager should then calculate the difference between the debit and credit columns on the income statement columns. This figure is the net income for the period (or net loss if the debit column is larger than the credit column). The manager should record the net income figure in the debit column of the income statement column immediately below the previously computed total.

Then the manager should calculate the difference between the debit and credit totals in the balance sheet columns. This difference is the increase in capital (if the debit column is larger than the credit column). This increase in capital is the increase to retained earnings (which is caused by the net income from the accounting period). The increase should be recorded as a credit to the balance sheet column on the same line as the net income was recorded in the income sheet column.

The account title for these newly computed figures is *net income*. Finally, the manager should compute and record the new totals for the income statement and balance sheet columns to verify that the debits and credits once again agree. An example of a completed trial balance worksheet is provided in Table 7-14.

FINANCIAL STATEMENT PREPARATION

The extended figures that were recorded on the income statement and balance sheet columns on the trial balance worksheet (Table 7-14) are used to develop operational financial statements. The following financial statements are presented:

- income statement
- balance sheet
- statement of sources and uses of funds.

Table 7-13 Trial Balance Worksheet

Acct. No.	Account Title	Trial Balance Dr.	Trial Balance Cr.	Adjustments Dr.	Adjustments Cr.	Income Statement Dr.	Income Statement Cr.	Balance Sheet Dr.	Balance Sheet Cr.
111	Cash	$44,077	$0						
120	Accounts receivable	$144,881	$0						
130	Supplies	$1,192	$0		$740				
140	Inventory	$6,950	$0	$8,675	$6,950				
150	Prepaid expenses	$0	$0						
160	Equipment	$48,216	$0						
165	Accum. depre.--Equipment		$18,000		$506				
170	Building	$90,000	$0						
175	Accum. depre.--Building	$0	$48,000		$250				
210	Accounts payable	$0	$137,630						

220	Salaries payable	$0	$0		$1,415
230	Long-term notes payable	$0	$0		
310	Retained earnings	$0	$126,300		
320	Income summary	$0	$0	$6,950	$8,675
410	Sales–Cafeteria	$0	$165		
411	Sales–Patient meals	$0	$49,986		
510	Purchases	$38,955	$0		
520	Supplies expense	$0	$0	$740	
530	Salary expense	$5,645	$0	$1,415	
540	Utility expense	$165	$0		
550	Deprec. exp.–Equipment	$0	$0	$506	
560	Deprec. exp.–Building	$0	$0	$250	
570	Misc. general expenses	$0	$0		
		$380,081	$380,081	$18,536	$18,536

Net income

Final verification

Table 7-14 Trial Balance Worksheet

Acct. No.	Account Title	Trial Balance Dr.	Trial Balance Cr.	Adjustments Dr.	Adjustments Cr.	Income Statement Dr.	Income Statement Cr.	Balance Sheet Dr.	Balance Sheet Cr.
111	Cash	$44,077	$0					$44,077	
120	Accounts receivable	$144,881	$0					$144,881	
130	Supplies	$1,192	$0		$740			$452	
140	Inventory	$6,950	$0	$8,675	$6,950			$8,675	
150	Prepaid expenses	$0	$0					$0	
160	Equipment	$48,216	$0					$48,216	
165	Accum. depre.–Equipment		$18,000		$506				$18,506
170	Building	$90,000	$0					$90,000	
175	Accum. depre.–Building	$0	$48,000		$250				$48,250
210	Accounts payable	$0	$137,630						$137,630

Acct	Account								
220	Salaries payable		$0		$1,415				$1,415
230	Long-term notes payable		$0						$0
310	Retained earnings		$126,300						$126,300
320	Income summary		$0	$6,950	$8,675	$6,950	$8,675		
410	Sales–Cafeteria		$165				$165		
411	Sales–Patient meals		$49,986				$49,986		
510	Purchases	$38,955				$38,955			
520	Supplies expense	$0		$740		$740			
530	Salary expense	$5,645		$1,415		$7,060			
540	Utility expense	$165				$165			
550	Deprec. exp.–Equipment			$506		$506			
560	Deprec. exp.–Building			$250		$250			
570	Misc. general expenses	$0		$0		$0			
		$380,081	$380,081	$18,536	$18,536	$54,626	$58,826	$336,301	$332,101
	Net income					$4,200			$4,200
	Final verification					$58,826	$58,826	$336,301	$336,301

The Income Statement

The income statement (also known as the revenue and expense statement or the profit and loss statement) reports the operational results over a period of time. The general sequence of line items is in the same order as listed in the trial balance worksheet.

Each line should be listed in the same order as it appears on the trial balance worksheet, beginning with sales. The exception to this is the reporting of the cost of sales. The cost of sales is reported on the income statement immediately after sales and is calculated from the trial balance worksheet as follows:

$6,950	(Amt of debit to income summary account for beginning invty)
+38,955	(Purchases)
45,905	Cost of goods available
−8,675	(Amt of credit to income summary account for ending invty)
$37,230	Cost of sales

The *gross margin* is derived by subtracting the cost of goods sold from the sales. The gross margin is recorded following the cost of sales. All of the other expenses from the trial balance worksheet are in the category of operating expenses and should be listed in the same order.

The operating expenses should subsequently be totaled and subtracted from the gross margin. The difference between the gross margin and the operating expenses is the net income. This figure must agree with the net income reported on the trial balance worksheet in the income statement column.

An income statement, using data from the trial balance worksheet (Table 7-14), is provided in Table 7-15.

Balance Sheet

The purpose of the balance sheet is to measure the value of the organization or operation at a specific point in time. This value, or net worth, is the total value of the assets minus the total value of the liabilities. The fully extended trial balance worksheet (Table 7-14) is used to generate the balance sheet.

The accounts are listed in the same order as on the worksheet, with the asset accounts listed first, followed by the liability accounts and the capital account. Within the asset section, the current assets are separated from the fixed assets. The current liabilities are also separated from any long-term liabilities.

Table 7-15 Income Statement for Month Ended 4/30

Sales	$50,151
Cost of Sales	$37,230
Gross Margin	$12,921
Operating Expenses	
Salary expense	$7,060
Depreciation expense–Equipment	$506
Depreciation expense–Building	$250
Utilities expense	$165
Supplies expense	$740
Miscellaneous expense	$0
Total Operating Expenses	$8,721
Net Income	$4,200

A schedule must be prepared to determine the end-of-period retained earnings in addition to the figures on the trial balance worksheet. An example of the retained earnings schedule is shown in Table 7-16. The ending balance for retained earnings in this Table is the figure reported on the balance sheet for retained earnings as of the end of the accounting period. The total assets must equal the sum of liabilities and capital. A balance sheet using figures from the trial balance worksheet and the retained earnings statement is provided in Table 7-17.

Statement of Sources and Uses of Funds

The purpose of the *statement of sources and uses of funds* is to disclose the causes of changes in either cash or the equivalent (i.e., working capital). *Working capital* consists of an organization's current assets. This statement gives the manager a method to study the department's (or organization's) net funds flow over a specific period of time. Attention is focused on the working capital generated by the normal operations of the department via the compilation of this financial statement. This helps the manager assess

Table 7-16 Retained Earnings Recap

Retained earnings (beginning balance)	$126,300
Plus net income for period	$4,200
Retained earnings (ending balance)	$130,500

Table 7-17 Balance Sheet as of 4/30

Current Assets		
Cash	$44,077	
Accounts receivable	$144,881	
Inventory	$8,675	
Supplies	$452	
Total current assets	$198,085	
Fixed Assets		
Equipment	$48,216	
Accumulated depreciation–Equipment	($18,506)	
Building	$90,000	
Accumulated depreciation–Building	($48,250)	
Total fixed assets	$71,460	
Total Assets		$269,545
Liabilities		
Accounts payable	$137,630	
Salaries payable	$1,415	
Total liabilities	$139,045	
Retained Earnings	$130,500	
Total Liabilities and Retained Earnings		$269,545

the viability and adaptability of the organization because these funds can potentially replace assets, acquire new assets, expand the capacity of the facility, and provide other opportunities for the organization.

The sources and uses of funds statement is of paramount importance in planning for the future needs for funds, both the nature and the timing of the potential uses: in other words, determining whether the increased capital investment is primarily intended for inventories, fixed assets, debt retirement, or other purposes.

The first step in preparing the statement of sources and uses of funds is to prepare a schedule showing the actual increases and decreases during the accounting period in the working capital accounts. This merely means to compare the current balance sheet accounts with the prior period balance sheet accounts. The current balance sheet was given in Table 7-17. A prior period's balance sheet is provided in Table 7-18.

The next step is to determine the change in every account. The most straightforward method to visualize this is to prepare a schedule similar to Table 7-19.

Table 7-18 Balance Sheet as of 3/31

Current Assets		
Cash	$36,350	
Accounts receivable	$112,960	
Inventory	$6,950	
Supplies	$629	
Total current assets	$156,889	
Fixed Assets		
Equipment	$48,000	
Accumulated depreciation–Equipment	($18,000)	
Building	$90,000	
Accumulated depreciation–Building	($48,000)	
Total fixed assets	$72,000	
Total Assets		$228,889
Liabilities		
Accounts payable	$102,589	
Salaries payable	$0	
Total liabilities	$102,589	
Retained Earnings	$126,300	
Total Liabilities and Retained Earnings		$228,889

Changes in the current assets and current liabilities figures do not represent sources and uses of funds. They represent only a change in the components of the working capital.

Sources of funds include transactions that reduced fixed assets and transactions that increased retained earnings. The transaction that increased retained earnings is net income. Accumulated depreciation decreases the value of fixed assets by the change in the accumulated depreciation during the period. The increase in retained earnings and the increase in accumulated depreciation are the sources of funds.

Uses of funds are the "flip side" of the sources. Working capital outflows have occurred if fixed assets have increased or if retained earnings have decreased. A decrease in noncurrent liabilities (i.e., mortgage note payable) is also indicative of a use of funds. An increase in fixed assets indicates the purchase of additional assets. A decrease in retained earnings would occur if the organization were to have a net loss during the accounting period.

Table 7-19 Worksheet: Changes in the Balance Sheet

	As of 3/31	As of 4/30	Increase (Decrease)
Cash	$36,350	$44,077	$7,727
Accounts receivable	$112,960	$144,881	$31,921
Inventory	$6,950	$8,675	$1,725
Supplies	$629	$452	($177)
Total current assets	$156,889	$198,085	$41,196
Equipment–Kitchen	$48,000	$48,216	$216
Accumulated depreciation	($18,000)	($18,506)	($506)
Building	$90,000	$90,000	$0
Accumulated depreciation	($48,000)	($48,250)	($250)
Total fixed assets	$72,000	$71,460	($540)
Total assets	$228,889	$269,545	$40,656
Accounts payable	$102,589	$137,630	$35,041
Salaries payable	$0	$1,415	$1,415
Total liabilities	$102,589	$139,045	$36,456
Retained earnings	$126,300	$130,500	$4,200
Total liabilities and retained earnings	$228,889	$269,545	$40,656

The other section of the sources and uses of funds statement summarizes all of the changes in current assets and liabilities from the prior period to the current period. The source for this information is also Table 7-19. The current asset component changes are listed first, followed by current liability changes. The resulting sources and uses of funds statement is provided in Table 7-20.

CLOSING AND REVERSING ENTRIES

After the preparation of the financial statements, closing entries are determined and posted to both the general journal and the individual accounts in the general ledger. Closing entries are initially recorded in the general journal following the adjusting entries. The determination of the closing entries is a two-step process.

The first step is to make a list of all income statement accounts that have credit balances on the trial balance worksheet, noting account names and balance amounts. In the general journal, debit these accounts, and credit the income summary account for these amounts. Table 7-21 shows these closing entries in a general journal.

Table 7-20 Sources and Uses of Funds (Funds Flow) for Month Ended 4/30

Sources of Funds		
Net income	$4,200	
Depreciation–Equipment	$506	
Depreciation–Building	$250	
Total sources of funds		$4,956
Uses of Funds		
Purchase of equipment	$216	
Total uses of funds		$216
Increase in Working Capital		$4,740
Changes in Components of Working Capital		
Increase (decrease) in current assets		
Cash	$7,727	
Accounts receivable	$31,921	
Inventory	$1,725	
Supplies	($177)	
		$41,196
Increase (decrease) in current liabilities		
Accounts payable	$35,041	
Salaries payable	$1,415	
		$36,456
Increase in Working Capital		$4,740

The second step is to make a list of the income statement accounts that have debit balances on the trial balance worksheet (these are usually the expenses) and again include account names and their balances. Debit the income summary account for the total of these balances. Then credit each income statement account for the amount of its listed balance. These entries are also initially recorded in the general journal. An example of these

Table 7-21 General Journal

Date	Description	Acct. No.	Debit	Credit
	Closing Entries (Closing All Credit Balances in Income Statement Accounts)			
4/30	Sales–Cafeteria	410	$165	
	Sales–Patient meals	411	$49,986	
	Income summary			$50,151

Table 7-22 General Journal

Date	Description	Acct. No.	Debit	Credit
	Closing Entries (Closing Debit Balances in All Income Statement Accounts)			
4/30	Income summary		$45,951	
	Purchases–Less inventory decline	510		$37,230
	Supplies expense	520		$740
	Salary expense	530		$7,060
	Utility expense	540		$165
	Depreciation expense– Equipment	550		$506
	Depreciation expense–Building	560		$250

entries is provided in Table 7-22. These two groups of closing entries should then be posted to the general ledger accounts as well, except for the income summary account lines. These postings to the general ledger will zero out all of the income statement balances in the general ledger.

The manager should then calculate the new income summary balance. The new balance is the net total of all debits to that account, as recorded in the general journal, less all the credits to the account.

The manager should then record a clearing entry to post this income summary amount to the retained earnings account in the general ledger. This posted amount is the change in the value of the operation caused by the activities during the current accounting period. If there was net income in the period, the entry will be:

- debit income summary
- credit retained earnings.

An example of this general journal closing entry is shown in Table 7-23.

Table 7-23 General Journal

Date	Description	Acct. No.	Debit	Credit
	Closing Entries (Closing Income Summary Account to Retained Earnings)			
4/30	Income summary		$4,200	
	Retained earnings	310		$4,200

Table 7-24 General Journal

Date	Description	Acct. No.	Debit	Credit
	Reversing Entry at Start of Next Accounting Period			
5/1	Salaries payable	220	$1,415	
	Salaries expense	530		$1,415

REVERSING ENTRIES

At the beginning of the next accounting period, certain adjusting entries from the prior accounting period are reversed. This ensures the proper matching in the proper period of revenues and expenses. The most commonly used reversing entry is for salaries. The adjusting entry for accrued salaries, the reversing entry, and the impact on overall salary expense are presented in Table 7-24.

The impact of these entries is readily identified. Although the total payroll was $2,830, half of the expense was for services rendered in April and half for services rendered in May. These entries properly allocated the cost of April services to the month of April, even though the payment did not occur until May. These entries are therefore in keeping with accrual basis accounting and properly match expenses to the time period in which the services were rendered. This entry is reversed at the beginning of the new accounting period. The actual salary expense incurred for the new period will be net of the amount incurred earlier. The liability for those seven days' pay still exists. It is just a matter of matching the expense to the accounting period in which it was incurred (rather than to the accounting period in which it was paid).

Once the reversing entries are posted at the beginning of the new accounting period, all of the transactional journals and the general ledger are ready for the new month's transactional posting. Before posting the new month's transactions, the journals should each be totaled, and debits and credits compared. The general ledger debits and credits should also be retotaled to check for accuracy in closing and reversing entry postings.

Chapter 8

Financial Analysis Tools for Financial Statement Interpretation

Preparing cost records and reports is only the beginning in the financial management of an effective foodservice operation. These data must be evaluated and trends monitored so that informed decisions can be made for the future. If these data are not used, it will be impossible to identify problems and implement appropriate corrective action. That is the primary focus of the control process.

A manager's performance (and career progression) is measured, to a certain degree, by the results achieved in managing the resources allocated to the operation. Therefore, it is in the manager's best interest to monitor the operation's financial performance continually. Profit-making organizations have long measured performance levels of line managers by their success at cost control and their contribution to the organization's overall profitability. Results are frequently used to recognize and reward managerial and departmental performance that equals or surpasses the budgeted performance.

The operational results (and the forecasted budgets) will take on new meaning with the skillful use of various measurement tools to clarify the true performance of the department. The foodservice manager should use the operational financial statements (and the budgets for the same time periods) as the basis for further in-depth analysis. If actual performance differs from planned performance, this analysis of the operation's financial statements can help the manager determine the reasons the operation is not on target and, as a result, highlight areas of concern for the future and provide clues to potential solutions.

There are several approaches to financial data analysis, including:

- cost trend analysis
- ratio analysis
- variance analysis
- common size statements.

179

This chapter explores these approaches and gives the manager techniques for identifying underlying problems, exploring implications, and making recommendations for corrective actions.

COST TREND ANALYSIS

There are several mechanisms available for monitoring cost trends in an operation. In addition, there are comparison data available from a variety of sources that can be used for evaluating the performance of a foodservice operation. Both internal and external comparisons should be made. The caveat is to evaluate external comparisons carefully, remembering that a number of factors may be different in external situations, making the comparisons invalid. That is not to say that external comparisons should not be done, but the results should be interpreted with care.

External Comparisons

Two primary sources of data exist for external comparisons:

1. *HAS/MONITREND™ System reports for hospitals:* Individual organizations collect internal data on standardized forms so that comparisons of performance can be made over time.
2. *Other published sources:* These include industry groups such as the NRA trade associations, government departments, chambers of commerce, and various financial publications.

HAS/MONITREND™

The Healthcare Administrative Services (HAS) Division of the American Hospital Association provides monthly and six-month statistical reports to hospitals subscribing to the service. Statistics on labor hours, expenses, revenues, and utilization are collected from all areas of the hospital and sent to HAS for the report preparation.

For dietary services, the following performance data are collected and computed:

1. Total meals per patient day $= \dfrac{\text{Number equivalent meals}}{\text{Total patient days}}$

2. Patient meals per patient day $= \dfrac{\text{Number of patient meals}}{\text{Total patient days}}$

3. Direct expense per adjusted patient day

$$= \frac{\text{Salary expense} + \text{Other direct expense}}{[\text{Total patient days}/\text{Overall ratio of charges to charges (RCC)}]}$$

$$\text{RCC} = \frac{\text{Total inpatient revenue}}{\text{Total operating revenue}}$$

4. Direct expense per 100 meals

$$= \frac{\text{Salary expense} + \text{Other direct expense}}{[\text{Dietary patient meals} + \text{Equivalent meals}]/100}$$

5. Salary expense per adjusted patient day

$$= \frac{\text{Salary expense}}{\text{Total patient days}/\text{Overall RCC}}$$

6. Salary expense per 100 meals

$$= \frac{\text{Salary expense}}{[\text{Dietary patient meals} + \text{Equivalent meals}]/100}$$

7. Other direct expense per adjusted patient day

$$= \frac{\text{Dietary other direct expenses}}{\text{Total patient days}/\text{Overall RCC}}$$

8. Other direct expense per 100 meals

$$= \frac{\text{Other direct expenses}}{[\text{Dietary patient meals} + \text{other meals}]/100}$$

9. Direct expense %

$$= \frac{\text{Dietary salaries} + \text{Other direct expenses}}{\text{Hospital's total operating expenses}} \times 100$$

10. Paid hours per adjusted patient day

$$= \frac{\text{Dietary paid hours}}{\text{Total patient days}/\text{Overall RCC}}$$

11. Paid hours per 100 meals $= \dfrac{\text{Dietary services paid labor hours}}{\text{Dietary meals served}/100}$.

The monthly statistical report prepared for the hospital has two sections: one for external comparison and the second for internal trends. The first provides median data for external comparison with hospitals of similar size in the state, region, and nation. An example of this portion of the report for dietary services is shown in Exhibit 8-1.

The second section provides internal trend data by comparing the current month indicators with the average of the 3 prior months, the average of the same 3 months from last year, the average of the prior 12 months, and

Exhibit 8-1 HAS/MONITREND™ External Trend Comparison

HAS/MONITREND
FOR

GENERAL SERVICES
GROUP MEDIAN DATA

PAGE 93

	YOUR PRIOR 3 MONTH AVERAGE	GROUP MEDIANS (PRIOR 3 MOS AVERAGE)								VARIANCE FROM MEDIAN	C O D E	EXTENSION
		NATIONAL (A) 138 INST		STATE (B) 30 INST		REGIONAL (C) 20 INST		SPECIAL (D) 18 INST				
1 DIETARY SERVICES												
2 TOTAL MEALS / PATIENT DAY	7.96	6.36	4	6.90	3	7.76	3	6 90	4	1.60	A	1,963
3 PATIENT MEALS / PATIENT DAY	2.81	2.80	3	2.85	2	2.81	2	2 81	2		A	
4 DIRECT EXPENSE / ADJ. PATIENT DAY	30.33	19.00	H	20.43	H	20.92	4	19 81	4	CHECK	B	
5 DIRECT EXPENSE / 100 MEALS	538.91	406.53	4	414.06	4	406.91	4	406 91	4	124.85	B	$12,110
6 SALARY EXPENSE / ADJ. PATIENT DAY	13.89	10.01	4	11.30	3	10.51	H	10 52	4		B	
7 SALARY EXPENSE / 100 MEALS	246.78	219.02	3	239.87	3	190.62	3	228 55	3		B	
8 OTHER DIRECT EXPENSE / ADJ. PATIENT DAY												
9 OTHER DIR EXPENSE / 100 MEALS	16.44	8.36	4	8.52	4	9.17	4	8 86	4	7.92	B	$13,749
10 DIRECT EXPENSE PERCENT	292.13	185.25	4	172.02	H	203.39	4	195 58	4	CHECK	B	$17,142
11 PAID HOURS / ADJ. PATIENT DAY	6.02	3.92	H	4.06	4	4.48	4	4 22	4	1.96	B	
12 PAID HOURS / ADJ. PATIENT DAY	2.19	1.43	H	1.65	4	1.55	H	1 63	4	CHECK	A	
13 PAID HOURS / 100 MEALS	38.85	31.70	4	34.46	3	27.74	3	35 74	3	7.15	A	693

HAS/MONITREND
FOR

GENERAL SERVICES
GROUP MEDIAN DATA

PAGE 94

		YOUR PRIOR 3 MONTH AVERAGE	GROUP MEDIANS (PRIOR 3 MOS AVERAGE)		VARIANCE FROM MEDIAN	C O D E	EXTENSION
			SPECIAL (E) 82 INST	SPECIAL (F) 6 INST			
1	DIETARY SERVICES						
2	TOTAL MEALS / PATIENT DAY	7.96	6.22 4	8.44 1	1.60	A	1,963
3	PATIENT MEALS / PATIENT DAY	2.81	2.83 2	2.71 3		A	
4	DIRECT EXPENSE / ADJ. PATIENT DAY	30.33	17.34 H	23.52 4	CHECK	B	
5	DIRECT EXPENSE / 100 MEALS	538.91	383.50 4	408.51 4	124.85	B	$12,110
6	SALARY EXPENSE / ADJ. PATIENT DAY	13.89	9.21 4	11.31 3		B	
7	SALARY EXPENSE / 100 MEALS	246.78	203.94 4	246.78 2		B	
8	OTHER DIRECT EXPENSE / ADJ. PATIENT DAY	16.44	8.40 4	8.99 4	7.92	B	$13,749
9	OTHER DIR EXPENSE / 100 MEALS	292.13	177.47 4	203.39 4	CHECK	B	
10	DIRECT EXPENSE PERCENT	6.02	4.05 H	4.66 4	1.96	B	$17,142
11	PAID HOURS / ADJ. PATIENT DAY	2.19	1.45 4	1.54 3	CHECK	A	
12	PAID HOURS / 100 MEALS	38.85	33.10 4	34.55 3	7.15	A	693
13							

Source: Reprinted from *Healthcare Administrative Services Monitrend System* with permission of American Hospital Association.

Exhibit 8-2 HAS/MONITREND™ Internal Trend Data

	CURRENT MONTH	AVG PRIOR INDICATOR	INTERNAL TREND DATA			AVERAGE PRIOR 12 MONTHS	SAME 12 MONTHS LAST YEAR
			3 MONTHS RAW DATA	SAME 3 MONTHS LAST YEAR	PERCENT CHANGE		
DIETARY SERVICES							
TOTAL MEALS / PATIENT DAY	6.56	7.96	9.773	6.28	26.7	6.75	5.68
PATIENT MEALS / PATIENT DAY	2.79	2.81	3,444	2.79	.7	2.88	2.79
DIRECT EXPENSE / ADJ. PATIENT DAY	25.31	30.33	52,668	23.12	31.1	24.75	22.45
DIRECT EXPENSE / 100 MEALS	503.39	536.91	52,668	489.46	10.1	491.02	518.01
SALARY EXPENSE / ADJ. PATIENT DAY	11.72	13.89	24,118	10.56	31.5	10.69	9.50
SALARY EXPENSE / 100 MEALS	233.15	246.78	24,118	223.52	10.4	211.98	219.20
OTHER DIRECT EXPENSE / ADJ. PATIENT DAY	13.59	16.44	28,550	12.56	30.8	14.07	12.95
OTHER DIR EXPENSE / 100 MEALS	270.24	292.13	28,550	265.94	9.8	279.04	298.81
DIRECT EXPENSE PERCENT	5.84	6.02	52,668	5.27	14.2	5.59	5.41
PAID HOURS / ADJ. PATIENT DAY	1.81	2.19	3,797	1.69	29.5	1.71	1.85
PAID HOURS / 100 MEALS	36.05	38.85	3,797	35.68	8.8	33.91	35.69

Source: Reprinted from *Healthcare Administrative Services Monitrend System* with permission of American Hospital Association.

the average of the same 12 months last year. The percentage of change for the 3 months of internal data is provided. The internal trend data from a sample report can be seen in Exhibit 8-2.

Interpretation of HAS/MONITREND™ System Indicators. These data can provide important information for the hospital and for the foodservice department. Hosptals may make changes based on the comparative information received from the HAS/MONITREND™ System.

The direct expense per adjusted patient day and the direct expense per 100 meals indicators provide information related to the cost control of the dietary department. If these ratios are high in relation to the hospitals in the comparative group, it may indicate that cost control measures are not being taken. Several causes for high costs include expensive menu items, purchasing products at too high a price, failure to obtain bids, overpurchasing, spoilage and waste of products, theft of products, overproduction, overstaffing, and poor scheduling. When these ratios are too high, management must identify problems areas and take corrective action to control the direct expenses.

The *direct expense percentage indicator* compares dietary expenses with the total expenses of the hospital. If this percentage is much higher than that for the comparative group hospitals, it may indicate that too much of the hospital's resources are being used by the dietary department in relation to other departments. If the percentage is lower, it may indicate that too few of the hospital's resources are being allocated to the dietary department, which may mean that the quality of the meals and dietary services are inadequate. Hospital administrators would need to determine if corrective action should be taken.

The *salary expense per 100 meals* indicates whether wages and salaries are in line with those of other hospitals. Because of variations in pay scales by area, the comparison with the hospitals in the state may be the most accurate. Even this comparison should be made with caution since many factors, such as local unemployment rates and the availability of skilled workers, influence wages. If this ratio is higher than for the comparison groups, it could be indicative of high wages, too many employee hours, and/or low productivity.

Productivity is also measured with the *dietary service paid hours per 100 meals.* When this number is higher than that for comparative group hospitals, it may indicate problems related to staffing, scheduling, and training. It may also be indicative of poor employee motivation. A lower ratio may mean that expectations placed on employees are unrealistic, which may lead to negative consequences for the organization, such as a high rate of employee turnover. Again, a warning about the interpretation of productivity comparisons: Many factors affect productivity, limiting the comparability of operations.

Other Published Sources

The NRA and other trade associations compile industry averages and other performance data. These are frequently more useful than industry or regional averages for a broader business category.

The Small Business Association, the commerce department in most states, and the secretary of state each compile business statistics, financial ratios, and projections for future performance on a regular basis. This information is generally obtainable by contacting the appropriate department. It may also be possible to participate in the collection of these data in the organization's area. Governmental agencies have grown more sophisticated in the computer age, and a broader cross section of data sources improves the financial measures and averages.

Local chambers of commerce compile general financial data for the level of business in the area. This information will give the manager an overview of the business climate rather than industry averages, unless the local area includes a sufficient quantity of similar businesses to make a reliable study possible.

A myriad of financial publications are widely available at most public and university libraries. Many of the ratios discussed later in this chapter are compiled by industry in Dun & Bradstreet's annual publication, *Dun's Review and Modern Industry*. Ratios for each industry are provided for various-sized operations in each industry and further broken into groupings by giving the ratios in quartiles. The Accounting Corporation of America publishes *The Barometer of Small Business* semiannually. This contains income statement and balance sheet data by sales volume for each region of the country. The large accounting firms, investment firms, and commercial banks also compile statistics and ratios for businesses that can give the manager a broad perspective of the business climate, even though the statistics may not be in precisely the same industry.

Internal Comparisons

The examination of departmental historical data over several accounting periods can frequently uncover a pattern in performance and can show deviations from usual performance. The compilation and examination of data over a number of accounting periods to determine the progression of revenue or expenses over time is *trend analysis*. It is a good idea to graph the progression of the historical figures. A graph is often more meaningful than endless pages and columns of numbers. Figure 8-1 is an example of a trend graph of the cost of sales.

Figure 8-1 clearly shows a spike, or peak, in cost of sales for the most recent period. The manager should investigate this situation, determine the cause(s), and take corrective action.

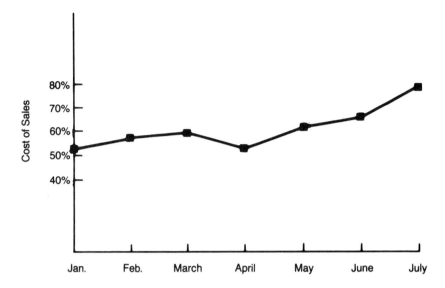

Figure 8-1 Trend analysis graph

Ratio analysis, variance analysis, and common size statement analysis are financial data analysis methods for which comparisons should be made between the newly calculated measure and the internal historical trends and figures. Another internal comparison should be made between the actual and budgeted measures for each method described in this chapter.

RATIO ANALYSIS

In-depth examination and study of the departmental or organizational financial status are essential to the success of the operation. The manager compiles the financial statements for the operation and plans for the future of the operation by studying the operational results. *Ratio analysis* involves the use of specific formulas to indicate an organization's financial position. These formulas use data from the financial statements to highlight various aspects of the organization. These ratios can be used both to compare the organization with similar organizations and to compare the organization's same ratios in prior periods or with budgeted ratios. These ratios fall into four categories:

1. liquidity ratios
2. asset management ratios

3. debt management (solvency) ratios
4. profitability ratios.

Liquidity Ratios

An organization's *liquidity* is its ability to conduct business and meet its short-term debts. This ability is determined by analyzing figures on the balance sheet. More specifically, it is measured by comparing portions of current assets with current liabilities. There are two measures of liquidity to examine:

1. current ratio
2. acid test or quick ratio.

Current Ratio

The *current ratio* provides a rough indication of the organization's ability to meet its current debt. It is calculated as follows:

$$\text{Current ratio} = \frac{\text{Total current assets}}{\text{Total current liabilities}}.$$

Both current and prospective creditors have a vested interest in the prompt settlement of their billings. One of the most reliable ways to determine liquidity is with the current ratio. In analyzing liquidity, the change in the current ratio from the prior period(s) to the current period is an important consideration. Then the manager should determine what strategy caused this change. This simply means that although the current ratio may have increased, the increase could have been attributable to a course of action that could ultimately have an unfavorable impact on the organization.

To determine the strategies causing the change in the current ratio, compare the line items on the current balance sheet with the same line items for the prior period. If the current ratio has increased, this would mean that either current assets increased, current liabilities decreased, or both. One way this could occur is by the selling of fixed assets and the use of the proceeds either to increase the current assets or to pay current liabilities. The second way this could occur is by the taking on of more long-term debt and the use of the newly borrowed funds to increase current assets or to pay current liabilities. The final way the current ratio could increase is if current assets had been sold or disposed of in order to pay current liabilities. This latter strategy is the most preferable, as it implies selling inventory, collecting on accounts receivable, or cashing in marketable securities in order to pay accounts payable or other current liabilities. If there has been a decrease in the current ratio from the prior period to the current period, the current assets would have decreased, current liabilities increased, or both. The opposite of these strategies would cause a decrease in the current ratio.

Tables 8-1 through 8-4 illustrate the concepts discussed in this section. Table 8-1 is an example of an operation's current and prior month's balance sheet reflecting the actual performance. Table 8-2 is the operation's current and prior months' actual income statement. Table 8-3 is the operation's budgeted balance sheet for the current and prior month. Table 8-4 is an example of the operation's budgeted income statement for the current and prior month. The current ratio for the current accounting period is:

$$\frac{\$45{,}073}{\$21{,}573} = 2.09.$$

This means that for every \$1 in liabilities, the operation has \$2.09 in assets.

Table 8-1 College Coffee Shop: Balance Sheet

	Current Month Actual Results	Prior Month Actual Results
Cash	$6,500	$8,500
Marketable securities	2,500	3,500
Inventory: Food	5,833	5,500
Beverage	3,000	3,000
Accounts receivable	27,240	29,500
Total current assets	$45,073	$50,000
Equipment	$125,000	$125,000
Accumulated depreciation	(25,000)	(22,500)
Total fixed assets	100,000	102,500
Total assets	$145,073	$152,500
Accounts payable	$14,255	$19,382
Salaries payable	5,818	6,618
Current portion of note	1,500	1,500
Total current liabilities	$21,573	$27,500
Note payable	$18,500	$20,000
Mortgage payable	0	0
Total long-term liabilities	$18,500	$20,000
Total liabilities	$40,073	$47,500
Capital	$105,000	$105,000
Total liabilities and capital	$145,073	$152,500

Table 8-2 College Coffee Shop: Income Statement

	Current Month Actual Results	Prior Month Actual Results
Sales	$127,771	$114,994
Cost of sales	54,779	49,500
Gross margin	$72,992	$65,494
Salaries and wages	$31,324	$27,950
FICA	4,380	3,700
Benefits	8,191	7,400
Utilities	3,697	3,200
Supplies	4,272	3,650
Depreciation expense	16,579	16,579
Net operating income	$4,549	$3,015
Interest expense on note	100	100
Taxes	2,224	1,457
Net income	$2,225	$1,458

This seems reasonable, since a typical guideline is $2:1$. The manager should compare the current performance with the prior period's actual current ratio:

$$\frac{\$50,000}{\$27,500} = 1.82.$$

This means that in the prior accounting period there was only $1.82 in assets for each dollar in liabilities. In other words, in the current accounting period the operation had more assets to cover the liabilities. The balance sheet in Table 8-1 indicates that accounts receivable and other cash were used to pay off some of the accounts payable.

The manager must compare the actual performance with the planned performance. The budgeted current ratio for the current accounting period is:

$$\frac{\$48,128}{\$24,628} = 1.95.$$

The actual current performance is 2.09 certainly compares favorably with the planned performance. The manager should also determine if the goal had been set too low. This can be investigated by comparing the historical

Table 8-3 College Coffee Shops: Balance Sheet

	Current Month Budgeted Results	Prior Month Budgeted Results
Cash	$10,500	$10,500
Marketable securities	3,500	3,500
Inventory: Food	6,000	6,000
Beverage	3,000	3,000
Accounts receivable	25,128	26,000
Total current assets	$48,128	$49,000
Equipment	$125,000	$125,000
Accumulated depreciation	(25,000)	(22,500)
Total fixed assets	100,000	102,500
Total assets	$148,128	$151,500
Accounts payable	$16,710	$18,382
Salaries payable	6,418	6,618
Current portion of note	1,500	1,500
Total current liabilities	$24,628	$26,500
Note payable	$18,500	$20,000
Mortgage payable	0	0
Total long-term liabilities	$18,500	$20,000
Total liabilities	$43,128	$46,500
Capital	$105,000	$105,000
Total liabilities and capital	$148,128	$151,500

budget with the historical performance. The prior period's current ratio performance is:

$$\frac{\$49,000}{\$26,500} = 1.85.$$

In the prior period, the actual performance of 1.82 fell short of the planned performance. So far, it appears that the manager is on the right track in setting the budget for and managing liquidity.

The Acid Test or Quick Ratio

The acid test or quick ratio is similar to the current ratio. However, this ratio gives a measure of the true strength of the previously determined

Table 8-4 College Coffee Shop: Income Statement

	Current Month Budgeted Results	Prior Month Budgeted Results
Sales	$124,000	$120,000
Cost of sales	54,500	53,700
Gross margin	$69,500	$66,300
Salaries and wages	$29,750	$28,350
FICA	3,850	3,825
Benefits	7,600	7,500
Utilities	3,400	3,200
Supplies	4,200	3,800
Depreciation expense	16,579	16,579
Net operating income	$4,121	$3,046
Interest expense on note	100	100
Taxes	2,010	1,473
Net income	$2,011	$1,473

current ratio. The formula is:

$$\text{Quick ratio} = \frac{\text{Total current assets} - \text{Inventory}}{\text{Total current liabilities}}.$$

Obviously, creditors prefer current liabilities to be covered by cash and other cash equivalent instruments such as marketable securities. This measure provides an even better indication of the management of operational liquidity as it examines solely the most liquid assets (i.e., cash or those assets that are quickly converted into cash).

The actual quick ratio for the current accounting period is:

$$\frac{\$45,073 - \$8,833}{\$21,573} = 1.68.$$

This means that for every dollar in short-term liabilities, the operation has $1.68 in highly liquid assets. Although this is significantly lower than the operation's current ratio, it is still near the safety zone of 2:1.

The next step is to calculate and analyze the prior period's actual quick ratio:

$$\frac{\$50,000 - \$8,500}{\$27,500} = 1.51.$$

This is significantly below the current period's quick ratio of 1.68. The manager apparently realized that payables were getting out of control and wisely took measures to correct the situation.

Comparisons with both the current period's and prior period's budgeted quick ratios should also be made. The prior period's quick ratio was:

$$\frac{\$49,000 - \$9,000}{\$26,500} = 1.51.$$

The prior period's actual performance was identical with the planned performance. Even so, the manager had realized that the liquidity situation had gotten out of control. The target for the current period was:

$$\frac{\$48,128 - \$9,000}{\$24,628} = 1.59.$$

The planned performance of 1.59 would have been a respectable improvement over that of the prior period. However, actual performance surpassed even the planned improvement.

Asset Management Ratios

Asset management ratios are computed to highlight the extent to which the organization is efficiently utilizing its assets to produce more income. Once again, the computed ratios should be compared with the organization's prior periods' ratios, the current period's budgeted ratios, and the applicable industry averages. Not only will this give management a better idea of current effectiveness or ineffectiveness but will also provide clues for future planning. This section presents four measures of asset management:

1. inventory turnover
2. average collection period
3. fixed asset turnover
4. total asset turnover.

Inventory Turnover Ratio

The *inventory turnover ratio* determines the frequency at which the operation uses its inventory:

$$\text{Inventory turnover rate} = \frac{\text{Cost of sales}}{\text{Inventory}}.$$

It would be more accurate to use the average inventory in this formula. Most of the external sources of comparison information, however, use the ending inventory instead of the average inventory. The computed inventory turnover is then compared with the industry average. Generally speaking, the larger the inventory turnover number, the more effective the organization is at using its inventory (and not overstocking). However, if the industry average for inventory turnover was 3, and the operation's rate was 9, this could indicate frequent stockout problems. Further investigation would be warranted. Conversely, if the industry average was 3, and the operation's inventory turnover was only 1, this could indicate that the operation has old inventory on hand, or at least the wrong mixture of items in inventory. Again, this situation would warrant further investigation.

Tables 8-1 and 8-2 provide data to calculate the actual inventory turnover rates for the current and prior periods. The manager should first calculate and analyze the current period's actual inventory turnover as follows:

$$\frac{\$54,779}{\$8,833} = 6.2 \text{ times.}$$

This seems high for a monthly turnover rate. A monthly rate of 3 or 4 would be more appropriate.

The manager should compare the current actual turnover rate with the prior month's rate:

$$\frac{\$49,500}{\$8,500} = 5.8 \text{ times.}$$

The turnover rate increased in the current month. The manager should investigate the sales data for specific products to determine whether inventory adjustments are needed.

The manager should compare the actual turnover rates with the planned turnover rates for the operation. Tables 8-3 and 8-4 provide data for the calculations. The current period's budgeted turnover rate is:

$$\frac{\$54,500}{\$9,000} = 6.1 \text{ times.}$$

The actual turnover rate is 6.2 times, which is not significantly higher than the planned rate. A review of purchases volume and sales volume should provide the manager with clues and possible solutions to turnover problems.

The prior period's budgeted turnover rate should be calculated as well:

$$\frac{\$53,700}{\$9,000} = 6 \text{ times.}$$

The prior period's actual rate of 5.8 times was only slightly lower than the planned performance.

Average Collection Period

The *average collection period* measures the average period of time between a sale and the receipt of the cash by the organization. The average collection period is determined using two formulas:

$$\text{Average daily sales} = \frac{\text{Total sales}}{360}.$$

$$\text{Average collection period} = \frac{\text{Accounts receivable}}{\text{Average daily sales}}.$$

Industry comparison data are based on average daily sales figures and collection period calculations based on a 360-day year. Even though the manager's operation may be open only five days a week, the measure should still be calculated using the industry standard. Of course, the manager could calculate additional measures that would reflect the actual number of days the operation is open.

Once the actual result for the period is determined, it should be compared with the official credit policy. For example, if for the current year the average collection period is 62 days, but the policy is that customers must pay within 30 days, some strong collection measures should be taken to correct the situation. The current period's results should be compared with the pro forma (budgeted) figures. Perhaps the original strategy was to reduce the average collection period from 90 to 80 days, and the actual result was 62 days. This would be a sign of success! In addition to comparing actual and budgeted figures, the manager should compare the actual results with the industry averages.

Tables 8-1 and 8-2 provide the data for calculating the current and prior periods' actual average collection periods. The current period's average daily sales are:

$$\frac{\$127,771}{360} = \$354.92.$$

The current period's actual average collection period is:

$$\frac{\$27,240}{\$354.92} = 76.8 \text{ days.}$$

An average collection period of nearly 77 days seems high. It certainly is in keeping with the lack of liquidity determined previously. The prior period's actual average collection period must be calculated and analyzed to find the answer. The prior period's actual average daily sales is:

$$\frac{\$114,994}{360} - \$319.43.$$

The average collection period is:

$$\frac{\$29,500}{\$319.43} = 92.4 \text{ days.}$$

The reduction in the average collection period from 92.4 days to 76.8 days decreased accounts receivable and thereby increased cash flow. A review of the balance sheet indicates that the funds from collected accounts receivable were used to reduce accounts payable.

The manager should next compare the planned performance for the current and prior periods with the actual performance for the average collection period. Tables 8-3 and 8-4 provide the data for the calculations. The current period's budgeted average daily sales is:

$$\frac{\$124,000}{360} = \$344.44.$$

The current period's budgeted average collection period is:

$$\frac{\$25,128}{\$344.44} = 72.95 \text{ days.}$$

The budgeted performance of 72.95 days in the current period was not achieved in actual performance. The actual average collection period was 76.8 days. The difference was almost 4 days. The manager should also examine the planned performance for the prior period.

The average daily sales budget for the prior period is:

$$\frac{\$120,000}{360} = \$333.33.$$

The planned performance for average collection period for the prior period is:

$$\frac{\$26,000}{\$333.33} = 78 \text{ days}.$$

The planned performance was 78 days, but the actual performance was 92.4 days. This is a serious deviation from the plan. The manager should review accounts receivable. There may have been an unresolved customer complaint that took longer than usual to correct, or there may have been a couple of larger accounts that paid more slowly than usual. The manager should investigate the situation so that another increase in the average collection period can be avoided.

Fixed Asset Turnover

The *fixed asset turnover* is a measure of the utilization of the organization's fixed assets. It becomes particularly useful when planning for future plant and equipment expansion.

$$\text{Fixed asset turnover} = \frac{\text{Total sales}}{\text{Total fixed assets}}.$$

By using this ratio and comparing it with the industry average, the manager can determine how the capacity utilization compares with that of the rest of the industry. For example, if the organization's ratio is significantly above the industry average, it could mean that additional capacity is needed to support the level of sales activity. If the fixed asset turnover has become very high, this could indicate either insufficient capacity or even obsolete, fully depreciated equipment. However, this higher capacity utilization is generally accompanied by higher profit margins.

On the other hand, if the organization's ratio is below the industry average, future fixed asset acquisitions should at least be reconsidered. Furthermore, comparison with the budgeted fixed asset turnover should be made to see if the operation is utilizing capacity as expected. If the operation is below the budgeted capacity utilization level, profitability could be substantially increased with only a small sales increase. This is because the existing unused capacity produces the additional output. The total cost of this increase in sales (and required output) would be an increase only in variable costs. The fixed cost would be spread over more units (meals served) and would decrease on a per-meal basis.

To have determined the possibility of insufficient capacity is only the starting point. The manager must then prepare forecasts and analyses indicating the costs of capital expansion and the impact on future costs. This topic is addressed in chapter 10.

To calculate the current and prior periods' actual fixed asset turnover, refer to Tables 8-1 and 8-2. The current period's actual fixed asset turnover ratio is:

$$\frac{\$127,771}{\$100,000} = 1.28 \text{ times.}$$

This compares quite favorably with the prior period's actual fixed asset turnover:

$$\frac{\$114,994}{\$102,500} = 1.12 \text{ times.}$$

The improvement from the prior period to the current period indicates that the fixed assets are generating more sales.

Budgeted turnover figures should be calculated to enable the manager to judge operational performance in relation to budgeted performance. The data for the calculations are provided in Tables 8-3 and 8-4.

The budgeted fixed asset turnover ratio for the current period is:

$$\frac{\$124,000}{\$100,000} = 1.24 \text{ times.}$$

The actual performance ratio for the current period is 1.28 times, which was slightly greater than the planned performance.

The budgeted fixed asset turnover ratio for the prior period is:

$$\frac{\$120,000}{\$102,500} = 1.17 \text{ times.}$$

The actual performance in the prior period was slightly less than the planned performance. Although the current and prior periods' performances did deviate from the plan, the deviation may be more indicative of a problem with the budgeting process than with performance.

Total Asset Turnover Ratio

The *total asset turnover ratio* is a measure of how efficiently the organization is utilizing all of its assets. The ratio also indicates the amount of sales that is being supported or generated for each dollar of assets. A low asset turnover means that there is excessive investment in assets for the current level of sales. The ratio is calculated as follows:

$$\text{Total asset turnover} = \frac{\text{Total sales}}{\text{Total assets}}.$$

This ratio should then be compared with the industry average, the organization's prior period's turnover, and the budgeted turnover. This will facilitate the manager's ability to see whether the department generates sufficient sales volume to justify the level of assets.

If the asset turnover is equal to or greater than the budgeted turnover and the industry average, there is justification for the level of assets. If the turnover is less than the budgeted or the industry average, assets are too high in relation to sales, and changes need to be made to create an appropriate balance. A wise strategy would be to find ways to increase sales rather than to start disposing of assets immediately.

The actual total asset turnover for both the current and prior periods is calculated using data in Tables 8-1 and 8-2. The current period's actual total asset turnover is:

$$\frac{\$127,771}{\$145,073} = 0.88 \text{ times}.$$

This measure seems low; perhaps the operation does have a higher investment in assets than the sales volume can justify. The prior period's actual total asset turnover is:

$$\frac{\$114,994}{\$152,500} = 0.75 \text{ times}.$$

The current performance certainly improved upon the prior period's performance.

The manager must also compare the actual performance with the planned performance. The data for the planned performance are provided in Tables 8-3 and 8-4. The current period's planned performance is:

$$\frac{\$124,000}{\$148,128} = 0.84 \text{ times}.$$

The current actual total asset turnover was slightly better than the planned performance for the same period. The prior period's should also be calculated:

$$\frac{\$120,000}{\$151,500} = 0.79 \text{ times}.$$

The actual performance was only slightly lower than this. The operation set the low target for these asset turnover ratios, but the manager should continue to investigate the level of sales and assets to determine the existence of excess capacity.

Debt Management (Solvency) Ratios

Some foodservice operations will take on debt in order to finance expansion of the facilities or the opening of the business. Examples of debt instruments include bond issues, installment purchases, and mortages.

In order to gain a fuller understanding of the financial health of the organization, the manager must examine both the long-term debt and the relationship between the debt and total assets. Two measures of debt management are described:

1. total debt to total assets
2. times interest earned.

Total Debt to Total Assets

The *total debt to total assets ratio* indicates the extent to which the assets are spoken for in terms of long-term debt. The debt to assets ratio is calculated as follows:

$$\text{Total debt to total assets} = \frac{\text{Total liabilities}}{\text{Total assets}}.$$

This measure should be compared with both industry figures and historical figures for the organization. This will give the manager a better handle on how well the organization is doing. For example, if for each $1 of long-term debt the foodservice has $5 of assets and the industry is averaging only $3 of assets for each $1 of debt, the organization is taking a more conservative approach. It is possible that the organization could afford to take on more debt if other analysis has indicated that expansion would be in order. However, caution should be advised, since in today's highly competitive marketplace, the below average debt level could give the company a competitive edge. This is because the organization could remain viable even if sales were to drop, simply because of the lower debt payments.

The actual total debt to total assets ratio is calculated using Table 8-1 for the current and prior periods. The current period's actual total debt to total assets ratio is

$$\frac{\$40,073}{\$145,073} \times 100\% = 27.62\%.$$

This indicates that during the current period, creditors have provided 27.62 percent of the financing of the assets.

The prior period's actual total debt to total assets ratio is:

$$\frac{\$47,500}{\$152,500} \times 100\% = 31.15\%.$$

The current period's creditor financing of 27.62 percent reflects improvement over the prior period's rate of 31.15 percent. This change is indicative of an improvement in the operation's debt management.

How did this stack up against operational goals? Table 8-3 provides the budgeted current and prior period's data. The current period's planned (budgeted) total debt to total assets ratio is:

$$\frac{\$43,128}{\$148,128} = 29.12\%.$$

Thus 29.12 percent was budgeted and only 27.62 percent was the actual result. This means that the operation relied on less debt than originally planned.

The prior period's budgeted total debt to total assets ratio is:

$$\frac{\$46,500}{\$151,500} = 30.69\%.$$

Although the operation budgeted only 30.69 percent of its funding to be provided by creditors, the prior period's actual performance was 31.15 percent. Comparison with both the industry averages and other prior periods can be especially helpful before forecasting future budget activity.

Times Interest Earned

The *times interest earned ratio* indicates how many times net income covers the required interest payments on long-term debt. Frequently, bankers and potential owners, contributors, or investors will focus on this measure because of its similarity to the liquidity ratios. The times interest earned ratio tells them how well the operation manages both its debt and its profitability. The times interest earned ratio is calculated as follows:

$$\text{Times interest earned} = \frac{\text{Net operating income}}{\text{Interest payments}}.$$

This measure should be compared with the industry average, as well as the organization's past historical figures for this measure.

The times interest earned ratio for actual performance data is calculated using data in Table 8-2. The manager should calculate and analyze the ratio for both the current and the prior period.

The current period's times interest earned ratio is:

$$\frac{\$4,549}{\$100} = 45.49 \text{ times.}$$

This means that the net income could have paid the required interest payments about 45 times. While there is no ideal ratio, creditors consider a high times interest earned ratio to be indicative of credit worthiness. In this case, the operation cleared close to $45 for each $1 of interest expense. Some creditors may specify a minimum level of times interest earned that the operation must maintain in order to obtain a loan.

The prior period's times interest earned ratio is:

$$\frac{\$3,015}{\$100} = 30.15.$$

The current period's actual performance was significantly higher than that of the prior period. However, since the operation is "covering its debt" so well in both of the accounting periods, this change in performance doesn't indicate a significant shift in strategy that would require corrective action.

The budgeted times interest earned ratio for the current and prior periods are calculated using data in Table 8-4. The ratio for the current period is:

$$\frac{\$4,121}{\$100} = 41.21.$$

The actual measure for the current period is 45.49, which is about 10 percent higher than the planned measure. Both the planned and actual ratios indicate that expenses are being controlled.

The prior period's time interest earned ratio must also be calculated and analyzed:

$$\frac{\$3,046}{\$100} = 30.46 \text{ times.}$$

The prior period's actual performance of 30.15 times was slightly below the budgeted performance, but this slight variation should not be a cause for concern.

Profitability Ratios

The *profitability ratios* describe and highlight the overall effectiveness of the business operation. These ratios are of particular importance, as they nicely dovetail with the figures analyzed thus far and tell the manager how successful the interaction of operational decisions and the "outside world" has been. There are three basic profitability ratios:

1. profit margin on sales
2. return on total assets
3. return on equity.

Profit Margin on Sales

An operation's profit margin is one of the most important measures of its effectiveness because it indicates the net result of operations for the period. Even in a nonprofit operation this is an important measure, as expenses must still be controlled to ensure that monies are spent in the most effective manner possible. The *profit margin* reflects the portion of sales volume remaining after paying all departmental expenses. The formula to calculate the profit margin is:

$$\text{Profit margin} = \frac{\text{Net income}}{\text{Sales}} \times 100.$$

Comparison of the profit margin with the industry average indicates expenses and/or sales prices in relation to the industry. In the event that the operation's profit margin is far below the industry average, it will be necessary to examine both the gross margin and the operating margin to determine the cause. Recall from chapter 7 that the gross margin is the difference between gross sales and the cost of goods sold, and the operating margin is the difference between the gross margin and operating expenses.

Data in Table 8-2 are used to calculate the actual profit margin on sales. The current period's actual profit margin on sales is:

$$\frac{\$2,225}{\$127,771} \times 100 = 1.74\% \text{ after taxes.}$$

The 1.74% after-tax profit margin is on the lower end of the typical profit margin of the foodservice industry. In order to gain a historical perspective, the manager should calculate and analyze the prior period's actual after-tax profit margin:

$$\frac{\$1,458}{\$114,994} \times 100 = 1.27\% \text{ after taxes.}$$

The current period's performance of 1.74 percent was a *significant* improvement over the prior period's performance.

The manager should determine how actual profit margin performance compared with the budgeted profit margin performance. Data in Table 8-4 are used to calculate the budgeted profit margins for the current and prior periods. The current period's budgeted, or planned, after-tax profit margin is:

$$\frac{\$2,011}{\$124,000} \times 100 = 1.62\%.$$

The current period's actual profit margin of 1.74 percent surpassed the budgeted performance, even though gross sales were lower than planned. This is a good example of the benefit of effective cost control methods.

The prior period's budgeted after-tax profit margin is:

$$\frac{\$1,473}{\$120,000} \times 100 = 1.23\%.$$

The actual performance in the prior period also surpassed budgeted performance. The manager should compare the budgeted and actual profit margins with the industry averages in order to determine whether the operation is in line with similar operations. Monitoring industry averages should provide the manager with general guidelines for reasonable expectations.

Return on Total Assets

The *return on total assets* (ROTA) is a measure of the combined effects that the profit margin on sales, the asset usage, and the debt usage have on the operation. The ROTA is calculated as follows:

$$\text{ROTA} = \frac{\text{Net income}}{\text{Total assets}} \times 100.$$

This measure highlights the impact of asset management, debt management, sales management, and expense management on operating results.

The comparison of operational results with external sources for industry averages is urged. The continual management of all facets of the operation is essential to the health and survival of the operation.

Tables 8-1 and 8-2 provide the data used to calculate the actual ROTA for the current and prior accounting periods. The current period's actual ROTA is:

$$\frac{\$2,225}{\$145,073} \times 100 = 1.53\%.$$

A return of less than 2 percent does not seem to be an outstanding result. However, it is in keeping with the profit margin of 1.75 percent.

For comparison purposes, the manager should then calculate the prior period's actual ROTA:

$$\frac{\$1,458}{\$152,500} \times 100 = 0.96\%.$$

The prior period's performance was poor, especially in comparison with the current period's performance. The manager should compare the operational results with the industry averages. The operation should at least aim for a return that is apparently acceptable to the rest of the industry.

The manager should calculate the budgeted ROTAs and compare them with actual performance. Tables 8-3 and 8-4 provide the data required to calculate the budgeted ROTAs for the current and prior periods. The current period's budgeted ROTA is:

$$\frac{\$2,011}{\$148,128} \times 100 = 1.36\%.$$

The current period's actual ROTA of 1.53 percent compares very favorably with the budgeted ROTA of 1.36 percent. Once again, effective management of both the cash flow and expenses is largely responsible for the better-than-expected performance.

The prior period's budgeted ROTA should be calculated and compared with both the current period's budgeted ROTA and the prior period's actual ROTA. The prior period's budgeted ROTA is:

$$\frac{\$1,473}{\$151,500} \times 100 = 0.97\%.$$

The prior period's actual ROTA of 0.96 percent was about the same as the budgeted ROTA of 0.97 percent. However, the current actual performance of 1.53 percent was about a 58 percent improvement in performance. The manager of the operation appears to be heading in the right direction.

Return on Equity

The *return on equity (ROE) ratio* measures the rate of return the owners (e.g., investors, stockholders) achieve on their investment. Recall from chapter 7 that the owners' investment in the firm is found in the capital, or net worth, section of the balance sheet. The ROE is calculated as follows:

$$\text{ROE} = \frac{\text{Net income}}{\text{Capital}} \times 100.$$

The ROE ratios should be compared with the industry averages. This will provide the manager with an indication of the level of ROE that prevails in similar organizations. Obviously, as with any investment, the investor will want the highest possible rate of return (or least negative return), given the level of risk acceptable to that investor. Foundations and governments also desire the best possible rate of return for their investments, or they will invest their funds elsewhere.

Tables 8-1 and 8-2 provide the data required to calculate the actual ROEs for the current and prior periods. The current period's ROE is:

$$\frac{\$2,225}{\$105,000} \times 100 = 2.12\%.$$

This return is lower than an investor would be able to make in a bank. However, the manager should compare the operation's ROE with the industry's average ROE. Investors in the institutional foodservice industry may find this to be an acceptable return on their investment. For comparison purposes, the manager should next calculate the prior period's actual ROE:

$$\frac{\$1,458}{\$105,000} \times 100 = 1.39\%.$$

The current period's actual ROE of 2.12 percent was a healthy improvement over the prior period's ROE of 1.39 percent. The manager is doing an effective job in maximizing profits.

The final step is for the manager to determine whether the operation is doing as well as planned in maximizing ROE. Tables 8-3 and 8-4 provide the data required to calculate budgeted ROEs for the current and prior periods. The current period's budgeted ROE is:

$$\frac{\$2,011}{\$105,000} \times 100 = 1.92\%.$$

The current period's actual ROE of 2.12 percent surpassed the budgeted ROE of 1.92 percent. Since the capital portion of the formula was the same in budgeted and actual performance, the improvement in actual performance had to come from the improvement in expense management. Effective expense management is, of course, always a wise strategy.

The prior period's budgeted ROE should be calculated to determine operational progress with one more comparison. This ROE is:

$$\frac{\$1,473}{\$105,000} \times 100 = 1.40\%.$$

The prior period's actual ROE of 1.39 percent was about the same as the prior period's budgeted ROE of 1.40 percent. The current period's actual performance was a solid indication of improved operational management.

As is the case with all ratios presented, it is important to test the operation's results by comparing them with the results of similar-sized operations in the industry.

VARIANCE ANALYSIS

Variance analysis is a particularily important managerial reporting tool to the savvy professional. This form of analysis can be thought of as a type of exception reporting. The premise is to analyze the financial statements one step further by comparing each line item with the budgeted figures. Frequently, upper management will require departmental reports with reasons and justifications for significant exceptions. Significant exceptions, or variances, are usually predefined as being above a specific dollar amount or percentage. Examples of significant exceptions are variances above 15 percent and variances above $5,000.

Variance analysis is generally done with worksheets (or on an electronic spreadsheet). The methodology involves the comparison of actual operational results with the budgeted or planned results. Once these figures are compiled, the manager determines the causes for any significant differences (variances). The definition of *significant differences* depends on the organization and the line item. Some organizations will perform variance analysis only on variances greater than a specific dollar amount. Other organizations will establish various requirements for different categories of income, expenses, or balance sheet items. The manager should discern which specific variances should be investigated and analyzed in addition to the predetermined analysis requirements.

Variance analysis in its most complete form analyzes both dollar variances and ratio variances. This means deriving the budgeted ratios as well as the actual ratios and then calculating the variances. Ratio variances are most logically performed at the same time as the ratio analysis. (Refer to the ratio analysis section in this chapter for examples of differences between budgeted and actual ratios.)

Variance analysis is a five-step process:

1. Format the variance analysis worksheet.
2. Post actual and budgeted figures to the worksheet.
3. Calculate and post variances to the worksheet.
4. Tie worksheet figures out.
5. Analyze significant variances and recommend changes.

Format the Variance Analysis Worksheet

The first time variance analysis is performed, the manager should set up a *template,* or master form, that can be copied for future use. (A computerized version is presented in chapter 12.) An example of a manual form is provided in Table 8-5.

Post Actual and Budgeted Figures to the Worksheet

Posting figures to the worksheet means to transfer the dollar amount for each worksheet line item from the same line item in the actual and budgeted financial statements. Table 8-6 gives the posted actual and budgeted figures for the current period. The source of the posted actual data is Table 8-2. The source of the posted budgeted data is Table 8-4.

Calculate and Post Variances to the Worksheet

Recall that a variance is the difference between actual and budgeted performance. Determining whether a variance is favorable or unfavorable is based on a simple rule. A favorable variance means that actual performance was *better* (more profitable) than budgeted. Table 8-7 outlines favorable and unfavorable variances for specific categories. When posting

Table 8-5 College Coffee Shop: Variance Analysis Worksheet

_____ Accounting Period

	Actual Results	Budgeted Results	Favorable (Unfavorable) Variance	Reason
Sales				
Cost of sales	_____	_____	_____	
Gross margin	══════	══════	══════	
Salaries and wages				
FICA				
Benefits				
Utilities				
Supplies				
Depreciation expense	_____	_____	_____	
Net operating income	══════	══════	══════	
Interest expense on note				
Taxes	_____	_____	_____	
Net income	══════	══════	══════	

Table 8-6 College Coffee Shop: Variance Analysis Worksheet for Current Accounting Period

	Actual Results	Budgeted Results	Favorable (Unfavorable) Variance	Reason
Sales	$127,771	$124,000		
Cost of sales	54,779	54,500	_____	
Gross margin	$72,992	$69,500	══════	
Salaries and wages	$31,324	$29,750		
FICA	4,380	3,850		
Benefits	8,191	7,600		
Utilities	3,697	3,400		
Supplies	4,272	4,200		
Depreciation expense	16,579	16,579	_____	
Net operating income	$4,549	$4,121	══════	
Interest expense on note	$100	$100		
Taxes	2,224	2,010	_____	
Net income	$2,225	$2,011	══════	

Table 8-7 Variance Posting Table

Favorable Variances	Unfavorable Variances
Actual gross sales greater than budget	Actual gross sales less than budget
Actual cost of sales less than budget	Actual cost of sales greater than budget
Actual other expenses less than budget	Actual other expenses greater than budget
Actual operating income greater than budget	Actual operating income less than budget
Actual operating loss less than budget	Actual operating loss greater than budget
Actual net income greater than budget	Actual net income less than budget
Actual net loss less than budget	Actual net loss greater than budget

variances to the worksheet, this table will be helpful to ensure posting accuracy.

Variances are calculated and subsequently posted to the current period variance analysis worksheet in Table 8-8. The favorable variances are posted as positive numbers, and the unfavorable variances are posted as negative numbers in parentheses.

Table 8-8 College Coffee Shop: Variance Analysis Worksheet for Current Accounting Period

	Actual Results	Budgeted Results	Favorable (Unfavorable) Variance	Reason
Sales	$127,771	$124,000	$3,771	
Cost of sales	54,779	54,500	(279)	
Gross margin	$72,992	$69,500	$3,492	
Salaries and wages	$31,324	$29,750	($1,574)	
FICA	4,380	3,850	(530)	
Benefits	8,191	7,600	(591)	
Utilities	3,697	3,400	(297)	
Supplies	4,272	4,200	(72)	
Depreciation expense	16,579	16,579	0	
Net operating income	$4,549	$4,121	$428	
Interest expense on note	$100	$100	$0	
Taxes	2,224	2,010	(214)	
Net income	$2,225	$2,011	$214	

Tie Worksheet Figures Out

Tying the figures out on a worksheet is an accountant's way of saying, "check your math!" The variance column should mathematically work the way a regular income statement works in that the net income variance should be the difference between the gross margin variance and the expense variance. Using the figures from Table 8-8, the following example will tie out the variance column.

Gross sales	$3,771
Cost of sales	(279)
Gross margin	$3,492
Salaries and wages	(1,574)
FICA	(530)
Benefits	(591)
Utilities	(297)
Supplies	(72)
Depreciation	0
Net operating income	$ 428

(*Proof:* 3,492 − 1574 − 530 − 591 − 297 − 72 = 428.)

Usually, if a variance has been calculated or posted incorrectly, the manager will easily spot it at this point. Frequently, the sign of the variance was posted incorrectly. Simply refer to the posting guide in Table 8-7 to determine whether the variance is favorable or unfavorable.

Analyze Significant Variances and Recommend Changes

Once the variances have been calculated, the manager should determine their causes. By doing this the manager can determine how either to "keep up the good work" for the favorable variances or to "fix it" for the unfavorable variances. A good initial source for this information is the records used to compile the performance and expense reports discussed in chapter 2. Table 8-9 shows the current period's variance analysis worksheet complete with reasons for the variances, as well as some future strategic changes.

The astute manager will perform the variance analysis each accounting period. The prior period's variance analysis is provided in Table 8-10. The source tables are the same as for the current period (Tables 8-2 and 8-4).

Variance analysis is a superb tool because it summarizes the results succinctly and can be used to generate management-level reports. It is far better for the foodservice manager to generate this report and inform upper

Table 8-9 College Coffee Shop: Variance Analysis Worksheet for the Current Accounting Period

	Actual Results	Budgeted Results	Favorable (Unfavorable) Variance	Reason
Sales	$127,771	$124,000	$3,771	New salad bar
Cost of sales	54,779	54,500	(279)	New supplier
Gross margin	$72,992	$69,500	$3,492	
Salaries and wages	$31,324	$29,750	($1,574)	Overtime
FICA	4,380	3,850	(530)	Overtime
Benefits	8,191	7,600	(591)	Maternity lve
Utilities	3,697	3,400	(297)	Rate increase
Supplies	4,272	4,200	(72)	Consulting
Depreciation expense	16,579	$116,579	0	
Net operating income	$4,549	$4,121	$428	
Interest expense on note	$100	$100	$0	
Taxes	2,224	2,010	(214)	
Net income	$2,225	$2,011	$214	Salad bar is bringing in new business

management proactively rather than to discover and investigage variances reactively only when upper management contacts the department.

Chapter 12 provides guidelines for automating most of the variance analysis report calculation and generation process.

COMMON SIZE STATEMENTS

Trend, ratio, and variance analyses need to be combined with another type of analysis. The manager should compare current financial statements with the financial statements from prior periods. However, to clarify the comparison, the *distortion* from volume differences should be removed. This can easily be done by expressing each line item as a percentage. *Common size statements* are the result of stating each financial statement line item as a percentage.

In the common size balance sheet, each asset, liability, and capital (net worth) line item is expressed as a percentage of the total assets figure. The

Table 8-10 College Coffee Shop: Variance Analysis Worksheet for Prior Accounting
Period

	Actual Results	Budgeted Results	Favorable (Unfavorable) Variance	Reason
Sales	$114,994	$120,000	($5,006)	See 1
Cost of sales	49,500	53,700	4,200	See 2
Gross margin	$65,494	$66,300	($806)	
Salaries and wages	$27,950	$28,350	$400	Fewer hours
FICA	3,700	3,825	125	Fewer hours
Benefits	7,400	7,500	100	Insignificant
Utilities	3,200	3,200	0	
Supplies	3,650	3,800	150	Lower sales
Depreciation expense	16,579	16,579	0	
Net operating income	$3,015	$3,046	($31)	See 3
Interest expense on note	$100	$100	$0	
Taxes	1,457	1,473	16	
Net income	$1,458	$1,473	($16)	See 4

1. Sales declined when new restaurant opened across street and conference was cancelled.
2. Smaller order.
3. Need new product to compete with new restaurant.
4. Watch future expenses for net income impact of competitor.

formula to determine the balance sheet's common size percentages for each line item is:

$$\text{Common size balance sheet percentage} = \frac{\text{Balance sheet line item}}{\text{Total assets}} \times 100.$$

Table 8-11 shows a common size balance sheet for the actual and budgeted figures for the current period. The data for the actual figures are from Table 8-1, and for the budgeted figures, Table 8-3.

The sections of the balance sheet should tie out just as they do when using the dollar values. This will probably require some rounding of percentages in order to get the balance sheet to balance. After the current period's common size balance sheet is compiled, it should be compared with the prior period's common size balance sheet. An example of this is provided in Table 8-12 (based on data in Tables 8-1 and 8-3).

Table 8-11 College Coffee Shop: Common Size Balance Sheet

	Current Month Actual Results	Current Month Budgeted Results
Cash	4.48%	7.09%
Marketable securities	1.72	2.36
Inventory: Food	4.02	4.05
Beverage	2.07	2.03
Accounts receivable	18.78	16.96
Total current assets	31.07%	32.49%
Equipment	86.16%	84.39%
Accumulated depreciation	(17.23)	(16.88)
Total fixed assets	68.93%	67.51%
Total assets	100.00%	100.00%
Accounts payable	9.83%	11.28%
Salaries payable	4.01	4.33
Current portion of note	1.03	1.02
Total current liabilities	14.87%	16.63%
Note payable	12.75%	12.49%
Mortgage payable	0.00	0.00
Total long-term liabilities	12.75%	12.49%
Total liabilities	27.62%	29.11%
Capital	72.38%	70.89%
Total liabilities and capital	100.00%	100.00%

In the common size income statement, each sales and expense line item is stated as a percentage of total sales. The formula to determine the common size income statement percentages is:

$$\text{Common size income statement percentage} = \frac{\text{Income statement line item}}{\text{Total sales}} \times 100.$$

An example of a current period's common size income statement is provided in Table 8-13 (based on data in Tables 8-2 and 8-4).

Table 8-12 College Coffee Shop: Common Size Balance Sheet

	Prior Month Actual Results	Prior Month Budgeted Results
Cash	5.57%	6.93%
Marketable securities	2.30	2.31
Inventory: Food	3.61	3.96
Beverage	1.97	1.98
Accounts receivable	19.34	17.16
Total current assets	32.79%	32.34%
Equipment	81.97%	82.51%
Accumulated depreciation	(14.75)	(14.85)
Total fixed assets	67.21%	67.66%
Total assets	100.00%	100.00%
Accounts payable	12.71%	12.13%
Salaries payable	4.34	4.37
Current portion of note	0.98	0.99
Total current liabilities	18.03%	17.49%
Note payable	13.11%	13.20%
Mortgage payable	0.00	0.00
Total long-term liabilities	13.11%	13.20%
Total liabilities	31.15%	30.69%
Capital	68.85%	69.31%
Total liabilities and capital	100.00%	100.00%

The common size income statement percentages should tie out just as the regular income statement did. Again, in order to balance the income statement percentages, some rounding may be required. The current common size income statement should be compared with that of the prior period to gain a historical perspective. This is provided in Table 8-14 and is based on the prior period's figures in Tables 8-2 and 8-4.

The analytical methods covered in this chapter can be excellent managerial tools. However, the manager must keep in mind the "big picture." Industry averages are not as meaningful as the financial condition and goals

Table 8-13 College Coffee Shop: Common Size Income Statement

	Current Month Actual Results	Current Month Budgeted Results
Sales	100.00%	100.00%
Cost of sales	42.87	43.95
Gross margin	57.13%	56.05%
Salaries and wages	24.52%	23.99%
FICA	3.43	3.10
Benefits	6.41	6.13
Utilities	2.89	2.74
Supplies	3.34	3.39
Depreciation expense	12.98	13.37
Net operating income	3.56%	3.32%
Interest expense on note	0.08%	0.08%
Taxes	1.74	1.62
Net income	1.74%	1.62%

Table 8-14 College Coffee Shop: Common Size Income Statement

	Current Month Actual Results	Current Month Budgeted Results
Sales	100.00%	100.00%
Cost of sales	43.05	44.75
Gross margin	56.95%	55.25%
Salaries and wages	24.31%	23.63%
FICA	3.22	3.19
Benefits	6.44	6.25
Utilities	2.78	2.67
Supplies	3.17	3.17
Depreciation expense	14.42	13.82
Net operating income	2.62%	2.54%
Interest expense on note	0.09%	0.08%
Taxes	1.27	1.23
Net income	1.27%	1.23%

of the actual organization. Thus, the average is not necessarily the ideal level of performance for a specific operation.

These financial analysis tools are the means to the end of understanding the organization's true financial condition. However, the tools are never the result. Therefore, the financial analysis is not complete until the manager understands the condition, formulates effective strategies for the future, and implements those strategies. Other financial indicators and strategic planning methods are discussed in the next two chapters.

Chapter 9

Financial Indicators

Financial indicators are specific managerial tools used to facilitate wise decision making. These indicators fall into the two broad categories of volume planning and capital budgeting. *Volume planning* concerns break-even analysis, and *capital budgeting* concerns an entire set of procedures known as the "capital investment decision-making process." The use of these powerful tools can improve managerial effectiveness, add to the upward mobility of the manager, and strategically position the operation for funding and recognition.

The astute manager will monitor both the department and the entire organization with these in mind. These tools can play a key role in positioning the department for the future and can often help the manager to be proactive rather than reactive

BREAK-EVEN ANALYSIS

The *break-even analysis* tool focuses on the interrelationship of costs, volume, and profits. The concepts of fixed, variable, and semivariable costs were discussed in chapter 2. This section explains the interrelationship of costs and volume and the impact that this interrelationship has on profit margins.

The *break-even point* is the level of sales volume at which the total sales and total costs are equal. This means that net income is $0, or that the operation neither made nor lost money. The calculation of the break-even point begins with the calculation of the contribution margin and the contribution margin ratio (CMR).

CALCULATION OF THE CONTRIBUTION MARGIN AND THE CMR

The contribution margin is the difference between sales and variable expenses. It can be stated as a percentage, a ratio, or as total dollars. The

219

contribution margin ratio percentage (CMR%) is the percentage of each sales dollar that is available to cover fixed expenses. Of course, after the contribution margin dollars pay the fixed expenses, the remaining income becomes profit. The contribution margin is similar to the concept of gross margin discussed in chapter 7. The similarity lies in the fact that the contribution margin is used to cover the remaining expenses. In the case of the gross margin, the remaining expenses are operating expenses.

The CMR% can be calculated in two ways:

$$\text{CMR\%} = 100\% - \text{Variable expense \%}$$

$$\text{CMR\%} = \frac{\text{Sales} - \text{Variable expenses}}{\text{Sales}} \times 100.$$

This CMR formula can be adjusted to state the CMR in dollars, percentages, or as a ratio. For example, assume that total sales are 1,000 units sold for a total of $1,000: a contribution of 0.20 per unit, 20 percent, $200 or .20 to 1 all mean the same.

Calculation of the Break-Even Point

The break-even point is the level of sales volume that will be equal to total expenses (both variable and fixed). Total expenses are calculated by multiplying the variable expense rate by total sales and then adding the result to fixed expenses. In the break-even formula, the CMR is stated in ratio form, not percentage form (i.e., as .70, not as 70 percent). The break-even formula is:

$$\text{Break-even sales} = \frac{\text{Total fixed expenses}}{\text{CMR}}.$$

For example, assume that variable costs have been running at 70 percent of sales, and that fixed expenses are $150,000. The break-even point is:

$$\text{Break-even sales} = \frac{\$150,000}{0.30} = \$500,000.$$

Thus, the break-even sales volume is $500,000. In other words, sales must exceed $500,000 before the operation would begin to make a profit. The result can be verified by plugging the figure into the following equation and then determining that net income is zero with the calculated break-even sales volume. For example:

$$\text{Total sales} - \text{Total expenses} = \text{Net income}$$
$$\text{Total expenses} = (.70 \times 500,000) + 150,000$$
$$\$500,000 - (\$350,000 + \$150,000) = \$0.$$

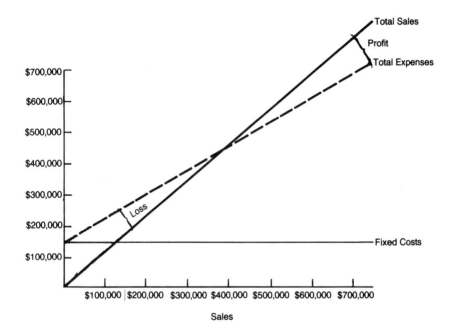

Figure 9-1 Break-even chart

The break-even point can also be identified with the use of a graph called the "break-even chart." Figure 9-1 is a break-even chart using the same fixed costs and variable expense percentage. The vertical axis is *expenses* and the horizontal axis is *sales*. The *total expenses line* is the sum of fixed expenses and the variable expense percentage times sales. The distance between the *fixed cost line* and the *total expenses line* represents variable expenses. The break-even point on the chart is located at the intersection of the *sales line* and the *total expenses line*. Examination of this break-even chart indicates the same break-even point that was determined using the formula.

Specific Applications for Break-Even Analysis

Although the starting point for this analysis was the calculation of both the CMR and the break-even point, these calculations are not the most important application or use of this analysis tool. Predicting, or forecasting, the impact that a *future* increase (or decrease) in sales will have on net income is one of the more typical applications of the break-even analysis tool. This application can be used whether or not variable costs are predicted to remain constant as a percentage of sales. If they are going to change, however, this change must also be taken into consideration when using the tool for the analysis of the forecast.

Using the CMR and the break-even point, it becomes relatively easy to determine the impact a change in the sales volume will have on operating expense. The impact of a change in the variable expense percentage can also be determined. Table 9-1 gives forecasts for various levels of sales and expenses and shows the impact these levels will have on profits.

Sales volume and variable rates that the manager may initially believe will maximize profits may not actually do so. For example, it may seem reasonable to expect that increasing sales while holding the variable expense percentage constant would maximize profits. However, in Table 9-1, forecast number 4 maximized profits. This sales forecast represented a decrease of 2 percent from the current level but also reflected a 2 percent decrease in the variable expense percentage (from 70 to 68 percent). This is an excellent example of how cost control can increase profits.

The break-even point formula can be adapted to calculate other variables in the formula. For example, the formula can be adapted to forecast the sales volume that would be required to provide the operation with a specified level of net profit given a specific variable expense. The formula would be:

$$\text{Required sales volume} = \frac{\text{Fixed expenses} + \text{Specified net profit}}{\text{CMR}}.$$

Thus, if fixed expenses were $150,000, variable expenses were 70 percent

Table 9-1 Break-Even Analysis: Forecasting Applications

	Break-Even Level	Current Period	Forecast 1[1]	Forecast 2[2]	Forecast 3[3]	Forecast 4[4]
Sales	$500,000	$600,000	$690,000	$690,000	$570,000	$660,000
Variable expense %	70%	70%	70%	75%	68%	68%
Variable expense $[5]	$350,000	$420,000	$483,000	$517,500	$387,600	$448,800
Fixed costs	$150,000	$150,000	$150,000	$150,000	$150,000	$150,000
Net profit[6]	$0	$30,000	$57,000	$22,500	$32,400	$61,200

[1]Forecast 1: Sales increase 15%; variable expense % unchanged.
[2]Forecast 2: Sales increase 15%; variable expense % increases.
[3]Forecast 3: Sales decrease 10%; variable expense % decreases.
[4]Forecast 4: Sales decrease 2%; variable expense % decreases.
[5]Variable expenses $ = Sales × Variable expense %.
[6]Net profit = Sales − [Variable expenses $ + Fixed costs].

of sales, and the manager wanted a net profit of at least $60,000, the required sales volume would be:

$$\text{Required sales volume} = \frac{\$150,000 + \$60,000}{0.30} = \$700,000.$$

Actually, the same formula can be adapted to forecast any value in the formula as long as the other variables in the equation are known. Simply use the equation to determine the unknown or unforecasted value based on the forecasted values for the rest of the formula. Using this approach, the impact of any cost or volume decision on operational profits can be readily identified.

CAPITAL INVESTMENT DECISION-MAKING PROCESS

The *capital budgeting process* is a set of selection and evaluation tools that involves the potential commitment of organizational resources for fixed assets in exchange for the opportunity to obtain additional income from the proposed fixed assets in the future. There are basic underlying principles, or rules, that are the basis for the entire capital budgeting/investment decision process. These include:

- the time value of money concept
- specific cash flow assumptions.

The Time Value of Money Concept

The premise of the *time value of money concept* is that $1 received today is worth more to the organization than $1 received at a future point. It is worth more today because in the intervening period the money could have been invested in the bank, in certificates of deposit, in the stock market, or in any number of other places. Thus, any financial decision about cash flows (inflows and outflows) must incorporate this principle to ensure that the most beneficial choice is made from a profitability standpoint. An example of this concept would be the choice between receiving $1 today or $1.12 from a project in one year. If the organization could invest the $1 elsewhere and earn more than 12 percent, that would be the appropriate choice. If, however, the operation could receive income of $1.05 from a project one year from now, or receive $1 today, the appropriate choice would be to take the $1 today.

Calculating the present value of a specific cash flow, or stream (series), of payments or revenues is based on this time value of money concept. A *cash stream* is defined as a series of cash flows to or from the operation. The purchase of capital equipment constitutes a negative cash flow. The additional income (from increased capacity and salvage flow) constitutes a positive cash stream. The derivation of any present value is based on the firm's *cost of capital.* This is the cost the firm must pay to borrow money. This cost of capital, then, is inherently the minimum return acceptable to the firm from a capital investment project. At the very least, an investment (whether it is in the stock market or in new equipment for the operation) must earn a return that equals the principal and interest. To determine the present value of a stream of payments over eight years is to say, "what lump sum today would be worth the same as the stream over time in the future?" This is just the "flip side" of the previous discussion of what premium should be required to accept a future stream in lieu of the lump sum today.

The present value of a cash stream generated by a project is calculated in three steps:

1. Calculate the cost of capital factor.
2. Calculate the present value factor.
3. Calculate the present value of the cash stream.

Cost of Capital Factor

The *cost of capital factor* is based on the firm's cost of capital. If the firm's cost of capital is 12 percent, then the base for the factor is 1.12. The reason for this is as follows: if the firm could earn 12 percent in one year on $1, then that dollar would be worth $1.12 in one year. The calculation of the actual cost of capital factor uses this base and then multiplies the base by itself. For year 2, the factor is 1.12×1.12, which is to say 1.12^2. The year 3 factor is 1.12^3. Thus, the year number becomes the power to which the base is raised. The manager should calculate a cost of capital factor for each year of the project or investment. Table 9-2 shows an example of calculated cost of capital factors for an operation with a 12 percent cost of capital.

Present Value Factor

The *present value factor* (PV factor) for each year is based on the cost of capital factor and is calculated as follows:

$$\text{Present value factor} = \frac{1}{\text{Cost of capital factor}}.$$

Table 9-2 also shows the calculations of the PV factors for the example.

Table 9-2 Present Value Calculations

Yr. No.	Cost of Capital Factor	Present Value Factor	Cash Stream	Present Value
1	1.12	0.8929	$2,000	$1,786
2	1.2544	0.7972	2,000	1,594
3	1.404928	0.7118	2,500	1,780
4	1.5735193	0.6355	2,500	1,589
5	1.7623416	0.5674	3,500	1,986
6	1.9738225	0.5066	4,000	2,026
7	2.2106812	0.4524	4,000	1,810
8	2.4759629	0.4039	5,000	2,020
			$25,500	$14,591

Present Value of Cash Stream

The PV factors for each period are multiplied by the cash inflow or outflow for that time period. The result of this calculation is the present value of each cash flow. The total of all of the cash stream's present values is the present value of the entire project.

Table 9-2 provides the data and calculations needed to determine the present values of the cash stream and the present value of the project. Referring to this Table, the present value of the total cash stream of $25,500 is the sum of the last column, or $14,591. The difference between $14,591 and $25,500 is the premium required for the firm to be willing to forego the $14,591 today in exchange for the stream of payments. If this premium is not possible, the firm should opt for the immediate payment rather than the stream of future payments. The cash stream present value also signifies that if a purchase of capital equipment were to provide $25,500 over the following eight years, this would be the same as receiving $14,591 today.

Cash Flow Rules and Assumptions

When making capital investment decisions, the manager should focus on cash flows since this is the measure of when the actual impact of the investment will occur. The cash flow to analyze is the cash flow after taxes. Depreciation is analyzed only in that it reduces taxes and thereby increases the after-tax cash flows. To highlight the impact of the potential investment, the manager should analyze only the incremental cash flows. The manager should assemble the forecasted cash flows for each project.

An example of data compiled for three potential capital projects is provided in Table 9-3. The incremental cash flow line was calculated by sub-

Table 9-3 Capital Investment Project Alternatives

	Project A	Project B	Project C
Initial outlay	$6,000	$9,000	$14,000
Life of asset	6 years	4 years	8 years
Salvage value[1]	$ 0	$1,000	$2,000
Annual depreciation	$1,000	$2,000	$1,500
Pre-Tax Cash Inflows			
Year 1–2	$2,400	$4,200	$3,800
Year 3	$2,400	$3,600	$4,200
Year 4	$3,400	$3,600	$4,800
Year 4 (salvage)	$ 0	$1,000	$ 0
Year 5–6	$3,400	$ 0	$5,800
Year 7–8	$ 0	$ 0	$6,400
Year 8 (salvage)	$ 0	$ 0	$2,000
Tax rate	50%	50%	50%
Cost of capital	12%	12%	12%
Pre-Tax Earnings[2]			
Year 1–2	$1,400	$2,200	$2,300
Year 3	$1,400	$1,600	$2,700
Year 4	$2,400	$2,600	$3,300
Year 5	$2,400	$ 0	$4,300
Year 6	$2,400	$ 0	$4,300
Year 7	$ 0	$ 0	$4,900
Year 8	$ 0	$ 0	$6,900
After-Tax Earnings[3]			
Year 1–2	$ 700	$1,100	$1,150
Year 3	$ 700	$ 800	$1,350
Year 4	$1,200	$1,300	$1,650
Year 5–6	$1,200	$ 0	$2,150
Year 7	$ 0	$ 0	$2,450
Year 8	$ 0	$ 0	$3,450
Incremental Cash Flows[4]			
Year 1–2	$1,700	$3,100	$2,650
Year 3	$1,700	$2,800	$2,850
Year 4	$2,200	$3,300	$3,150
Year 5–6	$2,200	$ 0	$3,650
Year 7	$ 0	$ 0	$3,950
Year 8	$ 0	$ 0	$4,950

[1]Salvage values are included in each asset's final year pre-tax earnings, after-tax earnings, and incremental cash flow.

[2]Pre-tax earnings = Cash inflows − Depreciation.

[3]After-tax earnings = Pre-tax earnings × 0.50.

[4]Incremental cash flows = After-tax earnings + Depreciation.

tracting taxes (50 percent of earnings before taxes) from the cash inflow line. This means that although depreciation is excluded from earnings, it is not excluded from the cash benefit or cash inflows. Salvage values are included in pre-tax earnings as well as in the incremental cash flows. Table 9-3 is referred to in the following sections as each capital budgeting evaluation and selection technique is discussed.

Evaluation and Selection Process

The manager's role in the capital budgeting process is to gather, evaluate, and select projects that are in keeping with the operation's goals. The manager should initially screen the projects by determining which ones will be profitable using the evaluation techniques to analyze the cash inflow and outflows and forecasted profitability of the investment. This criterion should be the initial requirement to classify a project as a candidate for selection. Five evaluation methods are explained:

1. payback period
2. net present value
3. profitability index
4. average rate of return
5. internal rate of return.

Payback Period

The *payback period evaluation method* involves determining the length of time it will take for the cash inflows from a project to equal the initial cash outlay. In other words, determine the time it will take for an investment to pay back the organization for the investment. The selection process using this method begins with ranking the projects by payback period, beginning with the shortest payback period, until the total capital budget is depleted. If the life of the project or asset is less than the payback period, the project will be immediately rejected.

Since this method stresses liquidity rather than profitability, an operation that is very short of cash could find this method particularly useful. The payback method is particularly useful for analyzing and selecting among a variety of proposals with the same general characteristics. Since this method stresses liquidity, in industries characterized by instability and uncertainty (such as the increasingly competitive health care field) this method can provide valuable decision guidelines.

The criticism of the method is that it ignores the time value of money, the salvage values of the potential new assets, and all cash flows beyond the payback period. The point is that the manager should not use the payback method as the only evaluation and selection method.

The figures in Table 9-3 were used to calculate the payback period for each project. Project A's payback period is for a $6,000 outflow. The payback period is determined by subtracting the expected future cash inflows for each period from the cost of the proposed project until the net cost is equal to zero.

Cost of project A	$6,000
Year 1 inflow	(2,400)
New net cost	$3,600
Year 2 inflow	(2,400)
New net cost	$1,200

The cash inflow in year 3 of $2,400 is more than the remaining net cost. The formula used to calculate the portion of year 3 to include in the payback period is:

$$\frac{\text{New net cost}}{\text{Inflow for year}}$$

Therefore, the project A payback period is:

$$2 \text{ years } + \frac{\$1,200}{\$2,400} \times 1 = 2 + 1/2, \text{ or } 2.5 \text{ years.}$$

The payback period for project B is:

$$\$9,000$$
$$(4,200) \text{ Year 1}$$
New net cost $4,800
$$(4,200) \text{ Year 2}$$
New net cost $600.

The total project B payback period = 2 + (600/3,600). This means that the payback period is 2 and 1/6th of one year, or 2 years and 2 months.

The payback period for project C is:

$$\$14,000$$
$$(\ 3,800) \text{ Year 1}$$
New net cost $10,200
$$(\ 3,800) \text{ Year 2}$$
New net cost $ 6,400
$$(\ 4,200) \text{ Year 3}$$
New net cost $ 2,200.

The total payback period for project C is:

$$3 + \frac{2,200}{4,900} = 3.45 \text{ years.}$$

The selection process for the payback period evaluation technique is a two-step process. The first step is to reject all projects that have payback periods that are longer than the estimated life of the asset. The second step is to rank the remaining projects in order by payback period, beginning with the project with the shortest payback period. Projects are selected, beginning with the shortest payback period, until the available funds for capital are depleted. This means that if the operation had more than enough funds to invest in the project that was ranked first but not enough left to invest in the project that was ranked second, only the project that was ranked first would be undertaken. Unfortunately, this means that even if there were sufficient funds to invest in the project that was ranked third, it would not be undertaken, even if this project would have been an acceptable alternative for the operation.

Average Rate of Return

The *average rate of return (ARR) evaluation method* is based on the average annual net profit and the average investment in the project. The measure is calculated in three steps:

1. Calculate the average profit after taxes on the project.
2. Calculate the average investment in the project.
3. Calculate the average rate of return.

The average profit after taxes for the project is calculated as follows:

$$\text{Average profit after taxes} = \frac{\text{Total of after-tax earnings for project}}{\text{Estimated life of asset}}.$$

The average investment in the project is calculated as:

$$\text{Average investment} = \frac{\text{Initial cost} + \text{Salvage value}}{2}.$$

The average investment is calculated by dividing by two based on the same reasoning used in calculating the average inventory.

The average after-tax profits and average investment are then used to calculate the ARR for a project:

$$\text{ARR} = \frac{\text{Average profit after taxes}}{\text{Average investment}} \times 100.$$

This measure is relatively simple to use and can be compared with the firm's return on investment (ROI), which was presented in chapter 8. The ARR does not adjust the profits or expenditures for the time value of money. The method does not base its logic on cash flows. In other words, it ignores cash flows generated by the recognition of depreciation expense and analyzes only the net profit dollars, even though the organization will have the depreciation dollars available for reinvestment.

The evaluation and selection method involves ranking the projects after calculating each project's ARR. The projects are ranked in descending ARR order. Then the projects with the highest ARRs are selected until the capital budget is exhausted, or until the project's ARR is less than the firm's cost of capital.

Data in Table 9-3 are used to show how the ARR can be used for capital budget decision making. The total profit after taxes for project A is:

$$\frac{\$700 + \$700 + \$700 + \$1,200 + \$1,200 + \$1,200}{6} = \$950.$$

The average investment for project A is:

$$\frac{\$6,000 + \$0}{2} = \$3,000.$$

Project A's ARR is:

$$\frac{\$950 \times 100}{\$3,000} = 31.7\%.$$

The ARR for project A is certainly higher than the operation's assumed 12 percent cost of capital. However, the manager must calculate the ARR for projects B and C before selecting the project(s) for the capital budget.

Project B's average after-tax profit is:

$$\frac{\$1,100 + \$1,100 + \$800 + \$800}{4} = \$950.$$

Project B's average investment is:

$$\frac{\$9,000 + \$1,000}{2} = \$5,000.$$

The ARR for project B is:

$$\frac{\$950 \times 100}{\$5,000} = 19.0\%.$$

Since the ARR for project B is less than the ARR for project A, project B will be ranked below project A when the manager evaluates the projects.

Project C must be analyzed before the final project selection can occur. The total after-tax profits for project C are:

$$[\$1,150 \times 2] + \$1,350 + \$1,650 + [\$2,150 \times 2] + \$2,450.$$

The average after-tax profits is the sum of this calculation divided by the life of the project:

$$\frac{\$14,500}{8} = \$1,812.50.$$

The average investment for project C is:

$$\frac{\$14,000 + \$2,000}{2} = \$8,000.$$

The ARR for project C is:

$$\frac{\$1,812.50}{\$8,000.00} \times 100 = 22.7\%.$$

The manager's selection process is begun by ranking the projects by ARR, with the highest project return being ranked 1 (first).

Project	ARR	Ranking	Project Cost
A	31.7%	1	$ 6,000
B	19.0%	3	$ 9,000
C	22.7%	2	$14,000

The number of projects eventually selected depends on the total funds available to the manager. For example, if the manager had $15,000 to invest, according to the ARR method only project A would be selected since the remaining $9,000 is insufficient to pay for project C (ranked second). This is a good example of one of the method's major weaknesses. Although $15,000 could have paid for both project A and B, project B was not selected. Project B was not selected because its ARR was less than C's, even though the ARR for project B may have been perfectly acceptable.

Net Present Value

The *net present value (NPV) evaluation method* applies the time value of money concept in analyzing the cash flows associated with each project. The NPV (also known as the "discounted cash flow") of a project is calculated by subtracting the present value of the cash outflows from the present value of the cash inflows. (The calculation of present values was discussed earlier in this chapter.) The present value of the *initial* investment is the same as the actual cost; no PV factor is required since the project is being evaluated as if it is to be undertaken today. Any salvage value is to be added to the other cash inflow in the final year of the project, and the total of the two figures is to be discounted by the appropriate PV factor for that year.

Table 9-4 evaluates projects A, and B, and C using the NPV method based on the project information in Table 9-3.

The project selection process once again involves ranking the projects. The projects are ranked in descending order beginning with the project with the highest NPV. The projects with the highest NPV are selected until

Table 9-4 Net Present Values

		Project A		Project B		Project C	
Yr.	PV Factor	Cash Flow	PV Cash Flow	Cash Flow	PV Cash Flow	Cash Flow	PV Cash Flow
0	1.0000	($6,000)	($6,000)	($9,000)	($9,000)	($14,000)	($14,000)
1	0.8929	$1,700	$1,518	$3,100	$2,768	$2,650	$2,366
2	0.7972	$1,700	$1,355	$3,100	$2,471	$2,650	$2,113
3	0.7118	$1,700	$1,210	$2,800	$1,993	$2,850	$2,029
4	0.6355	$2,200	$1,398	$2,800	$1,779	$3,150	$2,002
4	0.6355	$0	$0	$1,000 (salvage)	$636	$0	$0
5	0.5674	$2,200	$1,248	$0	$0	$3,650	$2,071
6	0.5066	$2,200	$1,115	$0	$0	$3,650	$1,849
7	0.4524	$0	$0	$0	$0	$3,950	$1,787
8	0.4039	$0	$0	$0	$0	$3,950	$1,595
8	0.4039	$0	$0	$0	$0	$2,000 (salvage)	$808
Project's net present values			$1,844		$647		$2,620

the capital budget is either insufficient to select the next ranked project or is depleted.

Although this method analyzes the actual cash streams and incorporates the principle of the time value of money, it still has limitations. This is not to say the method should not be used but rather that the manager should be aware of the limitations. The method assumes that the cash inflows can be reinvested at the organization's cost of capital and that the cost of capital will be constant. This may not always be the case. The NPV method does not differentiate based on the size of the investment, it evaluates only the NPV. The manager should always look at the size of the projects, too, and commit the organization only to the size of investments it can handle.

Profitability Index

The *profitability index (PI) evaluation method* is performed by dividing the present value of all the cash inflows by the present value of all the cash outflows. One note of caution: Be careful not to use NPVs. Divide the sum of the cash inflow present values by the total current value of the cash investment (outflows). This measure is similar to an ROI.

The selection process is to rank the projects in descending PI order and then to select projects with the highest PI until the available capital is gone. Any project with a PI less than 1 is rejected because this means that the present value of the inflows is less than the present value of the outflows. Obviously, in this case the funds would be better invested elsewhere.

Use the present values computed previously to compute the PI for each project.

$$\text{Project A's PI} = \frac{\$7,844}{\$6,000} = 1.31.$$

$$\text{Project B's PI} = \frac{\$9,647}{\$9,000} = 1.07.$$

$$\text{Project C's PI} = \frac{\$16,620}{\$14,000} = 1.19.$$

The ranking for project selection would rank project A first, project C second, and project B third. If only $15,000 were available for capital projects, only project 1 would be selected since there would be insufficient funds to undertake the other two projects.

Internal Rate of Return

The *internal rate of return* (IRR) is the rate of return that will make the future stream of cash inflows equal to the outflows. This is similar to the NPV approach except that the manager is solving the equation for the cost of capital. The procedure is to find a cost of capital rate that will provide factors that will sufficiently reduce the present value of the cash inflows so as to end up with an NPV of $0. This is done by trial and error. The method assumes that proceeds (inflows) can be reinvested at the same internal rate of return. This is often very unlikely.

The project selection process is to list projects in descending IRR order and to select projects until the capital budgets are exhausted. Any project with an IRR less than the firm's cost of capital is automatically rejected since this would mean that the investment would not make enough to pay for the principal and interest if the funds for the project were borrowed.

The data in Table 9-3 provide the cash flow information necessary to calculate the IRR for each project.

Table 9-5 shows the trial-and-error process used to derive project A's IRR. From the iterations in Table 9-5, project A's IRR is 21.65 percent. Assuming that the firm's cost of capital is 12 percent, the project would be a viable investment candidate since the return is higher than the cost. The other projects' returns must also be calculated before the investment selection decision can be made.

The iterations to determine project B's IRR are shown in Table 9-6. The calculations derived an IRR of 15.29 percent.

Assuming that the cost of capital is still at 12 percent, this project would also be a viable investment candidate. However, since the IRR is less than

Table 9-5 Internal Rate of Return Iterations for Project A

		22%			21.7%		21.6%		21.65%	
Yr.	Cash Flow	PV Factor	PV Cash Flow[1]	PV Factor	PV Cash Flow	PV Factor	PV Cash Flow	PV Factor	PV Cash Flow
0	($6,000)	1.0000	($6,000)	1.0000	($6,000)	1.0000	($6,000)	1.0000	($6,000)
1	1,700	0.8197	1,393	0.8217	1,397	0.8224	1,398	0.8220	1,397
2	1,700	0.6719	1,142	0.6752	1,148	0.6763	1,150	0.6757	1,149
3	1,700	0.5507	936	0.5548	943	0.5562	946	0.5555	944
4	2,200	0.4514	993	0.4559	1,003	0.4574	1,006	0.4566	1,005
5	2,200	0.3700	814	0.3746	824	0.3761	827	0.3754	826
6	2,200	0.3033	667	0.3078	677	0.3093	680	0.3086	679
Net present value[2]			($54)		($8)		$7		$0

[1]PV cash flow = Cash flow × PV factor.
[2]Net present value = Sum of PV cash flows.

Table 9-6 Internal Rate of Return Iterations for Project B

		15%		15.5%		15.3%		15.29%	
Yr.	Cash Flow	PV Factor	PV Cash Flow[1]	PV Factor	PV Cash Flow	PV Factor	PV Cash Flow	PV Factor	PV Cash Flow
0	($9,000)	1.0000	($9,000)	1.0000	($9,000)	1.0000	($9,000)	1.0000	($9,000)
1	3,100	0.8696	2,696	0.8658	2,684	0.8673	2,689	0.8674	2,689
2	3,100	0.7561	2,344	0.7496	2,324	0.7522	2,332	0.7523	2,332
3	2,800	0.6575	1,841	0.6490	1,817	0.6524	1,827	0.6526	1,827
4	2,800	0.5718	1,601	0.5619	1,573	0.5658	1,581	0.5660	1,585
4	1,000	0.5718	572	0.5619	562	0.5658	566	0.5660	566
Net present value[2]			$54		($40)		($3)		$0

[1]PV cash flow = Cash flow × PV factor.
[2]Net present value = Sum of PV cash flows.

Table 9-7 Internal Rate of Return Iterations for Project C

		16%		16.5%		16.53%		16.52%	
Yr.	Cash Flow	PV Factor	PV Cash Flow[1]	PV Factor	PV Cash Flow	PV Factor	PV Cash Flow	PV Factor	PV Cash Flow
0	($14,000)	1.0000	($14,000)	1.0000	($14,000)	1.0000	($14,000)	1.0000	($14,000)
1	2,650	0.8621	2,285	0.8584	2,275	0.8582	2,274	0.8582	2,274
2	2,650	0.7432	1,969	0.7368	1,953	0.7364	1,951	0.7365	1,952
3	2,850	0.6407	1,826	0.6324	1,802	0.6320	1,801	0.6321	1,801
4	3,150	0.5523	1,740	0.5429	1,710	0.5423	1,708	0.5425	1,709
5	3,650	0.4761	1,738	0.4660	1,701	0.4654	1,699	0.4656	1,699
6	3,650	0.4104	1,498	0.4000	1,460	0.3994	1,458	0.3996	1,459
7	3,950	0.3538	1,398	0.3433	1,356	0.3427	1,354	0.3429	1,354
8	3,950	0.3030	1,197	0.2947	1,164	0.2941	1,162	0.2943	1,162
8	2,000 (salvage)	0.3030	606	0.2947	589	0.2941	588	0.2943	589
Net present value[2]			$256		$10		($5)		$0

[1]PV cash flow = Cash flow × PV factor.
[2]Net present value = Sum of PV cash flows.

Table 9-8 Project Selection: Project Rankings by Evaluation Method

Project	NPV	IRR	PAYBACK	ARR	PI
A	2	1	2	1	1
B	3	3	1	3	3
C	1	2	3	2	2

project A's, project B would be ranked below project A in the selection process.

The project C iterations are provided in Table 9-7. The IRR for this project is 16.52 percent. Thus, project C would also be a viable candidate. As a matter of fact, it would be ranked higher than project B but lower than project A, based on the IRR selection method.

Different organizations use each of the capital budgeting evaluation methods, and many operations use more than one of the methods to evaluate proposed projects. When an operation is highly strapped for cash, and therefore concerned with liquidity, the payback method may be heavily relied upon.

The manager should determine the long-run impact any capital budgeting decision will have on operational performance. This is determined by calculating all of the project evaluation measures, paying particular attention to the NPV measure.

Once all the measures are computed, the manager can most easily compare the calculations by summarizing the results in a selection chart. An example of a selection chart is provided in Table 9-8. Ranking the projects in a selection chart will help the manager focus on the impact of the investment. The selection chart shows the highest ranked project using a specific evaluation method with a ranking of 1 and the lowest ranked project with a ranking of 3.

Finally, before a lease or buy decision can be made, the purchase alternatives should be evaluated. If the alternatives do not provide an adequate return on the investment, the project would not be worth the risk. In this case, the manager would be better off simply leasing the equipment and investing the funds during the life of the lease until each lease payment is due.

Chapter 10

The Strategic Plan: Design, Techniques, and Implementation

The manager's most crucial planning tasks include the selection of the specific products and services to offer, the choice of markets in which to operate, and the development of the road map that will help the organization most effectively meet these goals. Frequently, the overall organizational goal is called the "corporate mission." The strategic plan, then, is the way the manager has decided will most ensure that the organization will achieve the corporate mission.

The general requirement is for the manager to establish consistent strategies for each of the functional areas that will help the organization reach the corporate mission. Specific strategy formulation begins with choosing longer term, all-encompassing objectives for the organization. For example, the manager should define desired ranges of growth and profits. Effective strategy formulation should define acceptable and unacceptable levels of risk and should set goals for changes in key ratios. The effective manager is not only responsible for strategy formulation but also influences the success of these longer term objectives throughout the organization.

STRATEGY DESIGN

The process of strategy formulation and planning requires a combination of intellectual and administrative skills. Identifying problems that affect the long-term position of the firm calls for the ability to select and relate disparate bits of information so that an inclusive statement of key problems can be made. Making this inclusive statement requires the intellectual skill involved in analyzing the impact that environmental trends and data will have on internal corporate operations. It also requires the ability to articulate problems in such a way that identifies viable alternatives that can then be tested using various quantitative and qualitative tools. This ability

237

is indicative of an administrative sense. Similarly, setting objectives and formulating a plan of action require both the sense of what is needed and the sense of what will work.

Since objective identification is an ongoing process, the manager must continually redefine the appropriate organizational objective(s). The manager should determine how to achieve an objective only after the completion of the objective identification process. Obviously, these overall organizational objectives are not static, nor does the organization operate in a vacuum. Rather, the organization operates within the confines of the overall external environment, continually affected by changes and events in this competitive environment. Furthermore, the organization is continually affected by the impact of the organization's reputation, community and consumer expectations, and changing legal requirements.

Another facet of strategy formulation is determining the means to achieve the selected objectives. An analysis of the selected objectives should help the manager identify the key factors in achieving them. For example, an objective of a 5 percent growth in profits should lead the manager to set appropriate strategies for the factors that would contribute to increasing profits (e.g., increasing sales, decreasing cost of sales, and decreasing operating expenses).

Strategy formulation is an ongoing process of product/service definition and market identification. A key part of this is to search continually for ways to distinguish, or differentiate, the organization's products and services from similar competitive products and services. In this way the manager can make the organization's products and services more desirable by narrowing the gap between the product or service and the unmet market need.

Effective strategy identifies:

- the major steps to take
- the approximate time frame for each step
- the people responsible for accomplishing each step
- the amount of resources required for each step
- the potential sources of the resources required for each step.

The formulated strategic plan should address how the organization has decided to compete in the marketplace and specify potential adjustments attributable to trends in the environment. This includes capitalizing on the operation's strengths and compensating for its weaknesses, or even turning its weaknesses into strengths! The wise manager will never lose sight of the need to guide the organization in more than economic performance and ensure that the operation is meeting its purpose as perceived by the community within which it operates.

The overall responsibility of the foodservice manager is to ensure the provision of products to the clients of the operation in the most efficient, productive, effective, and satisfying manner possible. There are numerous quantitative tools available to help the manager determine the most efficient, productive, and effective strategies that will both satisfy the needs of the clients and maximize profits. These strategies are ultimately based on the manager's ability to combine the quantitative methodologies with qualitative considerations, which are based on overall experience and knowledge.

The evaluation, comparison, and selection of strategies and projects will depend on various criteria for acceptance set by management. For example, before launching a strategy of expansion, the manager must determine whether the current capacity is adequate to meet anticipated demand in a satisfactory, efficient, and cost-effective manner. Thus, forecasts should be made with and without the proposed expansion.

The foodservice industry is composed of many businesses (business segments). To define appropriate operational strategies, the manager must identify and analyze the organization's businesses. For example, a hospital foodservice department is concurrently involved in many businesses: in-house meal service, in-house catering, perhaps even external catering for daycare centers, or community services, perhaps providing mobile meals for senior citizens. After determining its current businesses the manager should determine appropriate strategies and current financial trends for each of these businesses.

In addition, this study of the operation's businesses can be a starting point for brainstorming on future product and service offerings and market niches. The organization's competition may not be only other hospital foodservices. The competition could also include caterers, restaurants, and contract foodservice companies. The strengths of potential competitors should be weighed and analyzed before new businesses are entered.

Obviously, the operational strategy must be formulated to match the *operation's* needs, goals, and capabilities, not the industry's, and not a competitor's. The success of the organization is based on its ability to strive to be, and become, the best it can possibly be. Each organization has its own distinct combination of competencies and strengths. The trick is to hone these into a uniquely successful operation. This strategy greatly helps minimize the threat that competitors pose because these strengths can become competitive advantages with the appropriate focus, attitude, and strategy.

Of course, the manager cannot overlook the organization's weaknesses. The set of the weaknesses and strengths of the organization should be combined with the opportunities in the marketplace to provide exciting, successful, and unique products or services. Strategies that incorporate these facets and that are still in keeping with the legal requirements, community expectations, financial requirements, and corporate mission of the operation have the best chance for success.

Another important element of the strategic plan is the marketing plan. The production, operations, financing, and marketing plans are interdependent in their functioning. Recall the sections in chapter 5 that explained product analysis based on contribution margins and sales volumes. This information fluctuates over time, depending on changes in the marketplace, new product opportunities, product and service obsolescence, and general changes in the economy. The astute manager is aware of the environment and the competition. This awareness helps the organization stay on the cutting edge by enabling the manager to realign it to meet the shifting needs of the market. This is a good reason to monitor and keep abreast of industry trends by attending trade association meetings and continuing education seminars, in addition to watching for general trends in the marketplace. By being prepared for change, the manager can help ensure the organization's survival and success.

MODELING AND STATISTICAL TECHNIQUES

Specific managerial quantitative tools are available to help the manager develop and formulate potential operational strategies. These techniques can be used to analyze all the potential strategies and point the manager toward the benefits of each. This can help narrow the choices so the manager can logically determine which strategy would most benefit the operation. Although there are numerous operational tools available, the following categories are discussed:

- linear programming
- "what-if?," or sensitivity analysis
- regression analysis.

Linear Programming

Linear programming is a mathematical tool frequently used by managers as a production/operations management tool either to maximize a goal (e.g., profits) or to minimize a goal (e.g., operating expenses). This goal is typically subject to a set of predefined limits and conditions. Linear programming, therefore, is a quantitative analysis tool that determines the most favorable alternative among various choices, with the most favorable defined as the alternative that comes closest to achieving the desired goal.

Linear programming is an optimization model. The targeted goal is called the "objective function." The limits and conditions are called the "linear constraints." Linear programming has two distinct phases. The first phase is to formulate the problem as a linear program. The second phase is to solve the formulated linear program.

Formulate the Linear Program

The first step in formulating the problem as a linear program is to define the decision variables. For example, if the manager is deciding the appropriate combination of two menu options to prepare, the decision variables could be defined as follows: Let X_1 = the total dollars in sales for menu offering 1, and let X_2 = the total dollars in sales for menu offering 2. Defining the decision variable helps the manager identify, define, and organize the information pertinent to the decision.

Once the decision variables are defined, the second step is to formulate the goal, which is called the "objective function." This is generally to maximize or minimize a specific mathematical relationship. Assuming that the profit contribution for X_1 is 15 percent and the profit contribution for X_2 is 21 percent, then the objective function to maximize profits is: Maximize profits where profits = $0.15 X_1 + 0.21 X_2$.

The third and final step in linear program formulation is to define the objective function's constraints, conditions, and limitations. Exhibit 10-1 shows a formulated linear program.

Solve the Linear Program

To solve the linear program, the manager follows the same procedure that is used to solve any system of simultaneous equations. The steps involved in solving the simultaneous equations for the sample linear program are shown in Exhibit 10-2. The technique involves solving for one variable at a time.

Multiple linear programming can be adapted to determine the optimal menu offerings. This could incorporate a fairly sophisticated scenario, including the following facets of the decision:

- dietary constraints
- occupancy rates
- capacity
- food prices
- available labor hours
- labor hours required for various menu options.

There are many software packages that include linear programming. It is fairly easy to solve a set of two simultaneous equations. However, most

Exhibit 10-1 Linear Program Formulation

Objective Function

Maximize profits where profits $= 0.15\ X_1 + 0.21\ X_2$

Constraints

$X_1 + X_2 \leq \$750$

$3X_1 + 6X_2 \leq \$2,700$

$X_2 \leq \$400$

$X_1 \geq 0,\ X_2 \geq 0$

Exhibit 10-2 Solving Simultaneous Equations

1. Extract the constraints from Exhibit 10-1 that contain both variables. State them as equations:

   (a) $3X_1 + 6X_2 = \$2,700$
   (b) $X_1 + X_2 = \$750$.

2. Reduce the first equation by dividing it by 3. List the new system of equations:

   (a) $X_1 + 2X_2 = \$900$
   (b) $X_1 + X_2 = \$750$.

3. Solve for X_1 by making $X_2 = 0$. Multiply the second equation by 2. Then subtract the second equation from the first:

   (a) $X_1 + 2X_2 = \$900$
   (b) $\underline{-2X_1 + 2X_2 = \$1,500}$
   $-1X_1 + 0X_2 = -\$600$, or $X_1 = \$600$.

4. Now solve for X_2. Return to the restated system in step 2. Subtract the second equation from the first:

   (a) $X_1 + 2X_2 = \$900$
   (b) $\underline{-X_1 + X_2 = \$750}$
   $0X_1 + 1X_2 = \$150$, or $X_2 = \$150$.

5. In the case of a two-variable system, the manager can solve for one variable and then substitute it into the equation to solve for the other. It is good practice, however, to solve for each variable.

models will be more complex than that and thus have more variables. These linear programming models can be solved quickly by using a microcomputer and an appropriate software package. Therefore, there is no reason to oversimplify the model since the computer can be used to optimize complex models.

"What-If?," or Sensitivity Analysis

Sensitivity analysis is a testing mechanism that evaluates the impact various changes would have on operational forecasts. The method is frequently known as "what-if?" analysis because the approach consists of a series of tests such as "what if sales increase by only 5 percent but costs still increase as forecasted?" Another example would be to determine the break-even point if inventory costs were to increase by 2 percent. Although the iterations of pro forma and related ratios can be calculated manually, the use of microcomputers and appropriate software packages is quicker and generates more iterations. The technique is called "sensitivity analysis" because the manager is attempting to determine just how sensitive the operational results are to the assumptions that were made by testing the impact of a change on various forecasts.

Many of the financial analysis and financial indicator tools can also be tested and analyzed using sensitivity analysis. A review of break-even analysis (chapter 9) will provide suggestions for types of sensitivity analysis. To test for the impact of simultaneous changes in multiple variables, it is almost essential to use appropriate software packages on a microcomputer.

Regression Analysis

Regression analysis is a statistical method that is widely used as a forecasting tool. The underlying assumption on which regression analysis is based is that there is a relationship between variables evident in the observed data. Regression analysis is used to forecast future values of a variable (called the "dependent variable") from the values of one or more other variables (called the "independent variables"). The assumption is that the future demand is related to the economic and competitive events that shape and affect that demand. The regression analysis technique calculates how the dependent variable has varied, on the average, with differences or changes in the other (independent) variables.

A specific example is forecasting food sales dollars based on forecasted changes in occupancy levels. In this case, *occupancy levels* is the independent variable, and *food sales dollars* is the dependent variable. The forecast is based on the relationship identified in historic observations.

Although regression relationships are inexact, the regression analysis tool does allow forecasts of future variables that are sufficiently accurate for decision-making purposes. Dependent variable forecasts are based on past observations of the dependent and independent variable(s) and the assumed future values of the independent variable(s). Using one variable to predict values of another variable is a type of statistical inference. The process of estimating a variable relies on finding the equation of a line that summarizes the average relationship between the dependent variable and the independent variable(s).

The manager must formulate the problem by identifying and defining the dependent and independent variables. Then the manager must gather historical observations of the variables. The next step is to use the *method of least squares* to estimate the equation for the relationship between variables. This method provides the closest possible estimate of the average relationship between the variables because it minimizes the sum of the square of the difference between the observed and estimated values of the variables.

The linear regression formula is $Y = a + bX$. The calculation of the linear regression equation is a multiple-step process:

1. Gather the historical data for the X and Y variables.
2. Record the data in a table and perform calculations.
3. Calculate the means (averages) of the Y and X values by dividing the column totals for each of the variables by the number of observations (n).
4. Calculate *a* and *b* using these formulas:

$$b = \frac{(\text{Total } XY \text{ column}) - [\text{n} \times (\text{mean of } X \times \text{mean of } Y)]}{(\text{Total of } X^2 \text{ column}) - [\text{n} \times (\text{Mean of } X)^2]}$$

$$a = (\text{Mean of } Y) - (b \times \text{Mean of } X).$$

Table 10-1 is an example of historical observations and the required calculations to determine the linear equation using the least squares method.

The primary purpose of regression analysis is to enable the manager to forecast future values of the dependent variable based on the average relationship of the dependent and independent variables. The linear equation calculated based on historical relationships show mean, or average, values of Y for given levels of X. Thus, forecasting is done by inserting forecasted X variables into the equation to derive the forecasted Y values.

Regression analysis assumes a linear relationship among the variables. After the line is estimated, specific tests must be performed to determine

Table 10-1 Regression Analysis[1-6]

Y	X	XY	X²	Y²
8	23	184	529	64
6	25	150	625	36
10	24	240	576	100
7	18	126	324	49
14	33	462	1,089	196
13	29	377	841	169
15	38	570	1,444	225
16	41	656	1,681	256
17	39	663	1,521	289
18	44	792	1,936	324
Totals 124	314	4,220	10 566	1,708

[1] Dollars are in 1,000s.
[2] $n = 10$.
[3] The mean of Y is $(124/10) = 12.4$; the mean of X is $(314/10) = 31.4$.
[4] $b = \dfrac{4{,}220 - (10 \times 12.4 \times 31.4)}{10{,}566 - (10 \times 31.4 \times 31.4)} = \dfrac{326.4}{706.4} = 0.4621$.
[5] $a = 12.4 - (0.4621 \times 31.4) = 12.4 - 14.51 = -2.11$.
[6] The linear regression equation is $Y = -2.11 + 0.4621X$.

the level of error in the estimate, that is, how reliable the calculated line is as a forecasting tool. The following measures are tests of the reliability of the estimate.

- standard error of estimate
- coefficient of determination
- correlation coefficient.

Standard Error of Estimate

The *standard error of estimate* measures the differences or variances between the observed values of Y (dependent variable) and the estimated values of Y that were obtained using the least squares method. The standard error of estimate is an analytical tool that determines the reliability of the regression equation. Specifically, it measures the differences between the observed and calculated Y values. This variation is called the "unexplained variance." While it is true that the least squares method provides the best possible fit of a line to the observed values of X and Y, the standard error of estimate reflects the degree of fit.

The larger the standard error of estimate, the more scattered the actual Y values will be from the regression line if the observed and calculated Y values were graphed for each actual observed X value and the regression line was then graphed.

Standard error of estimate =

$$\sqrt{\frac{\text{Sum of } Y^2 \text{ column} - (a \times Y \text{ column}) - (b \times \text{Sum of } XY \text{ column})}{n - 2}}$$

Theoretically, in the absence of regression data, the best estimate for a variable is the mean of the observations. Therefore, in analyzing the reliability of the regression equation, even though the equation will not perfectly match the *observed* values, the manager should determine how much closer the regression predictions for Y are to the observed Y values than is the mean of the observations.

Exhibit 10-3 shows the calculation of the standard error of estimate using the data previously used to calculate the least squares line. Remember that the example regression equation was $Y = -2.11 + 0.4621X$. Test the variation by substituting observed X values into the equation and computing the Y values. The Y values will be fairly close to the observed Y values but not equal to them.

Coefficient of Determination

Correlation analysis is the method used to determine the degree of association among the variables. Both the correlation coefficient and the coefficient of determination are used to measure the strength of the relationship between the dependent and the independent variables. This degree of correlation does not mean that there is a cause-and-effect rela-

---

Exhibit 10-3 Regression Analysis: Standard Error of Estimate

The total of the Y^2 column = 1,708.
The calculated a value = -2.11.
The total of the Y column = 124.
The calculated b value = 0.4621.
The total of the XY column = 4,220.
The number of observations, or n, = 10.
To calculate the standard error of estimate, first find:

$$\frac{1,708 - (-2.11 \times 124) - (0.4621 \times 4,220)}{10 - 2} = \frac{19.58}{8} = 2.45.$$

The standard error of estimate is the square root of 2.45, which is 1.56.

tionship between the variables. These two measures basically tell the manager the reliability of the estimate.

The *coefficient of determination* measures the proportion of variation between the mean of the observed values of Y and the observed Y values that is explained by the linear regression equation. The coefficient of determination is sometimes referred to as R^2. Recall from the discussion of the standard error of estimate that the overall, or total, variation was defined as the sum of the differences between each observed value of Y and the mean of those observed values. The coefficient of determination is the measure that shows the proportion of that total variation that the regression equation explains. This means: how much closer to the observed Y values did the regression equation bring the manager? One form of this formula is:

$$R^2 = 1 - \frac{\text{Total of } [(\text{observed } Ys - \text{calculated } Ys)^2]}{\text{Total of } [(\text{observed } Ys - \text{Mean of observed } Ys)^2]}$$

The calculations for this form of the formula can be very time-consuming to perform. There is another form of the formula that uses variables already calculated when the linear regression equation was calculated:

$$R^2 = \frac{(a \times Y \text{ column total}) + (b \times XY \text{ column total}) - (n \times \text{mean of } Y \text{ column})^2}{[(Y \text{ column total})^2] - [n \times (\text{mean of } Y \text{ column})^2]}$$

To state R^2 as a percentage, multiply the result of this calculation by 100. Exhibit 10-4 provides an example of the calculation of the coefficient of determination based on the regression calculations from Table 10-1.

How reliable is the example regression equation in estimating Y values based on the observed X values and their relationship to the observed Y values? An R^2 of 88.51 percent means that 88.51 percent of the variation in the forecasted values of Y can be explained by the relation between the dependent variable (Y) and the independent variable (X). This degree of reliability is usually acceptable.

The difference between estimated Ys and actual Ys is broken into two parts: observed Ys minus calculated Ys is the unexplained variation, while estimated (via regression) Ys minus the mean of the observed Ys is the variation that is explained by the regression equation. Thus, R^2 measures the difference between the estimates of Y using the regression equation and what Y estimates would have been if the manager had used the equation: $Y = $ Mean of observed Ys. The coefficient of determination is the proportion of the variation in the regression equation that is explained by the independent variable. R^2 is always stated as either a proportion or a percentage.

Exhibit 10-4 Regression Analysis: Coefficient of Determination

Figures used from Table 10-3
$a = -2.11$
$b = 0.4621$
$n = 10$
Mean of $Y = 12.4$
Y column total $= 124$
XY column total $= 4,220$
Y^2 column total $= 1,708$

$$\text{Coefficient of determination} = \frac{(-2.11 \times 124) + (0.4621 \times 4,220) - [10 \times (12.4)^2]}{1,708 - [10 \times (12.4)^2]}$$

$$= \frac{150.82}{170.4}$$

$$= 0.8851.$$

To state the coefficient of determination (R^2) as a percentage, multiply the calculated measure by 100: 88.51%.

Correlation Coefficient

Exhibit 10-4 showed the required calculations for the coefficient of determination using the same data originally used to estimate the regression line. The *correlation coefficient* is simply the square root of the coefficient of determination (before stating R^2 as a percentage); that is, because the coefficient of determination is R^2, the correlation coefficient is R. The correlation coefficient will always be between negative one and positive one. The advantage of using the correlation coefficient is that it shows the direction and strength of the relationship between the dependent and independent variables.

If the correlation coefficient is negative, an inverse relationship exists between the independent and dependent variables. This means that as the independent variable increases, the dependent variable decreases. Conversely, a direct relationship exists if the correlation coefficient is positive. A direct relationship means that as the independent variable increases, the dependent variable increases.

NETWORK PLANNING

Network planning is a production/operations management technique. Network planning develops a project network that is based on estimates of activity times. These estimates are used to develop a diagram showing each step involved in completing the proposed project activity along with the completion times. Network planning is usually used to plan and manage large projects. Large projects are composed of both activities and outcomes. The activities are the pieces of the project that require time, resources, or both. The outcomes are the results of the activities.

Two network planning tools are in general use today:

1. critical path method
2. project evaluation review technique.

Critical Path Method

The *critical path method* (C.P.M.) uses deterministic or constant activity times. Therefore, C.P.M. is used to analyze and diagram a project that is sufficiently similar to prior organizational projects to allow the accurate estimation of activity time frames.

The networking technique for C.P.M. is a six-step process:

1. Formulate the network parameters.
2. Draw the project network.
3. Enter early dates and activity times.
4. Enter latest dates.
5. Ascertain the critical path.
6. Analyze project criticality.

Formulate the Network Parameters

The *network parameters* are formulated by compiling an activity list for the project. The manager should determine how much time is needed for each activity. Since C.P.M. is used for projects that the organization has undertaken before, this should be fairly easy to do. The manager must add to the activity list the order in which each activity must be performed. This includes determining which activities require the completion of another activity before they can be started and which activities can be performed simultaneously. An example of an activity list is provided in Exhibit 10-5.

Draw the Project Network

The manager should draw the project network as indicated by the activity list. The network drawing begins with a box on the left to indicate time zero, which is when the project begins. The next step is to draw an arrow pointing to the right on the right-hand side of the box for each activity that does not have a predecessor activity. Below the center of each arrow,

Exhibit 10-5 Activity List

Activity	Description	Predecessor Activity	Time (wk)
Project: Install salad bar in coffee shop			
Network method: C.P.M.			
A	Submit building permit application to city		1
B	Obtain building permit	A	4
C	Do remodeling	B	3
D	Obtain bids for and order the salad bar (fixture)	B	2
E	Salad bar shipped and received	D	6
F	Salad bar installation	C, E	3
G	Submit and receive supply and condiment order	E	2
H	Run advertising campaign for grand opening	G	1

enter the letter corresponding to the activity from the activity list. On the right end of each arrow, place a box to indicate the completion of the activity. Then, on the right side of that box place another arrow to indicate the activity to be completed next. Again, enter the activity's letter below the arrow. This process continues until the final activity arrow and the box to indicate its completion are drawn.

Some projects will have an activity that has predecessor activities on multiple sections of the network. In this case, an additional arrow must connect the predecessor activities to a box before the arrow for the activity can be drawn. This arrow will not have a label below it referencing an activity. Instead, it will be labeled *MP* to indicate multiple predecessors, and the label will be placed to the left of the arrow.

The activity list from Exhibit 10-2 is diagrammed in a network diagram in Figure 10-1. The numbers on the diagram are explained in the next section.

Enter Early Dates and Activity Times

The manager's next task is to enter early dates and activity times on the project networks. The methodology is to begin on the left-hand side of the model and work across the model. For this step, all times are placed above each activity arrow or to the right in the case of vertical arrows. The first arrow(s) to leave the beginning box cannot begin earlier than time zero. Record a *zero* on the left end closest to the first box above each arrow

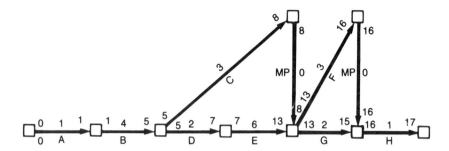

Figure 10-1 Network diagram using the C.P.M. method

leaving this box. The earliest completion date for each of these activity arrows is recorded on the right end of the arrow before the next box. The earliest completion date is the sum of the earliest start date plus the activity time for the activity arrow.

If there is only one activity arrow *leading into* a box, then the earliest start date of the arrow(s) *leaving* that box will be the same as the earliest completion date of the arrow leading into the box. If there is more than one arrow leading into a box, then the earliest start date of the arrow(s) leaving that box will be the same as the latest of the completion dates above the arrows leading into the box. The earliest completion date for each activity arrow is the sum of the earliest start date and the activity time.

In the case of the MP arrow, the only difference is that the activity time will always be equal to zero. This means that the MP arrow's earliest completion date will be the same as its earliest start date since there is no activity time to add to the earliest start date.

Figure 10-1 provided an example of a network diagram, complete with activity times and the earliest start and completion dates for each activity. The earliest completion time for the project is 17 weeks (found above the final activity arrow).

Enter Latest Dates

The latest dates are the activity dates that are as late as possible but that will still ensure that the last activity in the project will be completed by the same date as was calculated in the previous step.

The manager begins this step at the end of the project network and works backward to the beginning. All of the activity completion and start dates are recorded below each activity arrow, directly beneath the earliest start and completion dates that were recorded above the arrows. In the case of the MP arrow(s), or any other vertical arrows, the start and completion dates are placed to the left of the arrow.

The ending activity arrow (at the end of the project) must be completed at the same time as the earliest completion date for the final arrow. Record the same completion date below the ending arrow as above it. To calculate the latest start time, subtract the activity time from the latest completion time.

Record this latest calculated start date at the left end of the arrow directly after the preceding box. This latest start date also becomes the latest completion date of the next preceding activity. Remember, the manager is working backward toward the project start. If there are multiple arrows leading into a box, the latest completion date for each of these arrows will be the latest start date of the subsequent arrow. Of course, for any MP arrows, the latest completion date and latest start date will be the same because there will be no activity time for the arrow since it is not an actual activity.

The example of the project network is continued in Figure 10-2. The figures below (or to the left of) each arrow reflect each activity's latest start and completion dates.

Ascertain the Critical Path

A *critical path* is the set of critical activities along the project network. To determine which activities are critical, review each activity arrow. If both the start and completion dates below an arrow are the same as the start and completion dates above the arrow, that activity is defined as critical. This implies that the latest the activity can be performed in order to finish the project in the earliest time frame is also the earliest it can be done. In other words, if a critical activity is delayed, the entire project will be delayed.

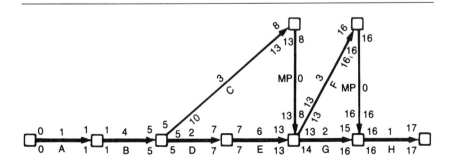

Figure 10-2 Network diagram using the C.P.M. method

Refer again to Figure 10-2. The following activities are critical: *A, B, D, E, F,* and *H*.

Analyze Project Criticality

The manager must do much more than identify the critical path. If there are financial penalties for a late project, the manager may need to take steps to shorten the duration of some activity or activities along the critical path. The wisdom of this strategy depends on the penalty for a late project compared with the cost of expediting the project. In the event the manager wants to shorten the project's time frame, the critical activities must be shortened. Of course, if some of these activity times change, other activities may become critical. The network times will need to be recalculated to adjust for the new situation.

Project Evaluation Review Technique

The *project evaluation review technique* (PERT) is another production/operations management tool. PERT uses probable activity times. PERT should be used if the project is a new kind of project for the organization or if the time frames cannot be accurately estimated.

PERT project networking is very similar to C.P.M. networking in many respects. The manager still compiles an activity list, draws the project network, places earliest and latest dates on the network, and determines the critical path. However, the times for each activity on the network are forecasts and are found using a specific method. This forecast for the activity times is subsequently used to determine the expected project completion time.

Forecasting Activity Times

Since the manager is uncertain of the exact time frame for each activity, the forecast is "hedged" by including a range of estimates. The forecast for each PERT activity time is determined in three steps:

1. Estimate a worst case (WC), most likely case (ML), and best case (BC) time frame from each activity.
2. Put these activity time forecasts on an activity list.
3. Calculate the forecast time (FT) for each activity using this formula:
$$FT = \frac{WC + 4ML + BC}{6}.$$

An example of an activity list is provided in Exhibit 10-6. This activity list is for the same project shown in Exhibit 10-5; however, the assumption

Exhibit 10-6 Activity List

Activity	Description	Predecessor Activity	WC Time (wk)[1]	ML Time (wk)[2]	BC Time (wk)[3]	Forecast Time (wk)[4]
	Project: Install salad bar in coffee shop					
	Network method: PERT					
A	Submit building permit application to city		2	1	1	1.5
B	Obtain building permit from city	A	7	4	3	4.3
C	Do remodeling	B	5	3	3	3.2
D	Obtain bids for and order the salad bar (fixture)	B	3	2	1	2.0
E	Salad bar shipped and received from supplier	D	9	6	4	6.2
F	Install salad bar	C, E	4	3	2	3.0
G	Submit and receive supply and condiment order	E	3	2	2	2.2
H	Run advertising campaign for grand opening	G	1	1	1	1.0

[1]Worst case time is longest expected time.
[2]Most likely time.
[3]Best case time is shortest expected time.
[4]Forecast activity time formula = (WC + 4ML + BC)/6.

has changed. The manager is now assuming that this project is so dissimilar to any other project the operation has undertaken that the activity times can only be estimated.

Plotting Activity Times

The network diagram is the same as Figure 10-1. However, the activity times recorded above the activity arrows are the forecasted activity times calculated and provided in Exhibit 10-6. Then the manager calculates the earliest start and completion dates using the same methodology as in

C.P.M. The latest start and completion dates are subsequently calculated, and the critical path is determined.

The project in Exhibit 10-6 is diagrammed in Figure 10-3 and includes all project times (earliest start and completion times, forecasted activity times, and latest start and completion times). The forecasted project completion time is 18 weeks.

Analyze Criticality

The manager then examines the diagram and determines the critical activities in the same way as with C.P.M. Referring to Figure 10-3, the project's critical path includes activities *A, B, D, E, F,* and *H*. The forecasted project completion time was 18 weeks. However, since the activity times are only forecasts, the manager must determine how likely it is that the project will be completed in the forecasted time. This is determined by calculating the variance for each activity in the project and then totaling the variances in the critical path. This variance total will indicate the range of time within which the project should be completed. Remember: Estimates are necessary because management cannot be certain of activity times.

The activity variances for each activity are always derived using the formula:

$$\text{Activity variance} = \frac{(\text{WC} - \text{BC})^2}{36}.$$

The PERT activity list with the forecasted completion times and variance calculations for each activity is provided in Exhibit 10-7. Recall that the expected project duration was 18 weeks. The critical path consisted of

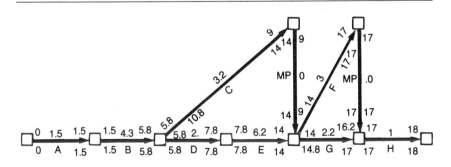

Figure 10-3 Network diagram using PERT method

Exhibit 10-7 Activity List

Activity	Description	Predecessor Activity	WC Time (wk)[1]	ML Time (wk)[2]	BC Time (wk)[3]	Forecast Time (wk)[4]	Variance Time (wk)[5]
	Project: Install salad bar in coffee shop						
	Network method: PERT						
A	Submit building permit application to city		2	1	1	1.5	0.03
B	Obtain building permit from city	A	7	4	3	4.3	0.44
C	Do remodeling	B	5	3	3	3.2	0.25
D	Obtain bids for and order the salad bar (fixture)	B	3	2	1	2.0	0.11
E	Salad bar shipped and received from supplier	D	9	6	4	6.2	0.69
F	Install salad bar	C, E	4	3	2	3.0	0.11
G	Submit and receive supply and condiment order	E	3	2	2	2.2	0.03
H	Run advertising campaign for grand opening	G	1	1	1	1.0	0.00

[1]Worst case time is longest expected.
[2]Most likely time.
[3]Best case time is shortest expected time.
[4]Forecast activity time formula = (WC + 4ML + BC)/6.
[5]Variance time = (WC − BC)^2/36.

activities *A, B, D, E, F,* and *H*. The sum of the calculated variance of these activities is calculated as follows:

0.03	Activity A variance
0.44	Activity B variance
0.11	Activity D variance
0.69	Activity E variance
0.11	Activity F variance
0.00	Activity H variance
1.38	Total critical path variance

This means that the project duration is expected to be between 16.62 and 19.38 weeks. This is merely the initial forecasted activity time for the critical path plus or minus the calculated critical path variance of 1.38.

The manager must still balance costs and benefits in making decisions regarding the expedition or delay of activities in the project. If more information becomes available to the manager that will affect forecasted activity times, the activity times and earliest and latest dates must be recalculated. This may change the critical path and, in all probability, will have some impact on the variance as well.

STRATEGY IMPLEMENTATION

The strategy must be designed to meet the needs of the customers and owners of the organization; that is, the manager's challenge is to design strategies that will support the corporate or organizational mission. All components of the strategic plan should work together as a cohesive system. The marketing plans should help maintain or increase market share, identify potential new market niches, and concurrently maximize profits or income. The production plan should minimize expenses, maximize capacity utilization, and still meet the product quality and timeliness of delivery requirements. The human resources plan should ensure maximum utilization of staff resources at the least possible cost. It should also provide a stable, high-performance staff. Of course, the financial plan should maximize profits and allow the organization to remain competitive.

Obviously, there are countless permutations of strategy systems that can be developed for a particular organization. Once the general strategy direction is identified, how can the manager help ensure that viable solutions are identified, and how can the manager systemize the evaluation of these solutions? Finally, what are the potential pitfalls of strategy design and implementation?

Management by Objectives

Management by objectives (M.B.O) is a technique that is used to involve line managers actively in goal setting. This has a dual benefit. First, since the managers are a part of the goal setting process, they are more likely to strive for those goals since they feel they had a say in their development. The second benefit is that with more input, a potentially terrific solution or strategy is far less likely to slip through the cracks!

The foodservice director or general manager must be aware of the significant opportunities and pitfalls facing the organization. By enlisting the help of line managers (through M.B.O.) in collecting and interpreting information, the line managers become a part of the strategic planning process. Through M.B.O., the director can ensure that the line managers and supervisors are working toward consistent goals. Since line managers become a part of the strategic planning process, they are more likely to support the choices and goals of the organization visibly and actively. This is especially true if the performance review and reward system depends on a manager's success at meeting the agreed-upon goals and objectives.

The goal of M.B.O. is to break problems into manageable components. Then, objectives, strategies, tasks, and procedures are formulated to solve these problems. Through the M.B.O. technique, the general manager is trying to coordinate all of the individual goals so that when combined into a system with an overall strategy, the individual efforts will work together rather than compete.

By designing a reward and incentive system based on M.B.O., less corporate level involvement is required on a day-to-day basis. This is because individual goals are more likely to be in the corporate interest and still meet the needs and goals of the subunit. The actual level of involvement by senior management and the level of detail in goal setting depend on the overall needs of the business and the corporate culture.

Many Japanese management tools are similar to M.B.O. The most common one in use today is *work groups,* or quality circles. These work groups usually brainstorm to generate solutions to problems that they have encountered in their immediate environment. Frequently, the group dynamics become as much a part of the solution as any actual strategy suggested by the group.

Feasibility Studies

A *feasibility study* is the process of estimating the impact of a proposal on the overall operation from every possible angle in order to determine its desirability. This proposal could be a change in product mix, a change in productive capacity, or a change in staffing, among other things. The aspects considered would include, for example, staffing, service levels, operating costs, revenues, and profitability.

The process can be divided into three parts. One part consists of pulling together quantitative information, such as forecasted pro formas, relevant costs, and the estimated time to complete a project. The manager should determine the capital investment required and develop a financing plan and a pro forma income statement for each proposal.

Another part of the feasibility study is to gather and summarize qualitative information. This would include additional justification for the proposal based on managerial experience. Examples of questions that might be considered are:

- What would this proposal do to the organization's competitive position?
- How will this proposal affect the operation's reputation in the community or industry?
- Is this proposal consistent with the corporate mission?
- If the proposal is not consistent with the corporate mission, has the mission changed, or should it be changed?

Finally, once all the information has been gathered, the manager must evaluate the information using decision criteria that are consistent with the organization's goals to determine whether it would be feasible (or desirable) to proceed with the proposal.

Caveats and Limitations of Techniques

Of course, the purpose of the strategic planning techniques (and all of the analytical methods discussed in this book) is to help in the decision-making task. There is a strong tendency to make management and strategic decisions based only on these tools. A more appropriate way would be to incorporate trade-offs and judgment into the decision-making process, since this would make it more likely that all relevant variables had been considered.

Typically, alternative solutions are generated and then analyzed based on predetermined decision criteria using modeling and analytical techniques. This results in the identification of the apparently optimal, or best, solution. In everyday practice, the manager may feel that this optimal solution must either be accepted or rejected. This is actually not quite right. The manager should generate a range of solutions, and since there are always trade-offs, the trade-offs and estimated costs should be included with the alternatives. These trade-offs, as well as the general knowledge and instincts of the seasoned professional, should be considered along with all of the scientific and quantitative tools. Through the inclusion of these factors, the manager is likely to make an even more effective decision or strategic plan.

Recap of Systems Theory

Recall that the overall basis or emphasis of this book has been the systems theory. The various chapters of this book have examined the components and inner workings of the system. Some of the benefits of the system are not derived simply by adding together the system components. The expression "the whole is greater than the sum of the parts" states the truth about systems theory; that is, part of the strength of a system arises from the combination of its components. The ongoing, or operative, goal is to design and manage a system that will maintain an appropriate balance between competing goals or that will improve that balance.

The strategic plan should never lose sight of this, and neither should the manager who designs and oversees the implementation of this strategy. The manager must look at each component as a part of the system and should therefore design the component's operation so that it will play a contributory role in the efficient achievement of the system goals. The ever-present challenge is to design a system that will coordinate management goals with environmental opportunities based on the resources, history, goals, and values of the operation.

STRATEGIC CONCERNS BASED ON THE LINE OF BUSINESS

There are a number of specific subgroups in the institutional foodservice industry functioning in various arenas. The major subgroups (and their strategic concerns) that are addressed include:

- colleges and universities
- school systems
- business and industry
- governmental units
- health care organizations.

Although there are large areas of commonality, each market has unique needs, requirements, and characteristics. Some institutional foodservice operations will operate in only one of these arenas, and others will operate in more than one.

Colleges and Universities

Most colleges and universities conduct their financial affairs using the fund accounting rules. This methodology heavily influences the purchasing, record keeping, and budgeting procedures for the operation.

The foodservice's budget will depend on the number of students, faculty, and staff members to be serviced. Waste control, menu quality, and variety have different emphases than in a hospital cafeteria. The market on many college and university campuses is fairly stable since the size of the student body tends to stay the same throughout the school year.

School Systems

Most school systems are limited in their menu offerings by governmental regulations. There is not usually the potential to bring in new customers. Strong customer loyalty, however, can be built by emphasizing quality and nutrition. One of the strongest strategic considerations that will face the school system market in the future will be an increasing student body but a tighter school budget. Productivity and financial management will therefore become increasingly important to the foodservice and the school system. Effective vendor and supplier selection strategies will be crucial to the survival of the foodservice in the school system.

School systems will determine the future of their foodservice operations by analyzing their options. If it is determined that an outside company can provide the same foodservice at a lower cost, that company will undoubtedly end up doing so. The manager must, therefore, stay abreast of both internal costs and the costs of competitive foodservice operations.

Business and Industry

Business and industry markets include many that are similar to those served by the hospitality industry and caterers. Many major corporations have on-site cafeterias for their employees. The major goal of the operation, however, may not be to make a profit. In this situation, the corporation subsidizes the cafeteria, so the prices are low. The goal may be to keep employees on-site, provide a gathering place, or keep the employees healthy at a reasonable cost.

The corporation makes an initial decision as to whether it makes sense to provide the foodservice itself or, alternatively, to contract with an outside foodservice company (or caterer) to provide this service. This decision should be made using the same data gathering and decision-making criteria as any other strategic alternative in the business world, typically with a feasibility study. Bids from contract services are compared with the forecasted cost of the corporation undertaking its own foodservice. Of course, the quality of food and the control of the operation must be considered along with the financial factors.

Businesses that *provide* foodservice for a corporation must also forecast costs based on the requirements of the potential client. Judgments should be made regarding how easy or difficult it would be to work with the potential client and whether the provider's ability to standardize the client's operation would be in keeping with the foodservice operation's standard operating procedures.

Submitted bids should be based on the forecasted costs. Budgets, pro formas, and feasibility studies should be a part of the bid package. Marketing savvy must also be a part of the bid and the proposal presentation. The outside company should be prepared to prove why, *besides* the financial considerations, they should get the bid. These reasons could include:

- nutritional counseling for employees
- a variety of healthy foods
- the reliability and reputation of the foodservice
- the quality of the food and services
- cleanliness
- the security-mindedness of the foodservice.

In many cases, the outside company may be attempting to woo a client in an industry that is highly competitive. If a bidder has a proven reputation for protecting a client's trade secrets, it could provide a real competitive edge. Since the on-site cafeteria is there to provide a gathering place, the employees will be "talking shop" during meal times and catered meetings. The last thing the client wants to worry about is a security leak from the people providing the foodservice.

Governmental Units

There are countless governmental organizations that require a foodservice operation. These units include armed forces' mess halls and commissaries, congressional cafeterias, and prison cafeterias. These governmental foodservice operations are generally provided internally. For each of these operations, just as for any other governmental unit, an enormous amount of paperwork is required in connection with its business. Most of the regulations, and related paperwork, involve complex bidding and procurement procedures, cost justification and policies and procedures manuals.

In the case of a foodservice operation in a prison, the nutritional needs of inmates is still a consideration. Government procedures and budgeting systems will generally be required. The clients served by the foodservice, however, cannot take their dining business elsewhere since they are the true "captive market."

Health Care Organizations

The health care field is in the midst of an unprecedented "shake-out." Hospitals are experiencing market share problems, low occupancy, and increased costs. New diseases and an aging population base will provide new challenges to the health care industry. The 1980s and 1990s will bring new problems (and solutions). The astute foodservice manager will be prepared to shift gears and provide foodservice products and services in new ways. These may include catering meals, serving hospice centers, Meals-on-Wheels, frozen meals, and bakery outlets or providing for day care centers (for both children and adults).

STRATEGIC CONCERNS BASED ON THE FORM OF BUSINESS

Strategies, concerns, and implementations vary depending upon the form of the business. The form of the business depends on the answer to two questions:

1. Is the business for-profit or nonprofit?
2. Is the business a corporation, a partnership, or a sole proprietorship?

For-Profit Operations

Any foodservice operation that is a *for-profit* operation has as its primary mission or strategy the goal of maximizing the wealth of the owner(s). Thus, major strategic considerations will include maximizing income and minimizing expenses. Increasing market share, being innovative in product and service offerings, and similar strategies are typical choices made by the operation.

Nonprofit Operations

Nonprofit organizations are typically in business to provide a social purpose or meet a societal need. Examples of these organizations include philanthropic foundations, private hospitals, nursing homes, religious organizations, orphanages, halfway houses, and hospices. Nonprofit operations have an overall strategy of providing a service that meets an existing need. Just because the operation is organized as a nonprofit operation does not mean that there are no financial, production, or marketing strategies to develop and implement. On the contrary, the manager must be particularly attentive to these functions so that the organization can continue to fill the needs of the clients and customers.

Other strategic concerns include conducting fund-raising activities, complying with government regulations, and effectively serving the operation's clients.

Corporations

In the corporate setting, the manager has a fiduciary responsibility to the owners. This fiduciary responsibility means there is an implicit trust that the manager will place the owners' interests (profit maximization) above personal or departmental goals. Therefore, the strategy design and implementation should evolve from, and be consistent with, this fiduciary responsibility. Nonprofit corporations face a particularly tricky strategic design problem. This type of operation has two corporate missions: to meet a societal need and to remain financially healthy so that it can meet that need.

Sole Proprietorship

A *sole proprietorship* has one owner. The distinction here is who owns the business; the size of the organization can range from one employee to thousands of employees. If the foodservice manager is also the owner, the manager will probably have no problem focusing on the need to maximize profits. The owner-manager, however, may have a serious problem in effectively delegating responsibility for the myriad of necessary activities. The lack of delegation, or the lack of the ability to select other effective managers, can make or break the organization. The other major concern facing the owner-manager is sufficient protection from personal litigation since the operation is not a separate entity. In the case of the corporation, the business is legally considered to be a separate entity; in the case of a sole proprietorship, since there is no legal distinction between the business and the owner, severe business losses can quickly become personal financial losses.

The manager that is employed in a sole proprietorship faces other strategic considerations. Some of the owner's decisions may seriously limit the potential for career progression, if for no other reason than the size of the operation. The organizational structure may be much less defined. This can be both a strength and a weakness. The level of informality may make strategic planning and budgeting less structured and time-consuming. By the same token, the lack of structure may also mean much more chaos. The foodservice operation will, of course, still need to continue to justify its existence by achieving the prescribed performance goals.

Partnership

The strategic considerations and legal ramifications facing a partnership are much the same as those facing a sole proprietorship. The difference is that there are two (or more) owners. The partnership is an association of owners who combine their skills and resources in order to achieve mutual goals. Although the partnership is a legal entity, the entity does not shield the owners with limited liability. This means that if the partnership incurs more losses than can be covered by the assets it has, the personal assets of the partners must be used to satisfy the partnership's debts. One of the key considerations facing a partnership, therefore, is the selection of appropriate partners. The division of labor and the delegation of responsibility can also be a time-consuming strategic consideration.

The manager who is employed by a partnership but who is not actually a partner may face the same situations as the nonowner-manager in a sole proprietorship. The key will be to understand operational goals clearly, acquire the tools and resources to meet them, and ensure that the performance achieves the stated goals.

UNIVERSAL CONSIDERATIONS

It is safe to say that whether the manager is the business owner or merely an employee, the overriding strategic concern is to ensure that operational goals are met using methods and strategies that are acceptable to the owners, clients, and community. The size, type, and form a particular operation takes may make the achievement of this task more or less complex with varying degrees of formality and structure. The astute manager will monitor the operation and the environment so as to be continually aware of shifting contingencies, power bases, and market needs and will utilize all possible tools to ensure that actual performance meets operational objectives.

Chapter 11

Policies and Procedures

Policies and procedures are plans that are made for an operation that serve as guides for decision making and action. *Policies* are general guidelines for action in an organization developed by the top level management or by the governing/decision-making body of the organization. *Procedures* are specific step-by-step actions that should be taken to implement a policy. The steps are usually ordered in the sequence in which they should be performed.

THE POLICY AND PROCEDURES MANUAL

The purpose of compiling a policies and procedures manual for an operation is to develop a dynamic tool that is in accordance with the goals and objectives of the foodservice operation. The policies and procedures in the manual should guide decision making by defining the areas in which decisions may be made and providing direction for action to employees in the performance of their duties.

This section discusses the design and development of the policies and procedures manual, the accreditation and inspection requirements regarding the manual, and the external sources to guide the manager in the compilation and development of the manual.

Development Process

The initial development of the policies and procedures manual is a three-step process:

1. Observe employees.
2. Examine and analyze tasks.
3. Determine and design the most effective procedures.

Observe Employees

The manager should observe the employees in action and compile information regarding all of the tasks and activities that are performed. The aspects to include in this study are who performs each task, when it is performed, why it is performed, and how it is performed.

Examine and Analyze Tasks

After compiling the list of all the organizational tasks, the manager must examine and analyze these tasks. This includes breaking down each task into the components that make up the task.

Determine and Design the Most Effective Procedures

The manager must then determine the most efficient and effective way to perform each task. This includes the determination of the most natural and effective division of labor. Compiling procedures for each duty forces the manager to examine and analyze each activity that occurs in the operation. After this analysis, the manager may determine that some of the current tasks are unnecessary. Compiling the manual through study, observation, and analysis helps uncover current strengths and weaknesses as well as potential problems.

Although the manager may almost automatically perform many of the analytical and reporting tasks, it is still important to have instructions for these tasks in the policies and procedures manual. Then the manager can systematically train the staff to collect and analyze at least some data for these reports.

Typical Components

Policies and procedures manuals should state the corporate strategy and mission so that all who use the manual will be made aware of the purpose for the organization's existence. Each section of the policies and procedures manual should include these basic elements: a statement of each policy, the purpose for each policy, who is responsible for carrying out each policy, the date developed and reviewed, and the procedures. The manual may include additional information, such as the policy number, its classification, primary and secondary responsibilities, special information related to the policies and procedures, and special equipment needed to perform the procedures.

Accounting and Record Keeping

There should be a section in the manual with step-by-step instructions for completing all accounting transactions: purchase orders, requisitions, receiving shipments into inventory, posting transactions to journals, posting journals to the general ledger, making deposits, verifying cash receipts, and making cash disbursements. These instructions should explain the specific steps and show examples of completed forms.

One of the more universal accounting policies to determine is the calendar used for accounting purposes. Some operations choose to run their accounting year on a fiscal year basis, and others on a calendar year basis. An example of a fiscal year calendar is an accounting year that begins on July 1 and ends on June 30.

Within the accounting year, the cutoff for each accounting period must be determined. Some operations run on a 4-4-5 basis. This means that in each quarter, the first two months are four weeks long and the third month is five weeks long. Other operations use the calendar month as the accounting period. Still others choose to break the year into 13 equal accounting periods of four weeks each. The decision is based on the need for financial reports and the general level of business throughout the year. The goal is to report the data in the most meaningful way possible.

A separate, but related, decision is how often employees will be paid. The most common method is to pay exempt employees one way and nonexempt employees another. Exempt employees are usually the salaried employees. This means that they are paid the same amount regardless of the number of hours worked. Nonexempt employees' wages are usually calculated based on an hourly rate times the number of hours worked, with a premium rate for any overtime hours. Local custom and labor laws play a major role in determining the frequency of pay. One method is to pay the nonexempt staff bi-weekly and the exempt staff monthly. Whatever method is used, the details should be described in the manual. The manual, however, should *not* contain salary information for specific jobs. The wage policy for work dates covered in each paycheck should be determined, that is, whether the paycheck covers the time period up to and including the pay date or some other interval. For example, the operation could delay the first check an employee receives. This is a fairly typical arrangement, particularly since it makes the record keeping much easier. Of course, when the employee leaves the organization, the final paycheck (which includes the last days worked) is received one pay period later.

If accounting records are maintained on a computer, procedures for system security and file backup must be included in the policies and procedures manual in addition to the procedures for entering the transactions into the computer.

Inventory Management

Policies and procedures for inventory management should be determined and placed in the manual. Specific aspects of inventory management that should be covered include receiving and storage procedures and procedures for the issuance of inventory from storage to the operation. Other procedures should include how to order new inventory (food, beverage, and supplies), when purchase orders are required, and the level of approval required based on the size of the order.

An example of a receiving policy and procedure used in a small nursing home chain is shown in Exhibit 11-1.

Vendor Selection

Procedures should be included in the manual that identify the appropriate steps to be taken in soliciting vendor bids. The vendor and supplier selection policies and procedures should identify and recommend the time frame in which to solicit and select bids from potential vendors and suppliers. Specific criteria for supplier selection should be defined. These criteria could include:

- volume discounts
- payment policy
- quality of goods guarantee
- lead time from order placement to delivery
- minimum order size
- extra charges for expedited delivery.

Specific criteria, procedures, and policies should also be established regarding the vending commission. This includes establishing policies and procedures for dealing with the company that provides and services the vending machines and any other contract services.

Business Ethics

Other company rules, such as the business ethics involved with accepting "gifts" from vendors or suppliers, should be covered in full in the manual. Generally, to avoid any hint or implication of bribe acceptance or favoritism, the acceptance of vendor gifts should be strictly forbidden.

Policies should be established that define any other ethical stances of the organization. These could include:

- conflict of interest
- confidential information

Exhibit 11-1 Receiving Policy and Procedures

Policy: All deliveries made to the operation will be checked when received.
Purpose: To assure that all items delivered are of the quantity, quality, and cost ordered
Responsible Employee: Dietary manager
Procedure:

1. Check all products listed on the invoice against the product received.
   - Count all items that can be counted (i.e., number of cases).
   - Weigh all products that are ordered by weight.
2. Compare invoices to the purchase order. This ensures that only the products ordered were delivered.
3. Check prices on the invoice against the prices on the purchase order or bid forms (daily price quotations).
4. Check that items delivered are of the quality desired. Make sure that all products meet the predetermined specifications.
   - Check produce items for freshness. If the produce is *not* fresh, *do not* accept it.
   - Check the count of produce items that are ordered by count (e.g., baking potatoes, apples, oranges).
5. Check cans for dents or bulges. The seal of dented cans may have weakened to the point that would allow microorganisms in. The use of these products could lead to foodborne illness. Bulging cans indicate that microorganisms have penetrated the container and are forming gas, thus food from these containers is *not* safe for use.
6. Spot check cases to ensure that they are full and that all products in the case are of the same quality.
7. Store all perishable items promptly. This ensures that the appropriate temperatures will be maintained to retain quality.
8. Store all items in their proper location, changing all appropriate inventory records.
9. Record all purchases on a monthly food purchases form (Exhibit 2-9) or an invoice spreadsheet (Exhibit 2-10).
10. Send all invoices and credit memos to the administrator's office promptly.

Date Developed: _____

Date Reviewed/Revised: _____

- sexual harrassment
- disclosure of trade secrets.

Facilities Management

Specific policies and procedures should be established to ensure the safety of employees, suppliers, and customers. These procedures include OSHA regulations and Health Department regulations.

Standards must be established regarding the required frequency for cleaning equipment, tools, counters, and floors. Energy conservation measures should be established and placed in the manual. Procedures should also be established for periodic review to determine the adequacy of insurance protection, particularly liability and workers compensation insurance.

Cash Control

It is imperative to develop and implement procedures to ensure the control of cash. These procedures should include instructions on cash register readings and the receipt of payments in the form of cash, checks, and charges. The manual should identify who performs the count, who takes cash register readings, and who verifies the count and readings.

Procedures should be established that identify how cash payments are to be handled as well as when and by whom deposits are to be made. Procedures should also be developed to identify who verifies and audits for compliance. Policies and procedures for nonadherence and irregularities should be established and implemented.

There should be controls and procedures developed and implemented to help ensure that guests do not leave without paying. This could mean a policy that all guests pay at the exit or that guests pay for the meal when served.

Financial Management and Analysis

Throughout this book, specific financial management and analysis tools have been presented. Policies and procedures should be established to ensure that the staff uses these tools to understand and manage the operation. Specific procedures should be established that explain the details of the budgeting process, including deadlines and assignments.

Guidelines for cost determination and menu pricing should be incorporated into, and become part of, the operation's standard operating procedures. The application of forecasting methods, and other analytical tools, should be described in the manual to provide insight into cost determination and pricing strategies.

Instructions and guidelines for any periodic reports should be included in the manual. Although the manager may compile all of these reports, the procedures, the sources of data, and the calculation instructions should still be provided in the manual.

Personnel Policy

The policies and procedures manual should include a complete job description for every position in the operation. These descriptions should include the duties and responsibilities of each position and the experience and education required for each position. The job description should also include where each position fits in the organizational chart and the job grade or classification of each position.

Performance evaluation procedures should be included along with the consequences of poor performance. Overtime, vacation, and sick policies should be covered. Generally, advance approval of any overtime should be obtained from the employee's immediate supervisor. The purpose of this policy is to keep productivity up and to control salary expense. The supervisor needs to be aware of trends in overtime and the need for it so that decisions about staffing can be made. For example, it is generally more cost-effective to have a part-time employee work some additional hours rather than have a full-time employee work overtime.

Other personnel policies are mandated by law. Examples of these include compliance with the Equal Employment Opportunity Law, the Civil Rights Act, and all other nondiscrimination laws. Furthermore, policies that prohibit sexual misconduct, sexual harrassment, and the possession or use of illegal substances must be included in the manual. (Notices of compliance must be visibly posted in the workplace.)

Foodservice Process

Of course, specific policies and procedures should be established that address the foodservice process. These include instructions on how to:

- place orders
- stock nourishments
- manage inventory
- follow standardized menus
- establish food checking systems.

There is not a universal procedure for any of these areas. Rather, the manager should establish and implement procedures that will be the most effective for the individual operation. The procedures should be consistent with the goals and resources of the operation.

Separation of Duties

The manager must establish procedures that distribute over several workers duties that are interconnected in order to provide a reliable system of checks and balances. A well-designed system of checks and balances provides an audit trail and decreases the possibility of theft, loss, fraud, and collusion.

Duties in many areas should be separated. This means that specific duties should be performed by different individuals. These include:

- cash
- inventory
- food checking
- guest checks.

Separation of cash duties means that the same person should not be responsible for receiving the cash, reporting the cash, depositing the cash, disbursing the cash, and verifying the cash transactions. An example of procedures that separate cash duties is to have one person count the cash and a second person verify the count. The employees who count the cash could prepare the deposit slip, but another person must verify the deposit slip and make the deposit. Yet another person should review the deposit receipt and record the transaction in the appropriate journal. Any discrepancies must be reviewed.

Procedures that separate inventory duties mean that one person receives and approves the shipment while another person is responsible for verifying the receipt. A separate person is responsible for securing and storing the inventory. Yet another person is responsible for requisitioning inventory from storage to the kitchen.

Food checking systems and procedures should identify who is responsible for comparing the food orders with the prepared food. This should be done to protect the operation from pilferage of food, incorrect charges, or human error.

Guest checks can also be audited by separation of duties. The use of prenumbered guest checks and the control of these checks by number is the first step toward separation of duties. A comparison of the original guest check with the kitchen control copy provides an audit source to verify that the customer was charged for the food that was received. A comparison of guest checks with cash register tapes and totals provides an audit trail to determine that the guest paid for the food that was received.

Public Relations

Public relations policies encompass procedures employees follow in dealing with the public. *The public* is defined as customers, suppliers, the business community, and other departments in the organization.

There should be specific policies regarding the recommended types of advertising and promotion strategies. Permissible strategies should be described as well as those that will not be permitted.

The public relations policies could include specific procedures the employees are to follow in the event of customer complaints, vending machine mishaps, and spillage. The overall goal of the public relations policies is to ensure that employees are aware that every action they take, or do not take, conveys a message to the customer. The message that the manager wants to convey and the forms that it should take should be identified. Generally, positive attitude, professional behavior, and fair treatment should be stressed.

Marketing Management

There should be procedures in place regarding how to administer surveys and questionnaires for potential new product and service offerings. Instructions, guidelines, and forms for data collection on sales patterns for specific products should be provided. Guidelines should be established and put in the manual for identifying when the sales patterns may indicate that a product should be dropped.

There should be procedures that define the steps to take to identify the appropriate product mix as well as any other marketing strategies the manager wants to implement.

BENEFITS

There are many benefits to designing and using a policies and procedures manual, including:

- a training and orientation tool
- a smooth-running operation
- consistent products, service, and performance
- a methodology to manage growth
- perspective broadening.

Training and Orientation Tool

Since the policies and procedures manual contains instructions for the performance of every activity in the operation, it provides an excellent basis for employee training. The manual should be placed in an area that is accessible to all employees. During the orientation and training process, the manager should stress that employees should continually refer to this manual whenever they have questions. No one should be embarrassed by the need to use the manual. Instead, workers should be complimented on their ability to be self-directing when they consult the manual.

Smooth-Running Operation

The manual serves as a communications tool to the entire operation so that employees know how to handle situations when they occur. This helps ensure that things run much more smoothly and gives some autonomy to the staff. In this manner, the manual frees the supervisor from making routine decisions. This allows the supervisor to spend more time managing the total operation instead of supervising and explaining repetitive tasks.

Consistent Products, Service, and Performance

An important benefit of using a policies and procedures manual is that the design and implementation of the manual can help ensure that products, service, and performance are consistent. If the staff is made aware of the appropriate procedures and expected standards of performance, they should then perform as a cohesive group. Frequently, employees fail to achieve what is expected of them because they are misinformed about expectations, procedures, and standards. By using the manual, employees will become familiar with the policies and procedures that are necessary for the successful completion of their jobs.

Methodology to Manage Growth

As the business grows, it will become necessary for the manager to delegate duties to other staff members. By having instructions for data collection and analysis in the policies and procedures manual, the staff will be able to take over some of the report generation duties for the manager. It is important to prepare the operation for future growth so that the outcomes of that growth (increased paperwork, reporting requirements, and staff) do not stifle the organization.

If these methodologies are organized and placed in the manual, the clues and indications about new trends, potential market niches, and potential problems will more likely be detected.

Perspective Broadening

One of the seldom-recognized benefits of compiling and maintaining a policies and procedures manual is the impact this has on the thinking of the manager and the staff. Since the staff will have an informational source that explains all of the operational procedures, they will no longer have to try to remember everything. This can help the manager clarify the operational strategy and corporate mission for the staff. If the staff is aware of the "big picture," it should broaden their perspective, too. This can increase creative problem solving and thereby provide job enrichment.

ACCREDITATION AND INSPECTION REQUIREMENTS

Many operations are required to have an up-to-date policies and procedures manual in the facility. Nursing homes must keep these manuals in order to pass the state Title XIII inspections. Hospitals that are accredited by the Joint Commission on Accreditation of Healthcare Organizations are also required to have a current manual in use. Standard DT.3 from the *Accreditation Manual for Hospitals*[1] states that written policies and procedures must specify the provision of dietetic services, including the scope and the conduct of those services. To meet this standard, the policies and procedures must be subjected to timely review, revised as necessary, dated, and enforced. Furthermore, the manual must be available for all employees to review. Several areas are specified for which policies and procedures must be developed, including cost-related areas such as purchasing, storage, inventory, production, and service.

TOOLS TO HELP DESIGN POLICIES
AND PROCEDURES

Two sources that are invaluable to the foodservice manager in developing or revising policies and procedures are: *Policies and Procedures for Hospital Dietetic Services*[2] and *Foodservice Operations Manual: A Guide for Hotels, Restaurants, and Institutions.*[3] Both references provide actual policies and procedures statements that are formatted for use in a foodservice operation.

There are software packages specifically designed to prepare policies and procedures manuals, which are described in chapter 12. Word processing software can also save a great deal of time when used to prepare policies and procedures manuals because of the ease in making revisions.

POLICIES AND PROCEDURES MANUALS AS DYNAMIC TOOLS

The policies and procedures manual is not a static document. The operation continues to change and evolve in response to environmental changes. The manual should reflect this and be revised to incorporate organizational changes, duty realignment, legal changes, and marketing changes. The maintenance of the policies and procedures manual should be an ongoing process, and the manager should always be prepared for the need to change the division of tasks and the task determination.

NOTES

1. *Accreditation Manual for Hospitals* (Chicago: American Hospital Association, 1987), pp. 22–23.

2. James C. Rose, *Policies and Procedures for Hospital Dietetic Services* (Rockville, Md.: Aspen Publishers, Inc., 1983).

3. John C. Birchfield, *Foodservice Operations Manual: A Guide for Hotels, Restaurants, and Institutions* (New York: Van Nostrand Reinhold Company, 1979).

Chapter 12

Microcomputer Applications

Computers are revolutionizing America. Their impact can be seen in diverse settings from the television to the classroom, from the home office to the executive board room, and from small companies to multinational companies. Computers are integral to business operations as well as to the lives of individual users.

The use of microcomputers has become increasingly attractive as the prices have decreased, capabilities have improved, and an increasing number of user-friendly software packages have been developed. This is a far different situation from that of a few years ago when most software was available only for a mainframe computer. The only way a department or specific operation could automate their record keeping, report generation, and analysis functions was to have the data processing department design and write specific programs. American workers have also become more computer literate and thus more able and willing to use both hardware and software.

A recent survey[1] of health care executives found that personal computers are most often used, and that nearly 75 percent of executives believe that survival in the 1980s will be difficult without computerized cost-accounting capabilities. The major benefits these executives anticipate from computerized cost accounting are cost savings, improved productivity, improved service, and improved quality of care.

Microcomputer applications in foodservice have been available for a number of years. Specialized software developed specifically for foodservice is available at prices ranging from several hundred to several thousand dollars. Specific applications for software include inventory management, procurement, standardized recipes, recipe costing, production planning, financial record keeping, and recipe nutrient analysis.

The emphasis in this chapter is on general use software that has applications for foodservice. General use software is available to perform

279

functions such as word processing, spreadsheet preparation, time management, financial analysis, training, and policies and procedures manual
preparation.

SOFTWARE SELECTION

Managers must determine which software packages are appropriate for
their specific operation. This begins with defining operational requirements. The manager should determine anticipated uses and needs for specific features in order to evaluate the packages. Then the manager should
meet with various vendors to determine which vendors and packages are
compatible with the operation's needs. The manager should also find other
operations that use the software packages under consideration. Seeing the
software in action gives the manager a much more accurate idea of its
usefulness and user-friendliness.

The degree of user-friendliness desired will depend on the computer
literacy of the intended users. Software packages vary in both the amount
and depth of menus and promptings they contain. Most managers will
probably want the software to prompt the user for information whenever
an entry is required on the part of the operator. The more guidance the
software gives the user (in promptings or help indices on-line) the more
user-friendly and useful it will be. The software packages that are the most
useful for the operation will be those that are oriented to the level of the
intended users.

WORD PROCESSING

Word processing is one of the most common functions performed on
microcomputers in most businesses. Word processing software is used for
most typing operations in an office. The advantage of using word processing
for document preparation is that material need be typed only once, allowing
corrections and changes to be made quickly. Any document, form or report
that will be used more than once should be entered in a word processor.

Word Processing Packages

Several word processing software packages are currently on the market. WordPerfect, Display Write 3, AppleWriter, WordStar, MacWrite,
MultiMate, and Microsoft-Word are but a few of the choices. The choice

of software will depend on a number of factors including hardware, cost, capabilities, and quality of documentation.

WordPerfect provides some powerful features. These features include an on-line dictionary that checks spelling and grammar as the document is prepared. The package has advanced sorting, merging, and column formatting functions. In addition, the package permits the user to perform addition, subtraction, multiplication, and division. There is a macrofunction that lets the user design and automatically execute a series of commands to perform specific functions. Using the four-function math feature and text entries, the manager can set up and calculate financial statements in the body of a report without leaving the word processing program. WordPerfect even permits the user to set up a concordance of frequently used phrases. Other word processing software packages have similar capabilities.

Applications for Word Processing

There are a variety of word processing applications related to financial management in foodservice. Some applications to consider include:

- policies and procedures manuals
- employee handbooks
- menus
- standardized recipes
- price lists for cafeteria and catering
- blank forms
- employee telephone lists
- employee work schedules
- mailing lists.

TIME MANAGEMENT

There are numerous time management software packages. Many include a calendar and notepad function. Some of these programs allow the manager to computerize the planning of a major project, including all of the intermediate deadlines for the components of the project. The users should balance the need for time management with the amount of time they are willing to spend managing their time! Some of the packages are more complex than the average manager needs, and many of them take more time to use than they save.

ACCOUNTING

An intermediate stage between the manual system described in chapter 7 and a computer-based accounting system is an *integrated manual system.* These systems go by names such as One-Write. They are typified by carbonless forms and cards. The bookkeeper uses these to post a transaction (e.g., a purchase or credit sale) to the accounts payable or accounts receivable card. The bookkeeper attaches the card to the journal and writes on the card. The transaction is simultaneously recorded on a line of the journal as a carbon copy of the written information. Payments (whether for purchases or payroll checks) are handled in a similar fashion. Checks are provided in a strip that is laid over the journal. As the bookkeeper writes the check, the writing is posted to the journal through the carbon on the back of the check. Each of the journals are then totaled and posted to the general ledger. Of course, the financial statements must still be compiled manually, as discussed in chapter 7.

Accounting software packages automate some or all of the record keeping functions described in chapter 7. The income and the expenses are still recorded, but in many cases, the software package posts the entered data to the transaction journals. The manager has the computer post the journals to the general ledger at the end of each accounting period. Most software packages also allow the manager to enter (post) adjusting, closing, and reversing entries. The majority of the accounting software packages can generate financial statements after posting journals to the general ledger. The more automated and integrated the software package is, the more time it can save. With a completely integrated system, a specific transaction will need to be entered into the computer only once, and the computer will automatically post the transaction every place it should be posted. Most accounting system software packages are *application systems.* Applications systems allow routine clerical tasks to be automated and can handle large volumes of input and output, which allow an organization to keep track of money, goods, people, and materials.

Accounting can be automated using many various software packages. The following sections describe some of the more popular packages.

Dac-Easy Accounting

Dac-Easy Accounting (Dac Software, Inc.) is a completely integrated software package with modules for accounts payable, accounts receivable, purchase orders, billing, inventory, general ledger, and forecasting. The entire package fits on one floppy disk and currently sells for about $70.

The system is fully integrated. This means that an entry to any module in the system is automatically posted to all other relevant modules. In addition to the accounting features, there is a powerful forecasting feature.

Dac-Easy provides a multitude of forms to help plan and customize the manager's accounting system and reports. The general ledger function compares all reports with prior year or budgeted figures.

Dac-Easy can be used to forecast inventory based on past sales and issues warnings when inventory approaches or falls below the preselected levels. Forecasts can be performed for every module in the system. The forecasting methods and assumptions are selected by the operator or manager, not imposed by the system. It even permits forecasting using the least squares method after three years' data are accumulated.

The Dac-Easy system does not force the user to close out one month before posting transactions for the next month. The month to which transactions are posted is chosen by the user. This facet and the forecasting features of the system make the system more valuable than many of the other accounting packages on the market.

Books! The Electric Ledger

Books! is an accounting program designed for small businesses. Not only does the program perform the routine bookkeeping chores, but it also provides the operation with detailed accounting reports. The package includes a chart of accounts, but new accounts can be created. Books! tracks and ages accounts receivable and accounts payable. Reports can be generated that even summarize accounts receivable or accounts payable by client or supplier name or number. Books! has additional modules available that print invoices and checks. The package is highly interactive and guides the operator through the system by "asking" the operator action-specific questions throughout the session.

SPREADSHEETS

Electronic spreadsheets are like the traditional columnar accounting pads, with the computer replacing the highly sharpened pencil. The set-up of the electronic spreadsheet, like the columnar pad, is in rows and columns that intersect to form cells. Data are recorded in these cells as numbers, alphanumeric titles, or formulas. If a number or formula is changed, all related numbers will be automatically recalculated.

Spreadsheets can be used to create financial models. Financial models simulate, forecast, and explain the performance of an operation. If the model is correctly defined, the financial model will act as a powerful tool for decision makers by showing the consequences of various alternatives before a decision is made. A financial modeling system aids in determining what may happen given various circumstances. Financial modeling via the use of various spreadsheet programs gives the manager a tool to manipulate data, see the impact of the manipulations, and generate reports without depending on programming specialists in the data processing department.

Once the relationship among variables is determined, the spreadsheet model can help a decision maker see the effect that a variation in one or more variables would have on the business. For example, a manager might be interested in knowing what effect a change in the hourly rate of second-shift employees would have on the cost of goods sold and the organization's gross margin. New dimensions can be added as a financial model is expanded. For instance, the amount of money allocated to an advertising budget might be tied to the gross margin of the company. Thus, if the manager is able to reduce production costs by one percent, the financial model could help simulate the effect of these cost reductions on the cost of goods sold, the gross margin, and the advertising budget for the next year.

Spreadsheet Packages

There are several spreadsheet software packages available on the market, including Lotus 1-2-3, VisiCalc, Multiplan, Open Access, Supercalc, Visicalc Advanced Version, and Symphony. The more popular spreadsheet programs can generate graphics, run regression analyses, and perform "what-if" analyses. This makes the programs especially useful not only for generating management reports but for forecasting and developing feasibility studies and the budget cycle. Many of these packages have a sensitivity analysis capability, can perform regression analyses, and can perform various built-in mathematical and financial functions, such as the net present value.

Template Design

Setting up a spreadsheet from the beginning may be more time-consuming than doing an operation or record keeping by hand. However, once the form is set up, subsequent spreadsheets can be produced with little effort. A *template* for a spreadsheet is the initial format set-up with all the formulas in place. This template is saved under a separate protected file name. The template is then called up for actual data entry. After the data entry, the new form of the report with the data entered is saved under a file name that is different than the template's. The template can be called up for new data entry and reused as needed.

Applications for Spreadsheets

There are many applications for spreadsheets in the financial management of foodservice operations. Payroll, daily reports, monthly summaries, food and labor cost analysis, budgeting, goal seeking, financial ratio development, and cash reconciliation can all be performed using spreadsheets.

Payroll

The payroll can be calculated and the payroll records maintained using spreadsheets. A template can be developed to calculate net income for each person based on the gross income by calculating income taxes owed, individual and organization Social Security taxes owed, insurance payments, and any other deductions that should be made.

A payroll record for the operation can be developed. A simple payroll record is shown in Exhibit 12-1.

Exhibit 12-1 Knox Hospital: Payroll Records

Name	Date	Total Hours	O.T.	Reg.	Gross Pay	Fed.	FICA[2]	State	Net Pay[3]
						Tax Deductions[1]			

Total Payroll

Tax Table

[1]To calculate federal and state taxes using Lotus 1-2-3, tax tables would be entered onto the spreadsheet. Using the LOOKUP function, taxes would be calculated automatically.
[2]FICA taxes would be calculated using the following formula: Gross pay × current FICA rate. In this spreadsheet, that would be $+F7^*.0751$.
[3]Net pay equals gross pay minus all deductions. In this example, the formula would be $+F7-G7-H7-I7$. This formula would go in cell J7. With spreadsheet software, the formula can be copied for each individual on the payroll.

A form can be developed that would summarize each individual's pay and deductions for a pay period for inclusion with the payroll check for the period. An example of an individual's pay summary is provided in Exhibit 12-2.

When salary review time arrives, the spreadsheet used for payroll could be quickly run to determine the total dollar impact potential raises would have on the organization. Remember, as wages and salaries increase, so do some of the benefit costs. Once the decisions are made, the new wage or salary would simply be added in place of the old one, and the new payroll would be calculated.

Monthly Cost Summaries

Monthly cost summaries can be developed with spreadsheet software. These cost summaries can be developed based on the individual needs of the operation. A monthly cost summary developed for a school foodservice is shown in Exhibit 12-3. Notice that the report contains specific information needed for a school, including the breakfast sales, the number of Type A lunches, and information about the school milk program. The real advantage to using a spreadsheet program is that it can be adapted specifically to the unique needs of an operation.

Another type of monthly cost summary is the foodservice performance summary. An example of a performance summary is provided in Exhibit 12-4.

Purchases Records

Records of purchases or invoices can be readily kept using spreadsheets. The total food cost, the food cost by category, and the percentages of total food cost by category can easily be calculated on the spreadsheet. This provides a useful way to track costs in the foodservice operation. An example of a blank template for a purchases record is shown in Exhibit 12-5. The record is shown in Exhibit 12-6 with actual data.

Sales Mix Analysis

The sales mix analysis and popularity index can be calculated and reported on a spreadsheet. An example of a sales mix analysis spreadsheet is provided in Exhibit 12-7.

Financial Statement Preparation

The development of spreadsheets that prepare financial statements begins with the design of the format. Chapter 8 gives examples of an oper-

Exhibit 12-2 Valley Nursing Home: Biweekly Earnings

Date: May 5, 1989
Name: Sue Smith

	Current	Year-to-date
Hours worked	80	160
Overtime hours	5	5
Gross income	$298.10	$566.10
Deductions		
Federal income tax	$44.72	$84.92
FICA (7.51%)	$22.39	$42.51
Health insurance	$21.00	$42.00
Net income	$210.00	$396.67

Exhibit 12-3 Knox Elementary School: Monthly Food Cost Summary for 1988–1989

	August	September[1]
Total student lunches		15987
Total adult lunches		803
Total lunches	B7 + B8[2]	16790
Income		$14,000.00
Food cost		
Beginning inventory		$6,959.00
Purchases		$11,400.00
Adjustments		
Ending inventory		$7,343.00
Total food cost	(B14 + B15) − (B16 + B17)	$11,016.00
Food cost per meal	B18/B9	$0.66
Gross labor cost		$7,225.00
Labor cost per meal	B21/B9	$0.43
Cost summary		
Total cost	B18 + B21	$18,241.00
Total cost per meal	B26/B9	$1.09

[1]Shows a month calculated using data.
[2]Formula for calculating cell value. This formula would be copied across the spreadsheet to calculate the total lunches for each month. All other formulas would be used in the same manner.

Exhibit 12-4 Performance Summary

Facility: ABC Hospital
Record Period: May 1989
Prepared by: J. Sneed

Meal Count		**Sales**	
Patient meals	B7	Cafeteria	E7
Cafeteria meals	B8	Catering	E8
Complimentary meals	B9	Total	+ E7 + E8
Catered meals	B10		
Other	B11		
Total meals	@SUM(B7. .B11)		

Food Costs

	Grocery	Meat, Fish, Poultry	Dairy	Frozen Foods	Bakery	Produce	Total Food Cost
Beginning inventory	B20	C20	D20	E20	F20	G20	@SUM(B20. .G20
Plus purchases	B21	C21	D21	E21	F21	G21	@SUM(B21. .G20
Minus ending inventory	B22	C22	D22	E22	F22	G22	@SUM(B22. .G20
Total gross cost	+ B20 + B21 − B22[1]						
% of total food cost	B23/H22						
Minus nourish- ments	B25						
Minus transfers	B26						
Net cost of food	+ B23 − B25 − B26						
Year-to-date food cost							

Supply Costs

	Disposables	China, Flatware, Utensils	Cleaning Supplies	Office Supplies	Other	Total Supplies
Beginning inventory	B37					
Plus purchases	B38					
Minus ending inventory	B39					
Total gross cost	+ B37 + B38 − B39/ G40					

Exhibit 12-4 continued

Supply Costs

	Disposables	China, Flatware, Utensils	Cleaning Supplies	Office Supplies	Other	Total Supplies
% of total supply cost	+B40/G40					
Minus transfers	B42					
Net cost of supplies	+B40−B42					
Year-to-date supply cost						

Labor Costs

Patient labor costs	B49
Nonpatient labor costs	B50
Allocated labor	B51
Total labor costs	@SUM(B49. .B51)
Patient labor hours	B53
Nonpatient labor hours	B54
Total labor hours	+B53+B54
Total FTE	+B55/173.33

Meal Cost Summary

	Patient Actual	Patient Budgeted	Nonpatient Actual	Nonpatient Budgeted
Total meal equivalents	B10		@SUM(B8. .B11)	
Total food cost	B64		C64	
Total supply cost	B65		C65	
Total labor cost	B49		B50	
Total cost	@SUM(B64. .B66)		@SUM(C64. .C66)	
Meals/Labor hour	+B10/B53		+B63/B54	
Cost per meal	+B67/B10		+C66/C63	

[1]Formulas would be copied across rows to calculate information for each column (category).

Exhibit 12-5 Purchases Record

Facility: _____
Record Period: _____
Prepared by: _____

Vendor	Date	Invoice Number	Grocery	Meat, Fish, Poultry	Dairy	Frozen Foods	Bakery	Produce	Total Food
									$0.00[1]
									$0.00
									$0.00
									$0.00
									$0.00
									$0.00
									$0.00
									$0.00
									$0.00
									$0.00
									$0.00
Total by category			$0.00[2]	$0.00	$0.00	$0.00	$0.00	$0.00	$0.00
% of total			ERR[3]	ERR	ERR	ERR	ERR	ERR	ERR

[1]The formula for this column is @SUM(D10. .I10). This formula would simply be copied down the column to repeat the function for each row.

[2]The formula for this row (Total by category) is @SUM(D10. .Dn). This formula would be copied across the row to repeat the function for each column.

[3]The formula for determining the percentages across the row is +D22/J22. This formula would be copied across the row. Using the dollar signs means that all rows will be divided by the value of cell J22, which is the total purchases that will result in the percentage of total purchases.

Exhibit 12-6 Purchases Record

Facility: Tex Hospital
Record Period: January 1988
Prepared by: J. Sneed

Vendor	Date	Invoice Number	Grocery	Meat, Fish, Poultry	Dairy	Frozen Foods	Bakery	Produce	Total Food
Food Vendors, Inc.	02-Jan-00	1236	$49.75	$221.32		$87.50			$358.57
Spring Green	03-Jan-00	45123						$96.73	$96.73
Hearty Bakery	03-Jan-00	99513					$58.75		$58.75
Elsie's Dairy	03-Jan-00	9530			$195.78				$195.78
ABC Wholesalers	04-Jan-00	67889	$234.65	$134.50					$369.15
J & K Meats	06-Jan-00	54312		$244.54					$244.54
Food Vendors, Inc.	10-Jan-00	3435	$132.45	$52.95	$18.75	$62.89			$267.04
Spring Green	13-Jan-00	33245						$123.45	$123.45
Hearty Bakery	15-Jan-00	12345					$123.45		$123.45
									$0.00
									$0.00
									$0.00
Total by category			$416.85	$653.31	$214.53	$150.39	$182.20	$220.18	$1,837.46
% of total			22.69%	35.56%	11.68%	8.18%	9.92%	11.98%	100.00%

Exhibit 12-7 Sales Mix Analysis

Month: October

Menu Item	Number Sold	Popularity Index
Entrees		
Prime rib	650.00	42.65%
Broiled shrimp	295.00	19.36%
Baked chicken	487.00	31.96%
Pork chops	92.00	6.04%
Total	1524.00	100.00%
Starches		
Baked potatoes	700.00	45.93%
Wild rice	695.00	45.60%
Buttered noodles	129.00	8.46%
Total	1524.00	100.00%
Vegetables		
Spinach Maria	312.00	32.50%
Green beans almondine	235.00	24.48%
Broccoli au gratin	413.00	43.02%
Total	960.00	100.00%
Breads		
Hot rolls	543.00	35.63%
French bread	321.00	21.06%
Onion rolls	660.00	43.31%
Total	1524.00	100.00%
Desserts		
Double chocolate cake	234.00	29.92%
Apple dumpling	513.00	65.60%
Key lime pie	35.00	4.48%
Total	782.00	100.00%

ation's financial statements in Tables 8-1 and 8-2. The template designs that produce this form are provided in Tables 12-1 and 12-2.

The preparation of the financial statement for a particular accounting period is a matter of copying the template from the diskette to the worksheet area and entering the operational results from the general ledger onto the template. A copy of the period's financial statements should be saved on the diskette.

Variance Analysis Reports

Variance analysis reports were discussed in chapter 8. An example of the format and an actual report were presented in Tables 8-5 and 8-9. The template to create this report is presented in Table 12-3.

Table 12-1 Balance Sheet

Row No.	Titles	Current Month Actual Results (Col. C) Input Values	Prior Month Actual Results (Col. D) Input Values
10	Cash	$,	$,
11	Marketable securities	$,	$,
12	Inventory: Food	$,	$,
13	Beverage	$,	$,
14	Accounts receivable	$,	$,
16	Total current assets	+ C10 + C11 + C12 + C13 + C14	+ D10 + D11 + D13 + D14
18	Equipment	$,	$,
19	Acc. depreciation	(,)	(,)
21	Total fixed assets	+ C18 + C19	+ D18 + D19
25	Accounts payable	$,	$,
26	Salaries payable	$,	$,
27	Current portion of note	$,	$,
29	Total current liabilities	+ C25 + C26 + C27	+ D25 + D26 + D27
31	Note payable	$,	$,
32	Mortgage payable	$,	$,
34	Total long-term liabilities	+ C31 + C32	+ D31 + D32
36	Total liabilities	+ C29 + C34	+ D29 + D34
38	Capital	$,	$,
40	Total liabilities and capital	+ C36 + C38	+ D36 + D38

The source of the data to calculate the report is the inputted values in the financial statement template. Therefore, these templates should be saved and filed on the same master spreadsheet. By doing this, the variance analysis report will be generated as soon as the data for the financial statements are entered with no further operator input.

Common Size Statements

Common size statements were presented and discussed in chapter 8. Examples of the common size statements were provided in Tables 8-11 through 8-14. Templates that can be used to calculate the appropriate data and generate these reports are provided in Tables 12-4 and 12-5.

Once again, the data used to calculate these reports are the data entered to generate the financial statement. Therefore, these templates should also

Table 12-2 College Coffee Shop: Income Statement

Row No.	Titles	Current Month Actual Results (Col. C) Input Values	Current Month Budgeted Results (Col. D) Input Values
56	Sales	$,	$,
57	Cost of sales	(,)	(,)
59	Gross margin	+ C56 + C57	+ D56 + D57
61	Salaries and wages	$,	$,
62	FICA	$,	$,
63	Benefits	$,	$,
64	Utilities	$,	$,
65	Supplies	$,	$,
66	Depreciation expense	$,	$,
68	Net operating income	(+ C63 – C65 – C66 – C67 – C68 – C69 – C70)	(D63 – D65 – D66 – D67 – D68 – D69 – D70)
70	Interest expense on note	$,	$,
71	Taxes	$,	$,
73	Net income	+ C68 – C70 – C71	+ D68 – D70 – D71

be created and stored within the same master template as used for the financial statement and the variance analysis.

Budgeting

Projecting income and expenses for the budgeting process is easy to perform using spreadsheets. One of the most efficient applications of spreadsheets for budgeting is goal seeking. Using goal seeking, the budget planner can project the profit goal in dollars and percentages and then project expenses based on that goal.

The spreadsheet will also help the budget planner do "what if," or sensitivity, analysis. Examples are to determine the impact on an operation if fixed costs were reduced by 1 percent, or if cafeteria prices were increased by 2 percent, or if absenteeism were reduced, thereby reducing labor costs.

COMBINATION PROGRAMS

There are software packages that are actually integrated modules. These modules consist of word processing, financial modeling, data base management, time management, and spreadsheets. The advantage of these

Table 12-3 Variance Analysis Worksheet for Current Accounting Period

| | | Income Statement Cell Reference Nos. | | | |
| | | Col. C | Col. D | Favorable | |
STMT. Cell Row No.	Titles	Actual Results	Budgeted Results	(Unfavorable) Variance	Reason
76	Sales	+C56	+D56	+C76−D76	
77	Cost of sales	+C57	+D57	+D77−C77	
79	Gross margin	+C59	+D59	+C79−D79	
81	Salaries and wages	+C61	+D61	+D81−C81	
82	FICA	+C62	+D62	+D82−C82	
83	Benefits	+C63	+D63	+D83−C83	
84	Utilities	+C64	+D64	+D84−C84	
85	Supplies	+C65	+D65	+D85−C85	
86	Depreciation expense	+C66	+D66	+D86−C86	
88	Net operating income	+C68	+D68	+C88−D88	
90	Interest expense on note	+C70	+D70	+D90−C90	
91	Taxes	+C71	+D71	+D91−C91	
93	Net income	+C73	+D73	+C93−D93	

integrated combination programs is that the information in each module can be used in the other modules. For example, a spreadsheet could be moved to the middle of a word processing document without rekeying the information.

20/20 Spreadsheet Modeling Program

20/20 is a combination package that combines graphics, data management capabilities, and spreadsheet modeling into one integrated environment. The package can be used on microcomputers, minicomputers, and mainframe computers. The package integrates the spreadsheet with word processing. 20/20 can schedule projects, calculate critical paths, and determine slack time. All of the usual spreadsheet modeling functions can be performed on 20/20, including budgeting, financial reports, and cash flow analysis.

Business Modeler Software

Business Modeler is a comprehensive financial modeling system. The package is a multispreadsheet system that helps managers develop their

Table 12-4 Common Size Balance Sheet

| | | Balance Sheet Cell Reference Nos. | |
| | | Col. C | Col. D |
Row No.	Titles	Current Month Actual Results	Prior Month Actual Results
171	Cash	+ (C10/C23)*100	+ (D10/D23)*100
172	Marketable securities	+ (C11/C23)*100	+ (D11/D23)*100
173	Inventory: Food	+ (C12/C23)*100	+ (D12/D23)*100
174	Beverage	+ (C13/C23)*100	+ (D13/D23)*100
175	Accounts receivable	+ (C14/C23)*100	+ (D14/D23)*100
177	Total current assets	+ (C16/C23)*100	+ (D16/D23)*100
179	Equipment	+ (C18/C23)*100	+ (D18/D23)*100
180	Accumulated depreciation	+ (C19/C23)*100	+ (D19/D23)*100
182	Total fixed assets	+ (C21/C23)*100	+ (D21/D23)*100
184	Total assets	+ (C23/C23)*100	+ (D23/D23)*100
186	Accounts payable	+ (C25/C23)*100	+ (D25/D23)*100
187	Salaries payable	+ (C26/C23)*100	+ (D26/D23)*100
188	Current portion of note	+ (C27/C23)*100	+ (D27/D23)*100
190	Total current liabilities	+ (C29/C23)*100	+ (D29/D23)*100
192	Note payable	+ (C31/C23)*100	+ (D31/D23)*100
193	Mortgage payable	+ (C32/C23)*100	+ (D32/D23)*100
195	Total long-term liabilities	+ (C34/C23)*100	+ (D34/D23)*100
197	Total liabilities	+ (C36/C23)*100	+ (D36/D23)*100
199	Capital	+ (C38/C23)*100	+ (D38/D23)*100
201	Total liabilities and capital	+ (C40/C23)*100	+ (D40/D23)*100

own models for decision making. Specific forecasting tools available in the package include projection on a linear, average, geometric, or least squares basis. Other tools include depreciation methods, discounted cash flow, internal rate of return, and production management. Interactive loops can be set up within any model to provide sensitivity analysis capabilities.

Open Access

Open Access is a sophisticated software package that includes word processing, spreadsheets, data base management, telecommunications, and

Table 12-5 Common Size Income Statement

		Income Statement Cell Reference Nos.	
Row No.	Titles	Col. C Current Month Actual Results	Col. D Prior Month Budgeted Results
210	Sales	+(C56/C56)*100	+(D56/D56)*100
211	Cost of sales	+(C57/C56)*100	+(D57/D56)*100
213	Gross margin	+(C59/C56)*100	+(D59/D56)*100
215	Salaries and wages	+(C61/C56)*100	+(D61/D56)*100
216	FICA	+(C62/C56)*100	+(D62/D56)*100
217	Benefits	+(C63/C56)*100	+(D63/D56)*100
218	Utilities	+(C64/C56)*100	+(D64/D56)*100
219	Supplies	+(C65/C56)*100	+(D65/D56)*100
220	Depreciation expense	+(C66/C56)*100	+(D66/D56)*100
222	Net operating income	+(C68/C56)*100	+(D68/D56)*100
224	Interest expense on note	+(C70/C56)*100	+(D70/D56)*100
225	Taxes	+(C71/C56)*100	+(D71/D56)*100
227	Net income	+(C73/C56)*100	+(D73/D56)*100

time management modules. Each module provides the manager with the same functions provided by similar packages. The graphics capabilities are highly sophisticated and include 3-D graphics.

TRAINING PACKAGES

Packages exist that can automate certain aspects of employee training. These include cash register operation as well as the use of specific software programs. These packages can be beneficial.

Specific interactive programs can be designed by automating standardized recipes, record keeping functions, and other basic training sessions. These programs can be designed so that the computer terminal "asks" the operator a series of questions and, thus, interactively teaches the employee the skill.

Some of the interactive training packages that teach the user how to use other software packages are called "tutorials." Having these packages available to employees can sometimes make the computer an interesting new tool that employees are eager to use. Being able to make mistakes anonymously in the learning process is often less intimidating to the employee than having to make a good impression on the boss.

An example of a training package on the market is one available from Arthur Young Business Systems. There are two courses available: Lotus 1-2-3 and Symphony. Each course is available in a basic form and a more advanced form. The courses consist of a videotape, a training diskette, and a manual. The purchase of this type of package will ensure that training is consistent and as nonthreatening as possible.

OTHER SOFTWARE PACKAGES

There is a software package entitled "A Company Policy and Personnel Workbook" that helps the manager quickly develop organizational policies. The package explains employment laws and helps identify policies for the specific company. The sample policies include a description of the purpose of each policy as well as the legal implications of it.

There are various strategic planning packages that simulate specific parts of the manager's operation. These include software packages that simulate various marketing plans such as product mix, pricing mix, and promotions. There are also countless production and operations management packages. Many of the specific decisions the manager will make can be designed on one of the spreadsheet application packages.

SYSTEM SECURITY AND BACKING UP FILES

The importance of system security cannot be overemphasized. *System security* includes protecting the equipment, the software, and the files. The equipment should be in a secure place where it cannot be damaged or stolen. The files should be backed up on a regular basis to minimize the impact of equipment failure. Any files or spreadsheets that contain confidential information should be protected by a password and kept in a secured file. File and disk backup procedures are explained in the owner's manual that accompanies the hardware. These procedures should be followed by all who use the equipment. The manager should ensure that all files are backed up regularly, especially the accounting records for the operation and any other records whose loss could impair the operation.

There are many excellent software packages on the market that restore lost, damaged, or inadvertently erased files. The manager of a highly automated operation with numerous records may find this kind of package to be a wise investment. Some operations may be legally required to have this capability, particularly if they are required to have hard copies of specific reports.

NOTE

1. "PCs Top Hospitals' Choice for Cost Accounting," *Hospitals*, April 20, 1986, p. 93.

BIBLIOGRAPHY

American Hospital Association. *Determination and Allocation of Food Service Costs*. Chicago: Author, 1979.

American Hospital Association. *Preparation of a Hospital Food Service Department Budget*. Chicago: Author, 1978.

Beer, Michael. *Organization Change and Development: A Systems View*. Santa Monica, Calif.: Goodyear Publishing, 1980.

Bell, Donald A. *Food and Beverage Cost Control*. Berkeley, Calif.: McCutchan Publishing Corporation, 1984.

Birchfield, John C. *Foodservice Operations Manual: A Guide for Hotels, Restaurants and Institutions*. New York: Van Nostrand Reinhold Company, 1979.

Brealey, Richard, and Myers, Stewart. *Principles of Corporate Finance*. New York: McGraw-Hill Book Co., 1981.

Brigham, Eugene F. *Financial Management Theory and Practice*. Hinsdale, Ill.: Dryden Press, 1979.

Buffa, Elwood S. *Modern Production/Operations Management*. 6h ed. New York: John Wiley & Sons, 1980.

Chaban, Joel. *Practical Foodservice Spreadsheets with Lotus 1-2-3*. New York: Van Nostrand Reinhold Company, 1987.

Christensen, William W., and Stearns, Eugene I. *Microcomputers in Health Care Management*. Rockville, Md.: Aspen Publishers, Inc., 1984.

Cleverley, William O. *Essentials of Hospital Finance*. Rockville, Md.: Aspen Publishers, Inc., 1978.

Coltman, Michael M. *Cost Control for the Hospitality Industry*. New York: Van Nostrand Reinhold Company, 1980.

Coltman, Michael M. *Financial Management for the Hospitality Industry*. Boston: CBI Publishing Company, 1979.

DeCoster, Don T.; Ramanathan, Kavasseri V.; and Sundem, Gary L. *Accounting for Managerial Decision Making*. Los Angeles: Melville Publishing Company, 1974.

Dittmer, Paul R., and Griffin, Gerald G. *Principles of Food, Beverage & Labor Cost Controls for Hotels and Restaurants*. 3d ed. New York: Van Nostrand Reinhold Company, 1984.

Figueroa, Oscar, and Winkler, Charles. *A Business Information Guidebook*. New York: Amacom, 1980.

Gass, S.I. *Linear Programming: Methods and Applications*. 4th ed. New York: McGraw-Hill Book Co., 1975.

Hemburg, Morris. *Statistical Analysis for Decision Making*. 2d ed. New York: Harcourt Brace Jovanovich, Inc., 1977.

Herkimer, Allen G. *Understanding Hospital Financial Management*. Rockville, Md.: Aspen Publishers, Inc., 1978.

Hillier, F.S., and Lieberman, G.J. *Introduction to Operations Research*. 2d ed. San Francisco: Holden Day, 1974.

Hoare, H.R. *Project Management Using Network Analysis*. Maidenhead, England: McGraw-Hill Book Co., 1973.

Horngren, Charles T. *Introduction to Management Accounting*. 5th ed. Englewood Cliffs, N.J.: Prentice-Hall, 1981.

Hughes, A.J., and Graiwog, D.E. *Linear Programming: An Emphasis on Decision Making*. Reading, Mass.: Addison-Wesley, 1973.

Keiser, James, and Kallio, Elmer. *Controlling and Analyzing Costs in Food Service Operations*. New York: John Wiley & Sons, 1974.

Krajewski, Lee, and Thompson, Howard. *Management Science: Quantitative Methods in Context*. New York: John Wiley & Sons, 1981.

Miles, Robert H. *Macro Organizational Behavior*. Santa Monica, Calif.: Goodyear Publishing Company, 1980.

National Restaurant Association. *Facilities Operations Manual*. Washington, D.C.: Author, 1986.

National Restaurant Association. *Uniform System of Accounts for Restaurants*. Washington, D.C.: Author, 1983.

Neter, John, and Wasserman, William. *Applied Linear Statistical Models*. Homewood, Ill.: Richard D. Irwin, Inc., 1974.

Rose, James C. *Policies and Procedures for Hospital Dietetic Services*. Rockville, Md.: Aspen Publishers, Inc., 1983.

Rose, James C., ed. *Handbook for Health Care Food Service Management*. Rockville, Md.: Aspen Publishers, Inc., 1984.

Shugart, Grace S.; Molt, Mary K.; and Wilson, Maxine F. *Food for 50*. 7th ed. New York: John Wiley & Sons, 1985.

Spears, Marian C., and Vaden, Allene G. *Foodservice Organizations: A Managerial and Systems Approach*. New York: John Wiley & Sons, Inc., 1985.

Stokes, Judy F. *Cost Effective Quality Food Service: An Institutional Guide*. Rockville, Md.: Aspen Publishers, Inc., 1979.

Wagner, H.M. *Principles of Operations Research*. 2d ed. Englewood Cliffs, N.J.: Prentice-Hall, 1975.

Whitehouse, G.E. *Systems Analysis and Design Using Network Techniques*. Englewood Cliffs, N.J.: Prentice-Hall, 1973.

Index

About the Authors

Jeannie Sneed is an assistant professor in foodservice systems administration at the University of Tennessee, Knoxville. She has been on the faculty at Oklahoma State University and the University of Georgia and has worked as a consultant dietitian for nursing homes and for a food distributor and as a manager of a testing company that served as consultants for allied health professions. She completed the B.S. and M.S. degrees in Dietetics at Oklahoma State University and a dietetic internship at the Indiana University School of Medicine. Her Ph.D. is from The Ohio State University with a major in Foodservice Systems Management and a minor in Organizational Behavior.

Kate Henderson Kresse is a consultant in strategic planning and financial and operations management. She has been a financial analyst and planning specialist for over ten years and has been employed in the computer industry by Wang Laboratories and the Burroughs Corporation (Unisys). During this time she wrote numerous policies, procedures, and operations manuals. In addition, as a management consultant, she assisted in the reorganization and restructuring of a variety of organizations. Her educational background consists of degrees from The Ohio State University (M.B.A. in Finance) and St. Mary's College, Notre Dame, Indiana (B.B.A. in Accounting and Economics).